MAYAN DRIFTER

MAYAN DRIFTER

*Chicano Poet
in the Lowlands
of America*

Juan Felipe Herrera

TEMPLE UNIVERSITY PRESS
Philadelphia

TEMPLE UNIVERSITY PRESS, PHILADELPHIA 19122
Copyright © 1997 by Temple University. All rights reserved
Published 1997
Printed in the United States of America

Text design by Gary Gore

Library of Congress Cataloging-in-Publication Data

Herrera, Juan Felipe.
    Mayan drifter : Chicano poet in the lowlands of America / Juan Felipe
Herrera.
        p.   cm.
    Includes bibliographical references (p.   ).
    ISBN 1-56639-481-3 (cloth : alk. paper). — ISBN 1-56639-482-1
(pbk. : alk. paper)
        1. Herrera, Juan Felipe—Journeys—Mexico—Chiapas. 2. Mexican
American poets—20th century—Biography.   3. Mayas—Mexico—Social
life and customs.   4. Chiapas (Mexico)—Description and travel.
5. Mexican Americans—Journeys—Mexico.   I. Title.
PS3558.E74Z469   1997
811'.54—dc20   96-16324
[B]

        ISBN 13 : 978-1-56639-482-6 (pbk. : alk. paper)

        111115P

    The Rigoberta Menchú excerpt on page v is from *Trenzando el futuro: Luchas campesinas en la
historia reciente de Guatemala* by Rigoberta Menchú and the Comité de Unidad Campesina.
    The excerpt on page 3, from "I Want to Write an American Poem: On Being a Chicano Poet in Post-
Columbian America" by Benjamin Alire Sáenz, is reprinted with the author's permission.
    The excerpt on page 21, from "On Touring Her Hometown" by Lorna Dee Cervantes, is reprinted
with permission from the publisher of *From the Cables of Genocide: Poems on Love and Hunger* (Houston:
Arte Público Press/University of Houston, 1991).
    The excerpt on page 96, from "Fever" by Víctor Martínez, is reprinted with the author's permis-
sion. The poem appeared in *El Andar: The Latino Magazine* 6, no. 12 (June 1996) (Santa Cruz).
    The excerpt on page 169, from "What Is Called Dreaming" by Margarita Luna Robles, is reprinted
with permission from the publisher of *Tryptich: Dreams, Lust and Other Performances* (Santa Monica,
Calif.: Santa Monica College Press, 1992).
    The excerpt on page 177, from *Temptation: A Play in Ten Scenes* by Václav Havel (New York: Grove/
Atlantic, 1989), copyright 1989, is reprinted with permission from Grove/Atlantic, Inc.

I crossed the border full of dignity.
My satchel flourishes with so many things
from the rainy earth.
                    —Rigoberta Menchú

You'll have to listen to those sounds.
You should hear the song of the sky crickets,
the passing of the sky, the abandonment of the earth.
                    —Viejo Chan K'in
                    Nahá, Lacandón jungle, Chiapas, Mexico

It will be born out of the clash between the two winds, it will arrive
in its own time, the coals on the hearth of history are stoked up
and ready to burn. Now the wind from above rules, but the one
from below is coming, the storm rises . . . so it will be.
                    —Subcomandante Marcos, EZLN
                    Lacandón jungle, Chiapas, Mexico

CONTENTS

III. JAGUAR HOTEL

IV. ANAHUAK VORTEX

V. MAYAN DRIFTER

ACKNOWLEDGMENTS

To all my Indian sisters and brothers, especially Ramón Medina Silva, Lupe Ruiz de la Cruz, and the Huichols from El Colorín, Nayarit; Severo San Martín and his family from Poza Rica, Veracruz; Maruch, Pasquala, Margarita, and Marianito from San Cristóbal de las Casas, Chiapas; and my Hach Winik friends from Lacanjá Chan Sayab and Nahá in the vestiges of the Lacandón rain forest. For Viejo Chan K'in, K'ayum Ma'ax, Nuk and family of Nahá; without their words and hospitality, I would not have undertaken this book.

To Tomás Mendoza Harrell for friendship and camera savvy and for his company on my first journey to the Lowlands of Chiapas in 1970; and to Roberto Sifuentes, Susana Racho, Ray Castro, Gil García, and Juan Gómez Quiñones, who made it possible. To my family—my life and soul partner, Margarita Luna Robles, and my stepchildren, Marlene Rene Segura and Robert Segura; and my own children, Almasol Azucena, Joshua, and Joaquín—it is my hope that their voices will become part of a chorus of and for the Americas. I also thank Roberto Alvarez for his care, healing, and intuitive sense of my project; Jorge Herrera for his own journeys and advice; and Ray González and Rubén Martínez for their steady support and for giving me a good read and a place to rest. For my cousins Alvina, Chente, and Rosita Quintana—they know how all this started. For his love for his family and Chicana and Chicano culture, this is for my brother in spirit, José Antonio Burciaga.

Much appreciation goes to the Chicano Studies Research Center at the University of California at Los Angeles for funding my first jaunt into Chiapas in 1970 and to Southern Illinois University at Carbondale for helping to get me there in 1993. To Rogelio "Smiley" Rojas and Maestro Andrés Segura Granados, for soul notes and homecomings, gracias. I give special thanks to "Las Fridas," who encouraged me along the way—Anita Leal-Idrogo, Ana Lucía Gómes, Olga Montes de Oca, and Susana Mata—as well as friends and poets Víctor Martínez, Stephen Kessler, Lorna Dee Cervantes, Joyce Jenkins, Lauro Flores, Hisauro Garza, and Benjamin Alire Sáenz, who backed my play.

At the risk of overstatement, for their wild and daring spirits I salute the students of my creative writing workshops at Southern Illinois University, the University of Iowa, New College of San Francisco, Norwich University, Cal State Fresno, and most recently, the Mani Krudo Ensemble. Special thanks go most of all to the poets, artists, and writers who have spoken of and for a true Indian America and to my sisters and brothers in Mexico, who have inspired me to keep walking and listening and speaking for its reemergence and liberation. I offer my gratitude to Carlos Enrique, Luz María, and José, Mexican university students whom I met in Nahá. For her golden patience and faith in my work, much appreciation goes to Janet Francendese, executive editor at Temple University Press. I thank my readers, especially Susan Bergholz for her insights at the beginning and Elizabeth Johns for her superb copyediting at the end; they moved me forward. The publishers from Broken Moon Press in Seattle were the first to encourage me to embark on the journey that became this book—gracias, John and Lesley. For my parents, Felipe and Lucha, may they rest in peace—I thank you for guiding me to the edge.

Although I have only touched the surface of their meditations and findings, I am indebted to the work of various poets, artists, novelists, and social scientists. I hope I have served my predecessors well. In particular, I owe abundant gratitude to George A. Collier of Stanford University for his friendship and critical feedback and for his research and lifetime dedication to the Tzotzil-Tzeltal peoples, cultures, and history of Chiapas. His various debates on energy development and economic restructuring in Mexico and their effects on campesino and Indian populations have been extremely helpful in clarifying the current situation in Chiapas. Much of these reflections have been incorporated into the first chapter of Part I, "Tuxtla Oil Float."

Gertrude Duby Blom's work, both her essays on deforestation and her photography, has kept me focused and charged. Notes via telephone from Barry Norris, photography archivist at Na Bolom, gave me a clear start for my journey to Chiapas. Jan de Vos's meticulous research on the history of the Lacandones and the logging industry in southeastern Chiapas provided the most in-depth chronology of intervention in the selva for the chapter "Lake Waters of the White Jaguar." I thank Ignacio March for conversations and a copy of the 1992 preliminary report of the milestone Lacandón jungle conservation research project, *Reserva de la biosfera*

Montes Azules, Selva Lacandona: Investigación para su conservación, under the auspices of CIES (Centro de Investigaciones Ecológicas del Sureste) in San Cristóbal de las Casas; this highly insightful collection gave me an ecological overview of the region and heightened my awareness of the endangered flora and fauna in the selva.

Research by the following scientists and social scientists was of major import in the report: Miguel Angel Vásquez-Sánchez, Mario A. Ramos Olmos, Richard C. Vogt, and Oscar A. Flores-Villela. Sonia Tello Toledo's dissertation on violence in the highlands municipality of Simojovel was pivotal to my chapter "Indian Corridos for Justice." Gary H. Gossen's work on Chamula birth occasions provided detail for the chapter "From the Mountain Face." I thank all of these researchers for their studies and findings. Naturally, I bear sole responsibility for the interpretation of their work.

Although this book is based on fact and experience, all named characters are to be viewed as fictional composites. From these investigations, my task has been to gain a sociopolitical perspective and, in some cases, a handful of statistics; but my true goal, most of all, was to write a personal poem, a manifesto from the heart.

American Prelude(s)

TO AMERICA WITH LOVE

I want to write an American poem.
—Benjamin Alire Sáenz

This book is my offering as a poet to Mexico's Indian peoples and to all those who want to think about and reimagine America. This is a set of meditations on a voyage to Nahá, a Lacandón Mayan village in Chiapas, at the outer edges of southeastern Mexico—a song of an often abandoned America, one that recently hurled itself into our consciousness with the courageous uprising of the Indian and campesino Zapatistas.

From late December 1992 to mid-January 1993, I embarked on a journey from San Francisco, California, to San Cristóbal de las Casas, Chiapas. After a brief stay there, and unaware of the groundswell of an impending revolution, I wandered into the Selva Lacandona in search of an old friend, K'ayum, whom I had met on my first trek to the Mayan lowlands in 1970 when I was twenty-one. In this second cycle, more than two decades later, I return to the same towns and villages. Although my focus is largely on the Lacandón Maya, a tiny fraction of the one million Maya in Chiapas and three million who live from Guatemala to El Salvador, I call attention to the stark realities of all Maya and the 95 percent of the non-Lacandón settler population of eastern Chiapas composed mostly of forced-out and impoverished Tzotzil and Tzeltal Indians. Guatemalan exiles rush into the figures. Displaced Ladino campesinos add on their suffering integers.

The seemingly simple task of revisiting K'ayum becomes problematic. Which K'ayum? In what village? What country? What borders? Another K'ayum appears, one who lives in Nahá, a small village with approximately two hundred Lacandón residents. In total, Lacandón Mayas compose an endangered group numbering about five hundred in both northern and southern villages of Nahá and Lacanjá Chan Sayab on the southeastern quadrant of Chiapas. Danger and endangerment are central to the reading of America. Danger invades the text too: Where is K'ayum? Terms and names blur, boundaries and categories collide,

3

landscapes reverse, and we must battle for passage: how do I go about this telling? What position do I occupy?

Irony and subterfuge gnaw at the center of this text: How can I speak of and for America if my entry is through the Na Bolom center in San Cristóbal de las Casas, a museum for research on the Lacandón Maya that has profited in many ways by the Othering of these people for almost half a century? Why the Lacandón—this tiny lowland tropical forest population, recipient of exclusive rights to timber revenues that in actuality are usually pilfered by the politicos? What of the fifty Mayan Highland municipios? I stumble for excuses: Because I want to be inside the phantasmagoria of "Indian museums," I say; because I want to dismantle the "Museum of the Americas." Smart quotations gnaw at me. I am retracing my steps, that is all—but they are not there.

The gloss of Spanish conquest and colony infiltrates the terms of place, perniciously reconnects them; even as I write this, an old project of European expedition and "discovery" frames the language that I utilize, which in turn orients my innermost self. "From San Francisco to *la selva*," I repeat with consternation. Colonial consciousness assaults my personal writing project.

Beyond the slogans in vogue, what are the exploitative relationships between the United States, Mexico, and Latin America? What are the proper terms for neocolonialism? What subterranean campesino stratum rumbles across the entire continent—from Mayas digging through famine to undocumented farm workers dodging armored helicopters in the Southwest? Chiapas serves Mexico as the Southwest serves the United States: undocumented labor and servitude. These are critical questions given the aggressive agendas in this country regarding "aliens" from the "South," whether they are perceived as Mexican, Latino, or Indian. Another angle: what are the proper terms for Indian tribute within Mexico and Latin America? The Berlin Wall is being reinvented in the United States and Mexico while everyone watches late-night comedy. As a Chicano, I am a member of a doubly alien culture and territory; I stand watch on warring turf. Could this book be a cartouche for my "alien papers"? What I say as much as "my speaking" is not easily accommodated in the traditional disciplines of social science or leisure canons of literary pleasure; what I say is *for* America.

In many ways this text is my spiritual practice where I meditate upon my own being and place in the world in relationship to the people sharing the same space. History, culture, and consciousness diffract as I "descend" into the "Lowlands"—a geopolitical, cultural, and psychic cosmos of unmitigated suffering and language loss. Terms for conquest become obsolete as we contemplate the Indian and campesino on their own ground; we must search for efficient and radical perspectives. Official discourse dissolves; we must find a new "American" language. At times the call requires quests into the self and its interconnections to the landscape. Figures appear: my mother in dreams, Mayas in the last vestiges of the rain forest, a sick woman selling tortillas in San Cristóbal de las Casas, the eerie, melancholy eyes of Tzotzil-Tzeltal Indians and Ladino campesinos—all with the gaze of Zapata. I cannot document my experience without recollecting my family's trials through the similar borderlands; Juárez, El Paso, Mexico City, Chihuahua, Texas, California, Mexico, United States. The search for authentic "American" descriptions and a way of speaking is a double quest, a journey into indigenous territories and a slippery trek into myself. An odd and illusory paradigm appears: the nearer I get to *la selva*, the further I enter into the strange figure and assemblage of my self.

This book is also my own contribution to the cause of Indian and campesino justice and social change. Writing tests my faith and responsibility: as I writer, I must attack a formidable cadre of adversaries: language, historical consciousness, traditional and obsolete patronal versions of the *indio;* I must challenge the very idea of "Social Inquiry of the Native"—the canonical ethnographic S.I.N. of the social sciences. To fall back on a stolid "minority poetics" is also another possible folly—that is, to call for a universal and automatic bond among Mexican, Chicano, Latino, and Indian peoples. The text wants to negate itself, yet I must keep on; a way to speak is possible and significant.

The road is wavy, wary: writing, culture, and justice, faces, voices, and histories implode; they remain incomplete, indeterminate. This is not an attempt to carve a Chicano or Mexican monument, a grand summation of "who we are" or a totalizing exhortation on "the real America." I do not want to add another tired volume to the racks of Chicano movement literature, the roots stuff of the sixties and also of minority nationalist narratives that tunnel through history in search of an ethnic essence to be conjured in a self-induced Ouija spell. This is not another torch song pitting Mexican non-Indians against Indians, "Americanos" against Mexicanos. In a similar fashion, I am not interested in melting-pot opera and other facile "multicultural" platitudes unaware of class relations, local interconnections, and culture history. This an affirmation of a complex set of cultural contradictions, political indictments, and personal awarenesses. I do not claim a pan-Indianist philosophy, I do not espouse an official political agenda. As a poet I am wary of these fragile platforms. Even though I support the Zapatista vision for Chiapas, Mexico, and, ultimately, for the Americas, I do not seek to build a revolutionary "character" either in the text, the reader, or in myself. Here questions of revolution must be posed by a deeper and more critical set of currents—the people themselves, across the Americas and the world. At best this is an unfinished poem of a desire; a return to America—in the present: a möbius-shaped trek backward and forward to a shattered realm of Indian and campesino villages and bodies, to an unsettled mestizaje that at every turn aims to subvert itself. Subversion, I say to myself, then—America.

I want to reinvent the Mexican southlands as much as I want to reinvent the position that I hold as a brown man from "El Norte." One of the functions of a poem—if, indeed we can say that a poem has a function at all—is to turn things on their head or on their side: inside out or concave is the ideal. This characteristic is central to my explorations and reflections in this book as a literary project as much as a spiritual quest and cultural investigation. Do not let words like quest and search fool you. I did not begin with the thirst for discovery, a plan for personal acquisitions, an academic map for professional careership, nor even a disciplined research objective. I want to say something called me. It is not enough, unfortunately—it smells of worship, revelation, and the old sentiments of religious-conversion campaigns in Mesoamerica. I wanted to leave and possibly arrive, that is all—to leave my station in the United States and arrive at another in a demarcated limbo called Mexico. My existential motion and puzzle through and around these two wavering points provide the opening for this writing of and for America. One of the things I fear is the voice that says: "You never arrived." Another says, "You never left."

The boundaries and borders of America, as with nations and cultures everywhere, are in a state of rupture, inevitable collapse, and new design. I am also interested in the New American Figure or, better stated, the New American Dis-figure—that is, the emerging face and body of political and cultural rupture, an intensive, experimental, and revolutionary world change as it is expressed throughout the borderlands of the Americas. Ironically, we rarely regard the United States as undergoing any deep change. We assume an impermeable cultural groundwork that is more inclined to measure how "everything falls around us" more than how "we are falling." We are the master form; that is all we know, it seems. Here, in a sense, I propose that what we may consider to be America may not match the actual phenomenon; this book is one tracer of the drift from America, one account of the fissures on this side of the globe. For the Indio, Latino, Mexicano, and especially for the Chicano, the categories of Mexico and America inhabit a poetics and metaphysics of self more than an official geopolitical location. The lesbian poet Gloria Anzaldúa has made key contributions to this debate on borderlands identity, the multilayered self, and a new feminist form of ethnopoetics. At the risk of hyperbole, I propose this work as a preliminary rough-cut contribution to the epistemology of the American self.

Hyperbole often falls short; I also fear that this text is an initiation ritual out of sync. A rite of passage into Chicano and American being cannot occur: The instructions are missing or the sacred songs or the shaman woman are absent, and the proper language and materials for the ordeal have been subverted; the full-bodied realizations cannot be accomplished. The self is severed from the community; the world is a fragment. Myth cannot marry cosmos; myth dissolves into trials and shambled shadows of separateness. Maybe this slippage is the subject, perhaps this is what I want to say—American slippage—our current experience as residents of a fin-de-siècle America. Can we grasp what America is? Is it too late, too splintered, too far?

Again, I cannot question the place of and for America if I do not question my own position. Therefore this is at heart an account of my internal struggle to become whole, to re-collect myself as a member of a disinherited Indian and American family, the Maya of the Lowlands, to reassign myself into a new, contradictory, fictive kinship system. Forms of language as well as cultural relationships are skewed at a metaphysical plane; ideas of ancestry and the verse of revindication are intertwined. I seek as I fight, I fight as I remember; my language, then, emerges as a possible re-cognition.

The current crises in the human sciences give me ample room for challenge and defiance. What once were seen as proper ethnographic and objective tellings of an "exotic" culture have become suspect as the subjective constructions of the speaker with few connections to the people and places "under" investigation. The subject that speaks has taken the floor. Moreover, the radical telling may truly reside in the interplay between both worlds: investigation versus revolution. If we can find and invent the fresh terms, this Other-speaking may become a new form, no longer Other but I. Also, the mediums may switch categories: a long free-verse poem might be spliced with theater, for example. A multimedia manifesto and autobiographical ethnography can dance on the head of a scientific description of reality. Evans-Pritchard, Frida Kahlo, a shaman dream, and Sor Juana Inés de la Cruz can meet at last. Form mesmerizes me, displacement authenticates me; but I do not seek form or the margin: I seek America, I seek indio/india, americano/americana—in *liberación*.

I am involved in a triple vision: to rethink America, to rethink myself, and to rethink American writing. Is this another false trinity: America—Self—Writing? The debate is welcome and exponential: I want to tackle concepts of nation, symbols of ethnicity, practices for cultural knowledge, systems of literary order, questions of the margin and the center, the border work between the observer and the observed, between loss and recovery, suffering and liberation, between the language of America and for America. I offer these preliminary questions to all American writers, to all Americans.

America, I have said—poetics, writing, subversion, language; indeed, these terms are central to my concerns in this book. A major part of my task is to dissassemble the reading of America and Mexico, to revolt against the lexicon of European Indianism—Gauguin-like escapes into a tropical scrim of berry-eaters and long-haired, silent, punk Quetzalcoatl incarnates. Yet, the revolt is ancient, cyclical, and at times hemispheric. This text pays homage to Chicano and Latino poetics and literature in the United States, and throughout the Americas, which in the twentieth century have taken on the mass enterprise of writing in and for America. This work also shares kinship with all "writers for the people," those with their writing eye on human and civil rights. African American writers of the Harlem Renaissance, such as Zora Neale Hurston and Langston Hughes, have been a beacon for me, as have the makers of the Latin American "new novel," which began its trajectory at the end of the Second World War. Miguel Angel Asturias, José María Arguedas, Mario Vargas Llosa, Joao Guimaraes Rosa, Alejo Carpentier, Gabriel García Márquez. Elena Garro, Rosario Castellanos, Mario Monteforte Toledo, Augusto Roa Bastos, and Juan Rulfo fall into this latter catagory; their collective literary enterprise and focus on the displaced *indígena* and campesino wastelands have been key to my thinking on the complex relationships between authorship, history, literary form, and how power, people, and culture may be positioned with language. Although many of these postwar authors, predominantly male, wrote about contemporary Mayan Indians, it is the Mexican poet Rosario Castellanos to whom I feel closest, both as a poet and a writer who devoted much of her literary project to the life experience of the Mayan Indians in Chiapas. In Maureen Ahern's critical and literary anthology, *A Rosario Castellanos Reader*, she notes an interview where Castellanos makes a key differentiation between "indigenista" writers and herself: "I am not an indigenist writer . . . Indians do not seem mysterious or poetic to me. What happens is that they live in atrocious poverty." More than twenty years after her death, this declaration resounds through me and, I hope, through this book.

The Quiché Maya poet Rigoberta Menchú recently provided us with a model for the new American writer. In *I, Rigoberta Menchú*, her harrowing autobiographical account of being Indian in the highlands and city centers of Guatemala, Rigoberta also outlines, indirectly, the role of the poet and the writer's enterprise. She seems to tell us to stare back at chaos, disaster, and death, be fearless in the face of relentless oppression, learn the languages of the marginalized as well as of the oppressor, remember to assist in organizing exploited communities, remember to break through assigned borders, always fight and always forgive—remember the secrets. Rigoberta's work inspires this text. Not long ago, at a creative writing residency, I proposed this idea—Rigoberta Menchú as a model for the poet of the twenty-first century. Most were baffled. Some hollered: "That is not poetry," or "Get serious, you don't know what you are talking about." Few smiled and agreed, "Rigoberta, the key proponent for a poetics of and for America?" As more American regions send their campesino and Indian tremors across the bordered lines of information, capitalist power, hydroelectric energy fincas, and culture warps, my workshop friends must speak louder.

As I have said earlier, the contending canons of writing, speaking, and reading are formidable opponents. In my case, I have chosen to enter into the text and battle as a poet. This book, then, is a poem. And yet even the poem must rage against itself or it will die; it must move, enlarge itself, change shapes, then dissolve. So, too, I go in this book from personal narratives to dream journals, from internal monologues to stories told in the hard light of lowland villages; we rush into signs propped up by PEMEX that warn the intruder not to poach in the forests or interfere with the environment while the petrochemical colossus erects new refineries in the jungle. Other signs come at us, the tiny prophecies of a deaf-mute Mayan boy. "Jaguar Hotel," a play, emerges in the middle of the book. This particular section calls you to get up and act out the book, a portion of America, as it were, to recognize and physicalize that which is barely visible to us on this side of "high" America. At the end, a letter appears—to my friend from la selva, K'ayum Ma'ax. If you read it, are you K'ayum Ma'ax too? Look everywhere for the possibility of fire, for the possibility of a poem—this is my personal maxim.

My goals? the culture and literary critics ask. To go into America as I go into myself, I respond. I have a particular historical and psychic possibility, given my place as a Chicano. It is a life and cultural riddle that I have at hand, an American poetics of and for the twenty-first century. I am intent on elaborating on what Benjamin Alire Sáenz, the poet and novelist, states in his essay, "I Want to Write an American Poem." I say, "I want to write America." Not a Joycean, Ulyssean epic; there is another probability—a writing from Other locations, as Rigoberta Menchú suggests. My audience? All those interested in these reflections are invited to join me in a collective conversation of and for America; find more precise quandaries, finer fractures, tougher intimacies.

THE THIRD CONVERSATION

"How can I write of Mexico?" Juan said. He had just returned to California from an arduous trek to Chiapas. "With my bare hands, my two fists—with the guts of the people and gravel bits from the crazy roads." The task punished him and left him without what he seemed to need most—words. Big words embossed with agile meanings that would travel far and land softly on the shoulders of a student, a little girl, maybe a young woman about to reconsider her life or a sturdy professional in the sundry course of office chatter. The silvery words would fall casually into their ears, and then, after a pause, these careful terms would unwrap and explode. Juan wanted this explosion, and yet he had no idea how to light the fuse of letters.

"What about the Indian? Can the writer truly speak of revolution?" Juan smiled a wry smile. He knew that he was about to collapse; there was little room for North American writers to speak of Mexico and its concatenation of Indian archipelagos in a neocolonial choke chain. Juan's very status as a writer prospering in the ganglia of a superpower sabotaged his literary claims.

It was starting all over, he could taste it; this uncanny inclination to say something true; to cast out his soul and let it fly in all its multicolored vapors—with language. "Mirrors and mirror games." He laughed and fidgeted.

Juan was well aware that when he talked of Mexico, he was actually talking about Latin America. Juan laughed again. "I must really be stupid," he said. As soon as he mentioned Latin America, he would slip; he knew this. The rhetoric would falter and soon enough he would end up referring to Malaysia or the Philippines; each landscape was interchangeable, Third World borders seemed to be illusory—the border work was more like an Escher pattern superimposed throughout various zones of exploitation throughout the globe.

Juan had just arrived from his journey: Mexico City, Tuxtla Gutiérrez, San Cristóbal de las Casas—the highlands, the lowlands. His lips

11

were parched. Reddish flecks dotted his forehead where the tropical sun of southeastern Chiapas had burned his skin. Was the language on his face?

He was at his desk inside an ordinary three-bedroom suburban house in a small California town. "I have all the clues in my hand, I've had them for God knows how long." It was only last night, after his plane landed in San Francisco, that the pieces of the puzzle finally fell into place. He finally saw how he would gather all his experiences and recast every tiny moment in Chiapas that had whirled through his blood: from San Francisco to San Cristóbal de las Casas, then to Ocosingo, the gateway into the lowlands, and finally to the Lacandón jungle, to Nahá, one of two major Lacandón Maya villages. Juan meditated on the last vestiges of the lowlands, the wiry and blackened forests; he could see the tawdry rope of slavery and sickness tied around the wrists of every Tzotzil-Tzeltal and Lacandón Maya Indian in the landscape. The double knot of Ladino usury and Indian dependence stood in bold relief. He brushed his dark hair back, propped his glasses over the bridge of his nose. What of the wealthy Ladinos sympathetic to the plight of displaced campesinos and oppressed Indians? And the new class of wealthy Indians who feared any change in the social order that would interfere with their hard-won status? The meditation dissolved.

What writing? What language? Even the term "native" irritated him. He had nothing to say. Pure and simple. Nothing. Juan would have to invent a conversation in order to solve his predicament. An old conversation?

During the early summer of 1970, while living in Santa Monica and attending UCLA, Juan had begun the task of finding the terms for Mexico. These were the acid days, the Chicano movimiento days—Molotov cocktails hurled at Greek frats, high school blowouts in East L.A., and antiwar rallies. These were the days of truth, Quaaludes, and jazzy verbs for liberation. Black Power and salsa-blues bands. Just like that and pow! Juan tasted the flavors of the early seventies: poetry in prisons with a Gibson guitar strapped across his back, riffing with saxophone and congas in Farmworker camps. "Pow! Just like that." This was the manner in which Juan headed south from Los Angeles, to the center of the world, Mexico, for the first time. Everything pasted onto his eyes: old volumes of anthropology and archaeology on the aesthetics of Bonampak, Frans Blom and Gertrude Duby's 1940s list of jungle expedition supplies, Viet Nam black and green canvas boots, bulk rolls of Ilford film, the degree charts of rain, and the hollow-eyed gaze of the last five hundred Lacandón Mayas.

Now he found it difficult to plow through that romantic jumble. He needed the second conversation, a deeper connection—the circle of native faces, men huddled around little fires at the heights of the Sierra Madre, women praying hard in slanted twig shelters, speaking to the goddess of corn; an odd-shaped Lacandón tortilla from Nahá brushed with chili paste and washed down with a gourd of lemonade. Juan needed these fragile images in order to find his proper stance.

In 1970 in Tepic, Nayarit, Juan had met Ramón Medina Silva, a Huichol shaman who had been waiting for him downtown at the Instituto Nacional Indigenista. "Tauyepá, Father Sun told me that you were coming," Ramón informed him in the outskirts of the mestizo city. "Come back and visit me after you return from Veracruz and Chiapas. When you come back we will look over these yarn paintings and we will talk of the fire, the earth, and the road to the stars, the crystal shapes of the soul. When you come back." Juan left for the Atlantic coast, to northern Veracruz. "Let's say we have a date with someone we forgot on the road long ago," he said to his buddy Tomás when they arrived in Tuxpam, in time for the Flying Pole Ceremony of the Totonacs. They stayed and learned about the pole and the ritual fasts of the Totonac youth who lived in Poza Rica, a metropolitan maze of refineries and Ladino merchants, restaurants, and Indian barrios. It was the end of July. The road was half ocean and half ancient shrines, the sea falling away to the left and the jagged trail to Chiapas rising on the right. "No one will believe us when we get back to the States," Juan said to his partner, Tomás. He did not know what awaited them in San Cristóbal de las Casas, in the deeper terrain of la selva.

After a month in Chiapas, Juan had set foot in reality. He could not recognize the taste in his mouth—ecstasy, or was it anxiety? Squalor? A buzzing chain of humped humans appeared, some better off than others, rough copper skin shot into black string sandals; men and women like handsome ants with high cheekbones and sleepless eyes, cut with the sharp point of foreign whips and silent centuries—rebellion or oblivion?

After a series of accidents and small triumphs in Mayan country, Juan returned to Ramón in the sierra. Then he lay in the back of a Volkswagen bus, yellowish, bony, and fevered; then back in Los Angeles, home, for a while. This was his initiation into the complex of his identities as Chicano, Latino, mestizo, Indian, American—most of all American. Powerlessness in human form: dark-skinned powerlessness at the frayed edges of America; no doubt about it, he had found his Other home too.

For years Juan wandered. "I spent the whole day daydreaming," he would say to his lover. "I found a flower and crushed it against my mouth." "You always do that," Maga, the somber woman with long dark hair, told him. "I wanted to dissolve its colors, to taste true red and true gold. Its little life in my little life." This is how he carried himself. His college friends liked him and confided in him; the rest thought he was a clown, a smart clown good at words. For the next two decades he went about putting up his photos of the distant villages where he had stayed: Nahá, Lacanjá Chan Sayab, Joigelito, Chamula. He spoke of José Pepe Chan Bol, the Mayan Baptist preacher of Lacanjá Chan Sayab, the southern Lacandón village, with his tattered tunic and fine wristwatch, and how they talked about the invasion of chicleros and the rape of their women by Ladinos, and how all the while they were talking they heard the Beatles on a box radio in the night.

"Ramón was different," Juan said. "He was killed in 1971 in the Nayar mountains near his village, El Colorín, a year after I met him. The authorities in Tepic were jealous of him because he was gaining an international audience. Anthropologists and students were flocking to his side. 'These are the secrets,' he would say as he told us the stories of the First Ones. A year later, five shots—dead."

Juan wrote in a frenzy. Poems and antipoems—antipoems most of all. He was fixed on tearing the new language out of the old structures. Juan crossed the streets writing; he stood and wrote holding a miniature paper pad in his hand; jazz and poetry, blues and politics. He wrote on napkins, posters, anything that would take the ink. "I must feed the conversation, the way the Huichol feed Grandfather Fire, Tatewarí, at night, the way the women dance under a full moon, their bare feet on the earth, opal light in their eyes," he told Maga again and again.

In the winter of 1993, Juan journeyed back to Chiapas. "I just have to go," he said to Maga. "I don't know why or what I am going to do when I get there." He had not the slightest inkling that he was about to step into the last days of Chiapas as he had known it. Juan smiled and ambled to the south again, carrying a few bags and a 35 mm camera. He did not know, as he worked himself into the Chiapas lowlands, that a few feet behind his conspicuous figure (as much as he attempted to humble himself in order to slip further into the yellow-green scrim of Indian country) a campesino and Indian revolution hiccuped in the shadows of his fancy-colored backpack.

After a short stay in Chiapas, Juan returned to the States. Again he was caught up with the questions: Where is America? What is an Indian? Who am I? It was an odd maneuver to be a Chicano, a person of color, en route to a "native" topography. The most formidable folly had to do with swallowing the master's conquest language in order to liberate oneself, to initiate the process of resolving one's cultural disenfranchisement in the United States. "I have to become a trickster, a language saboteur," he said. Maybe this was another mirror game. Did he have to become a cross-eyed seeker of self? The path required fracture. He knew, as he had long ago, that first he must disrupt the terms, figures, and images of colonialism if he dared search for the way into America, a path leading back home.

Juan rested his head on Maga's chest and listened to the beating of her heart. "The second conversation," he said softly. Juan realized that he had been lost in the first conversation—the one about loss, genocide, the multiple fissures of America and its native people; the conversation about split cultures and hybrid men and women kicked-in against their Indian selves. Where was their love? The other conversation had not occurred to him. "Machines make love too." Juan could not believe he said this to Maga. Love between machines, between corporate fax voice boxes and military bulldozer teeth. The digitized machine erotica of computer chips and resource exploitation profit lexicons. This was not a language of redemption and social transformation. The terms and channels were corporate and political, and yet it was a language of fire. It ran its yellow-red spikes beyond the borders that riveted America a thousand times over.

The term Indian was not necessary in the second language. "It's funny, Maga. I don't have a word for Indian either, and I am not a machine. How can that be?" No terms for native, America, not even for Mexico—they were all collapsible, they were all quicksilver placeholders for globalized corporate interests. "Useless," he uttered to Maga as he stood up and faced the windows to the southern skies.

"They are like stars," Juan said. Maga knew he was talking about the usurped ones, the sucked-out Indian children, the aged mothers, and the young men with wiry-tree torsos. She stared at him. "Falling stars, rising stars. By the time we see them in their true light, they have shifted

into another sky, drifted far out of our reach. Into an unimaginable cosmos of abandonment and power."

"You haven't changed," she said, looking out the window pane with
him. "You said you were different now that you are back. But you are
still the same man that not too long ago wanted to save a sparrow. Remember, you found it in our backyard? You put it in one of my shoe-
boxes with a bubble of bread and a small dish of water. You didn't see
the claw marks under the wings? Instead, you went to bed and made
wild love to me. In the morning, the tiny bird lay on its side, eyes shut,
the wings quiet and still. This is your Mexico?"

Juan loosened his shirt collar, peered to the south. He took Maga's
hand in his. "They are looking this way too," he said."From the edges of
every border, they look back—mud and cardboard kingdoms, from a
busted makeshift hotel they pace; huddled, caught by surprise, by their
own hunger and history; a broken hotel, made of smoke, revolution, and
the strange intersections of global invasions. In every room there is an Indian, one with a VCR, another with an ancient machete, a missile, a fighting woman, a Ladino on his knees—you and me. Outside, the future
lurks and stalks."

Maga nodded her head. "You are quoting yourself, Juan. It is an old
poem you wrote years ago. 'The Mexicanos were being lured into a gold
hotel,' you said. That's not enough, Juan."

"I suppose you want me to talk about Frida Kahlo?" he asked Maga.
"'We are all condemned to be Fridas.' Is that what you want me to say?"
He knew Maga's point of view; they had gone over all this with coffee
and toast, in blues bars. Juan knew that the central column of our cultural
vertebrae had been shattered—much in the same way as Frida's own
spine and pelvis had been dismantled in a horrible bus accident when
she was eighteen—that we have no unified and authentic discourse of
what we are. All we know is that we have been tightened into a cast, our
realigned foreign body. And yet, from the inside, we know that we inhabit a radically different space. Juan knew this about Latin America. He
also knew that this could be said of any peoples at the margin of power.
"Because of the cast and the terrible accidents to our historical selves, we
go about immersed in the enterprise of self-portraiture; at every juncture,
we seek our shape, our face—right, Maga? Paradox and parody over-
whelm us: what we paint is seen as minute and gracious in comparison
to the full-bodied enterprise of the master painter, who seems to walk

about freely, scale walls, and launch his mediums and letters with such public gaiety and historical intelligibility."

Maga stared: "I know that rap." Juan shrugged his shoulders, sighed. "We are up against everything," Maga said in a deep voice. "Words, concepts, the sly throat of the new Mexican president, our own bogus leadership, if I can use the term leadership at all—the last quarter-inch of topsoil on this continent, the World Bank, Mexican billionaires with NAFTA teacups, military machines in every village; the whole universe when it listens passively; we are up against that too," she said. "Every time we say 'Indian culture' we lose ground, Juan. Every time we say those words we encourage a white-bearded God to wake up, rise, and prowl the pyramids and the basalt shrines in search of tropical converts. We give permission to New Age technofriars and culture clerics in diplomatic body wraps to scurry late at night poring over what they have gathered from their devoted Indian informants and most of all from our language about ourselves. How can we speak of a fettered Indian Latin America barely breathing within the inherited boundaries and systems of servitude, finca and hacienda labor credit-debt relations and credit by female rape? Who talks about this? The PRI? Have you heard their shit lately? They are saying that Mexico must honor its cultural patrimony—'honor,' they say, as they divert U.S. antidrug money and World Bank environmental funds for sniper work in the villages. Is this the 'Indian culture' you are talking about? Sparrows? Indians? You would like to put them in the same poem, wouldn't you? How do you talk about your own taste for an Indian paradise? Isn't this what we must fight against too? Have you heard of 'imperialist nostalgia'? It is the modern scurvy of those who live at the margins of this country. You think you are a suburban Zapatista, don't you? Let's see your ammo." They both laughed out loud. Then they both played with their hands and grew silent.

Days passed. Juan began to write; Maga worked on a new set of performance art pieces. Maybe the first conversation was his utopian quest in 1970 to the tropical jungle villages of Nahá and Lacanjá Chan Sayab, the story of the last Lacandón in the smoldering forest of charred caoba. Maybe his most recent journey was his second. The third one was locked up in the occasion of a smoldering Mayan and campesino revolution, a Mexico broken and splintered by complex socioeconomic disparities and global interventions. Would he speak of the million Tzotzil, Tzeltal, Tojolabal, and Chol—all the Maya who in many ways were at the mercy of this Lacandón "elite of five hundred" empowered by government environmental concessions and the monetary promise of logging?

"Where is the third conversation, what is it?" Juan asked Maga outside on a city avenue." She gazed hard into his wide-set eyes. "There must be a way to speak, to act," he said. Maga stopped and turned to him. Juan pressed his lips against hers, and for the moment all the words that he had searched for welled up in his heart.

I

Gathering a Mayan Repertoire

TUXTLA OIL FLOAT

I am going to where I am from.
I am fleeing from visions, fences
grinning from the post. Give me
a hole with a past to it. Fill up
this mess with your wicked engines.
　　　　—Lorna Dee Cervantes,
　　　　from "On Touring Her Hometown"

Floating in a blue taxi. From Tuxtla Gutiérrez to San Cristóbal de las Casas. Eighty kilometers in two hours and I would begin again.

I was leaning into the central highlands of Chiapas at the edge of southeastern Mexico. I recognized the narrow asphalt strip; as I went farther I looked down over the edge. Was this the Mayan edge? One hundred and twelve municipios, two-thirds Mayan speaking; one million Mayas churned their lives and sought out their souls. They split into linguistic quadrants—Tzotzil speakers in the western highlands, Tzeltal in the eastern slopes, toward the Lacandón selva. Farther northeast, near Palenque, the Chol, and south, toward Guatemala, the Tojolabal. All below me in the last ring of a Mexican Indian and campesino inferno.

Nine thousand feet above the sea, I was looking for something I left behind twenty-three years before; a stone upturned, smashed against a tree, a shoestring, a hazy smoke pattern hovering over the greenness; searching for reflections and refractions. Breathing in and taking the pine-scented air, the oak tree sap, the speckled milpa colors; leaning in and searching for the cloud and cave music, the underbrush twisting into the earth.

Since 1970 the oil boom, the OPEC crises, and Mexican President López Portillo's leap into rapid energy and oil development in southeastern Chiapas had taken their toll. This surge of hunger for the deep-energy syrup drove the Indians out of their hamlets in the highlands and pulled them into construction jobs where the government erected new hydroelectric power plants and where builders laid out new housing near the

21

Gulf Coast oil fields. The Mayan edge dwellers took up commerce.
They became fast-trading shippers driving trucks along the transport
routes where the oil business set its projects. They learned the new work
formulas along the dams of Angostura, Chicoasen, and Malpaso, stretching along the Grijalva River toward the Gulf. They were sucked into the
metropolitan centers of Villahermosa, Tuxtla Gutiérrez, and San Cristóbal.
As these developments went into high gear, southeastern Chiapas began
to supply the rest of Mexico with 50 percent of its energy and oil for ex-
port. The neat and erect Zinacantecos and Tzotzil-Tzeltal Indians were the
hidden figures behind the GNP. A new Indian class gained momentum
and distanced itself from the older Indian generations and from the Indian
communities that did not have access to the new opportunities.

Behind the mountains, in the deep valleys, there was a new kind of
indio—one who had gone to the outer reaches of Tabasco, into the So-
conusco, the Pacific coastal strip, into the lowlands, and had smelled the
oil and poured it over the face, had felt the bright stumps of pipe blow
their newfound blood into tanks and trucks and tubing. The new indio
possessed an anteater snout, one reshaped by a global political and economic impulse for energy resources. These indios felt the boiling under
their feet—an underground sea of petrochemical channels and sewers
and the complex systems of hydroelectric power. The energy development web spread and pushed under and over them like wild cancer eating away at the forests of precious hardwoods and most of all,
tierra,
más tierra.

What had happened to the highland Mayas since I left in 1970? After the 1982 debt crises, many indios in the highlands came back with
new ideas, with new ways of seeking money, with new investments in
trucking and motorized transport, new agricultural practices, with herbicides and chemical fertilizers so they could cultivate their forest lands
season in, season out. As corn production in Chiapas swelled to more
than 1.5 million tons in 1993, the gap widened between the wealthy and
the poor indio.

Maybe this was the key—the land and its new year-round harness:
what used to lie fallow was now being exploited year round. The impacts
of energy development in southeastern Chiapas were pernicious and exponential. And the lowlands? A day's journey to the northeast, the land of
the Lacandón Mayas, with its ever-diminishing rain forests—overrun by

colonists, displaced campesinos, exiles, and new PEMEX campamentos—was about to shrink to the size of a dollar bill.

From inside the soft taxi all I could see were the bodies—either standing in the usual manner by the road watching us make the curb or ascending into the mountains on trails that carried them further into their own lives. The Zinacantecos still wore their traditional hot-pink striped gavanes and their muslin pants and huaraches. Their woven hats were thin from a distance, tilted and still. Now they were standing by little wooden tables selling servilletas, bright-colored placemats for the passing tourist.

Under all of this, under the plasma of the fresh trees, the corn and bean milpas and the asphalt, there was a slow cable of siphoned oil and hydroelectric energy cutting at the yellow roots, eating away at the tiny reddish oval cells of the breathing body that sustains us all. My destination flared before me in the shambles of pushed-out Indians and knocked-out campesino populations, in their crazy traces imprinted over the entire region, in a familiar yet foreign terrain of Indian communities sliced by new wealth, bank accounts, and corporate firms. I was the lost partner in this tango of dislocations, this swivel beat of migrations guided by socioeconomic power and resource exploitation.

Coming home, somehow. As the century closed, it was now my turn to complete the circle, to make the infamous Chicano metaphysical U-turn. The taxi spun toward "El Sur"—toward San Cristóbal, the highlands, thereafter the lowlands. I was cutting toward the southern front once again.

JUAREZ GYPSIES

On the run. I am a Chicano manchild hovering over the hushed Mayan highland chasms; I slip into their wild greenness. But whose fast strokes are these? What urges and pulls me in these directions?

As always, I am falling forward, my head bent, eyes caught up in the fast colors, the blur of familiar and strange shapes, as I have done since I was a kid in the early fifties wandering through the San Joaquín Valley and southern mountain villages of California—in motion, spinning and playing in farmworker camps where my mother, Lucha Quintana, and my father, Felipe Emilio Herrera, aged campesinos, hung onto the edges of small towns like Fowler, where I was born by chance, out of wedlock, on the run to Parlier, Delano, and MacFarland.

My father's "legitimate" family lived in southern New Mexico. He would visit them occasionally in the summer, take gifts, bring me T-shirts from Arizona, postcards from the Carlsbad Caverns. He hovered, in his own way, between families, the first and the second, between me, his last child, and himself. My mother accepted this arrangement; she knew he loved us and would stay with us. He was an older man, jovial, kind, wise, and branded by a desire to lead us from one town to another. "Every time you move, your cells change, your whole body changes inside," he would repeat, his hazel eyes moving with a burst of energy. And he had a knack for searching out particular mineral springs and the healing waters of the ocean: "Up there in the mountains, near the Ramona Indian reservation, there are ojos de agua, water springs, that will take care of your pains, Luchita." My mother loved the idea of magical waters for her ailments, and in the end she gave in to my father's quixotic visions.

We moved to Ramona one year and lived behind Mr. Weed's ranchhouse, facing ten acres of the driest dirt on the planet. You bought bottled spring water or walked through the orchards with an empty bucket to the nearest sundry-store faucet at the entrance to town. Absence, dislocation, abrupt movement, rose-colored fantasies, spiritual calls, and

24

Lucha Quintana, Juárez, Chihuahua, circa 1936.

Felipe Emilio Herrera (right) with José Barrera, Denver, Colorado, October 15, 1904.

the burning pull to return to sacred vistas were key emotional accelerators and creative triggers in my interior world. Later these early forces and psychic pulleys would power up as poems, theater work, and a foolhardy and feverish penchant for wild escapades and adventures. My travel fate was hidden in the tiny grapevines, the pungent tomato jungle, my father's separations, and vagabond campesino maps; my wondering theme was in the frosted morning onion patch and the forlorn corn milpas abandoned to the mysterious and intelligent spider spinning webs between the sweet dark leaves. I was being true to myself on this road into Mayan territory. My theme was still personal and campesino, still in the realm of family rupture and at the edges of national power and city ambitions.

As an undergraduate at UCLA in 1969, all I needed to leap to the southernmost regions of Indian Mexico was my anthropology professor's comment that there were only a few hundred Lacandón Mayas left in Chiapas. A year later, outfitted with old Army fatigues, miniature machetes, mosquito nets, antiviper first-aid kits, and Viet Nam tropical combat boots, I jumped out of a junky Cessna into Lacanjá Chan Sayab, one of the two major Lacandón Mayan villages in southeastern Chiapas. My school chum, Tomás Mendoza Harrell, followed me. (Himself a world traveler, he wrote me the last time we communicated from a small island near Sao Paulo, Brazil.) Yet what began as a personal and political quest into Lacandón land, a logical step in the process of cultural inquiry into one of Mexico's smallest Mayan groups pushed out to the edges of survival, became upon my arrival a radical life connection. From that point on I realized that I would not forget the Lacandón in the lowlands nor the Mayas in the highlands. To read about their "way of life" and spew Chicano "azteca" poetry jive was blasphemy, and to assign the oppressed Maya the honorable position of ancestors was a culture crime—if I did not take action. So I return to connect again, to speak again, to write again, to reunite with my other family, the bastard daughters and sons unclaimed and ignored by official Mexico and the uptown, buttoned, mainstream world of Indian lovers and Indian haters.

To roam, to wander, to dream, to lose myself, to break deeper into soulful worlds—the themes have not changed. Being a child of migrant farmworkers made sudden change a delicacy. I stayed in the labor camps only long enough to know the names of a few farmworker children: Esteban, with a crewcut and Levi's cut-offs; María Luisa, with braids and a big forehead, the girl who gave me my first kiss; Toña, the skinny tomboy who hated skirts; and little buck-toothed Sonny, who helped me bury a charred lizard that had burned in a shanty fire. After we patted down the lizard shrine with leaves and clumps of dirt, we sang "Silent Night" for its safe journey to the next world. I never stayed long enough to see blossoms on the crops my father and mother sowed. We were migrantes, simply. Motion and new travel stories and grape fields fed our hunger for life.

I go south to San Cristóbal bearing vestigial images belonging to another sphere. The hospital bedside of my father reappears. Gangrene from diabetes has mangled his legs, and one is amputated; his kidneys are failing; his campesino days have gone up in smoke to the big city of San Diego, where we finally settled after jaunting through the migrant camps of the San Joaquín Valley until I was eight years old. My father passes away at eighty-two with my mother at his side. Sixteen years old, midnight: I am holding my mother's tiny frame as she trembles and cries into my shoulder and the darkness of our two-room apartment on Eleventh Street, downtown. The relay of family jaunts comes to an end, and a new cyle begins.

Twenty years later, after moving from San Diego to San Francisco's Mission District, where my Aunt Lela and Uncle Beto lived, my mother dies from pneumonia. Since my mother's death in 1986, I have been busy going through my warehouse of locked secrets, unfinished business, and pain. The pain follows me, I write it, and it leaves. I am left alone. The task of unraveling my personal history, the flame that burns in the left side of my chest, begins; an orphan is by nature a seeker of other selves, a night gazer with fire in the blood.

My father, Felipe Emilio, and Lucha come to me now as we swerve past Joigelito, a few miles from San Cristóbal. They are with me in some way in this Chiapas Indian void. We would take long evening summer walks in San Diego, after we had left behind jeep rides, Army truck hauls, makeshift trailer nights. The walking was our urban migration shuffle. Instead of vineyards and orchards, we passed by storefront windows, stopping to inspect Schwinn bicycles and Sears and Roebuck furniture sales, to gawk at Swiss watches and emerald bracelets whose qualities and blemishes we would ably discuss as we passed into the next city block, the next field of asides, the boomcrash of truck traffic heading toward the piers at the end of Broadway. You could see them next to the shadowy profiles of Navy cruisers and destroyers, past the Spreckles downtown theatre and the orange lamplit boulevard studded with Navy lockers and neon tattoo parlors. This was my little drop of Mexican America in the early sixties. Our last walking stop was the Greyhound depot, that amazing, brilliant modern ranchería of poor travelers carrying tricolored jute bags to the south and flat-top white shirt and Levi's seekers to the north.

So there I am in "El Perro," as my father called the Greyhound station, yelling out like the announcer in the speaker box: "Oceanside, Bakersfield, door number five; Needles, Barstow, door number seven. The Los Angeles bus will be loading at door number one in ten minutes. Please have your tickets ready." At the jukebox, drop a dime for Elvis and another for Jackie Wilson, one more for Brenda Lee's "Sweet Nothings"; run over with a dime to the baseball machine with scuffed iron men swinging stiff bats at a large silver ball bearing rolling past second base. Now in the photo booth: spin the seat to my height and practice funny Jerry Lewis faces for five snapshots in sepia. Back on the woodgrain pews of the depot, which remind me of the ones at Our Lady of Guadalupe Church in Logan Heights, the Mexican and black barrio where I attended Lowell Elementary School and sang "Swing Low, Sweet Chariot" for Mrs. Sampson's third-grade class.

At the Greyhound pews my mother conjures stories about my uncles again. There was Uncle Beto, the hard worker who in the forties moved from El Paso to San Francisco. A warehouseman and a disk jockey. She says, "Your Uncle Beto created Radio KOFY in a busted garage somewhere in Chinatown in San Francisco, and he did the same in Juárez after we had come up from Mexico City. But it was your Uncle Geno's idea to travel to the North. The idea came to him when we were all living in 'El Niño Perdido,' a barrio in Mexico City. He wrote to the president of Mexico and requested a leave so that he could join the American Army and pull us out of our misfortune. It sounds crazy, but it worked." My mother nods her head in wonder. "And that's what happened. He was sent to Fort Bliss, in El Paso."

She reminds me of Uncle Beto's early discoveries: "In Juárez, your Uncle Beto had his own radio show called 'El Barco de la Ilusión.' You know, he's the one who introduced Tin-Tan to the public, the famous Mexican comedian and movie star."

"El Barco de la Ilusión," I mouth to myself. Sounds like magic, the "Ship of Illusion." While my father was away visiting friends and family

or leaving in search of "healing waters," my mother would take out her
Brownie Kodak camera and we would take snapshots in the park and city
streets. Later we would return to her photo album, where she had col-
lected family picture dating back to the late nineteenth century. My
mother traveled with silver print images and stories.

I still keep my mother's old photo album with its black feltlike paper
leaves, spotted and torn at the edges, missing its front and back covers
and some of the pages, loose and stuffed in one of her five-and-dime yellow plastic bags that I inherited. Like the Greyhound tales, the album stories captivated me, sparked my imagination, and nurtured my love for
language and fast changes. My mother reintroduces her family: "Here's
your grandmother Juanita, who you are named after. This is your grandfather, Alejo Quintana, a pulquería worker, who died of exhaustion at
the age of forty shortly after I was born in 1907." We pause a while, gazing at his dark features. "Here are my brothers: Geno, the oldest, who
joined the U.S. Army like I told you. I don't know what would have happened to us. I would never have met your father Felipe in El Paso." Another pause: "You wouldn't be here." Back to the picture stories: "This is
Roberto, who was always at work on a crazy invention, distributing
newspapers in a Model T, imagine. Here's your Uncle Vicente, the artist,
who made toys out of wood in El Paso, painted murals, carved figures
out of soap, clay, and plaster, anything, who dreamed of going to Paris
but settled in New York City for a while, where he drew cartoons for the
tourists and sold fast bullfighter paintings in the delis." My Aunt Aurelia is the stern sister. She is taller than my mother and possesses the ability to tell you the ugly truth directly to your face. She is standing behind
my mother and my grandmother Juanita, all dressed in black with sharp,
sad, angry eyes as they stop for a moment "en la linea" and are ordered
get their picture taken by the Juárez border officials in the early twenties.

My mother describes herself as a tiny baby. There is no photograph.
"I was so small that my father, Alejo, would say to my mother, 'You can
carry her in a tompiate.'" (A tompiate was a handmade basket used for
clothes or picnics in those days.) We laugh at the idea of a baby in a tompiate. In an oval brownish photo, grandfather Alejo is a handsome man
with a full mustache, dark eyebrows, and large sad eyes, an Emiliano Zapata face, a young man in deep thought. You could easily mistake him
for a Mexico City dandy, a classy gentleman, except his eyes are set on
something deeper or ancient or somber. Maybe it is the specter of Mex-

ico a few years before the revolution; maybe it is his own fate and that of his family of eight, about to begin the long and unexpected trek to "El Norte" not long after his death.

I go over these trails: my father's campesino path, my mother's jaunt north from the lowlands of America, my mother's Army family, my father's orphanhood. Once, at the depot, he recounted his fate as an orphan child to Will Kelly, a friend and former neighbor. The two still often met at the fountain in the plazita, the city's old town square, right across from Bradley's Burgers and the Cabrillo Theater. He said to Mr. Kelly, the Irishman dressed in a blue suit and white shirt, "I jumped a train from Chihuahua to the States at fourteen." Then he added, "My mother, Benita, died while giving birth," and his eyes watered. In the album I turn to a photograph where my father stands, maybe twenty years old, with a friend, José Barrera, posing in a dark, worn suit and a short tie, hat to the side, gazing into the studio camera's eye. The margin of the worn picture reads, "Denver, Colorado, 1904."

As I write I glance up at my mother's photo above my computer. She stands with both hands on her hips while her steel-string guitar rests on the ground, held in check by the tilt of her right hand. "Become an actor, a singer, how about a dancer? Yes, a dancer," my tiny mother would advise me, herself gazing at this very photo. "I always wanted to join the theater, sing and travel, but your uncles didn't want this. They warned my mother, Juanita, 'Don't let Lucha get mixed up with these oddballs doing vaudeville. Who knows how she'll end up?'" The guitar was the reservoir of her unfulfilled desires, the punishing repressions. To this day I have two guitars, a nylon string and a Fender electric. My first was my mother's gift when I was sixteen. I sing her corridos, I create my own tunes; more than anything else, my writing is my song. Our melodies resemble each other, and then they go their own way.

In the photograph my mother is dressed as a gypsy in a nameless and nondescript Juárez barrio alley: long pearl necklace, furled print skirt, puffed flowery blouse, a proud flamencolike stance, a curl of hair on her forehead. She looks away from the camera, à la Gloria Swanson and Libertad Lamarque; she is haughty on a harsh sun-drenched day in 1936. Juárez gypsy. As the Tuxtla taxi blurs through the narrow highlands road, the images burn above me and float below me.

I am en route to the homeland. Is it south? Is it north? Is it the motion in between? One hundred years of wandering, walking, sleeping, and waking up in the middle of the night, asking for directions to the next crop, the bus to the next small town, the next escape into fullness, a forgotten family in the center of things, toward another invention and intervention of places, art gadgets, jars of magic water, neon blue sailors dancing on strange piers, a Top 10 rock 'n' roll jukebox bopping through my teen romance head. My homeland shifts and disintegrates as soon as I touch ground, as soon as I name it. The narrative switches back into the corrido of the Colonial Culture Extractor, or should I say the postmodern Chicano road warrior in ragged pants and Coleman trail boots holding on to the Goddess of Fracture.

Grandfather Alejo's grave and grandmother Juanita's tomb are under me somewhere south of Mexico City, in a barrio appropriately named "El Niño Perdido," the lost child. I am that child, as San Cristóbal comes into view, as the taxi driver swerves past the Fray Bartolomé de Las Casas monument at the entrance of the city. San Cristóbal looks almost the same as it did in 1970—the short streets, the kiosk next to the smoke-daubed cathedral, a sweeping sky over the highlands mountains to the east, the hotels bristling with foreigners, and the carmine-colored muslin suit Indians; always the Indians. I want to take a photograph but I don't; instead I tell the driver to cut through the small talk and cobbled streets, straight to the House of the Jaguar, Na Bolom.

K'AYUM ON THE DOOR

I am facing the door of the dream Trudi Blom made with her bare
hands and Frans Blom's inner fire—a monastery, bought in 1950 for sixteen hundred pesos, at Avenida Vicente Guerrero no. 33, San Cristóbal
de las Casas.

Starting in the early forties, Frans and Trudi were the first to begin
and sustain the Lacandón research enterprise through this monastery reshaped as Na Bolom, a museum, cultural center, and tourist hotel named
after the native and nearly eradicated jaguar, Bolom. When I arrived here
for the first time in 1970, I was taken aback; the rough archives, the
boundless stacks on the "native" overwhelmed me. What was lacking in
the bookshelves at the UCLA library was abundant as bougainvillea at
Na Bolom. And the "native"? As I gazed around the hotel that year, I
noted that the Zinacantecos and Chamulas were accepted at the margins,
seen more as "folk" fodder for tourist consumption than as subjects with
wills of their own, residents of a territory laced with deities in their own
name, a people with an overarching history of oppressive visitations. Lacandón Mayas were kindling for the hearth of the Na Bolom enterprise;
"good acts" in the form of gifts and Western commodities had made the
villages more dependent on the culture and power of the touring "investigator" and his ilk of would-be Indian caretakers; the scrolls of "rescue" language uttered at academic and political campaign podiums had
merely stamped a fashionable liberal Indianism on the Bolom center and
possibly on its allys and opponents, the brokers and agents of govern-
ment-sponsored culture programs and projects in the region. Folk talk
and folk do-goodism rarely effect deep transformation for the "folk" in
question. Na Bolom was in many ways a Mayan folk castle. Was I walking into another Mayan museum machine—except, in this case, one that
props, stuffs, and displays the living? Perhaps I was wrong. An undergraduate in social anthropology must not rely on intuition or, most of all,
on what he sees. But now I was returning as a poet, and a poet does rely
on intuition and, most of all, on the eyes—all of the eyes.

33

The door was ajar. The lock was broken, and the house was quiet in the late afternoon. Took a few steps inside. Under a foyer: unseen and almost hidden, an arching entry with plaques, photographs, and documents on the walls enveloped me. The photograph to my right lured me with its frankness and casual faces. Evon Z. Vogt, the Harvard anthropologist and founder of the Harvard Chiapas Project in Zinacantán, stood with a group of students. George Collier, one of my Stanford professors, smiled in his white shirt and khakis, standing a few feet from the Mexican anthropologist and, at that time, local director of the Instituto Nacional Indigenista, Alfonso Villa Rojas. The typed date on the photo had faded. 1964? Not sure. Who read these photographs, who remembered?

To my left, higher up, a wide yellow parchment honors K'ayum Ma'ax with the prestigious Premio de Chiapas, an award made annually by the state government. Was K'ayum still there? Still in the lowland village of Nahá, where he played the flute and stood in front of a menacing puzzle of twisted vines and windswept twigs. He is the boy who pointed me to the gnarled flesh of a fallen Cessna engine propped up like a stele, a monument to a lost American civilization of progress and archaeological hunger—a native landscape in reverse.

K'ayum is the only one I think of—the others are nebulous, scattered throughout the Lacandón jungle. It wasn't that we played along the rough open trails of the village without a care in the world, or that I stood with him at the translucent green world milpa where his brothers cut and stacked cane for the making of arrows for the next season hunting the jabalí. And it wasn't because there I finally I met his father, Viejo Chan K'in, the elder and leader of the village, keeper of the sacred stories, histories, last in the line of the great *t'o'ohil* spiritual leaders and guardians of the Maya tradition; or that I followed K'ayum into his family's open-air kitchens and stood dumbfounded and awed at the familiar and strange connections between his world and my migrante campesino parents' life. Maybe my attraction for K'ayum simply had to do with being in his presence, in an abrupt jumpcut away from my Chicano machinations, my serious "culture work," my California-boy-in-search-of-his-roots game to my motion as a human being again. I could truly begin: a man filled with more contradictions than connections to K'ayum and his land. My journey started with him, those few days in the summer of 1970, at that moment. After a pause of almost a quarter century, I was going to begin again. But first, I thought, I must find him, somewhere in the new ruins, a few miles from Guatemala. Was K'ayum still there?

A receptionist greeted me, a Chamula woman dressed in a dark blue Chamula skirt that had been trimmed and made to look Ladino. "My name is Martina," she announced in a quick flurry of words, and led me to my room in the back of the building. "I am going to give you the Chamula room," she said, adding, "If the toilet doesn't work, let me know." Then she handed me two large bronze keys, one to the main door and the other for my one-room house.

A little museum of Chamula photos was displayed on the walls of the room, which also contained Indian rugs, a large red bed framed by thick black wooden beams, an antique armoire, and a fireplace filled with wood and kindling. Next to the bed was a short wooden desk over-looking a window to the east.

The air was cool. I knew that I was going to burn wood every night until the time came for me to leave in mid-January. Time had stood still in the museum machine. The colossal timepiece monastery-museum was constructed with an exoticized web of Mayas, always on the verge of extinction, always banished from the policed and authentic beat of "civilized" time and space. This was the starting point, my headquarters.

RAIN FOREST DONATION BOX

After a few days in San Cristóbal, I met Nelly Maldonado, for many years one of Trudi's close Ladina friends. Nelly reminded me of my Aunt Lela living in the blown-out sections of San Francisco's Mission District. Nelly wore a black embroidered shawl, a striped jersey dress, and a dark sweater. Her face was kind and had the peculiar ingrown mercy and hushed strength that most Mexican women of her generation displayed. I recognized this smoldering power imbued with religious piety as my mother's gift to me—a gift that I had fought with, honored, detested, and, in rare moments of forgiveness, accepted. Nelly wore her hair in a woven bundle covered by a light scarf. She whispered and moved her eyes from one side to the other.

We were alone in the main office. The light was feathery, the large windows wide open near the high ceiling behind her. Listen:

> *El Viejo Chan K'in lives and still works la milpa. They say he's one hundred years old. I don't know; maybe it's true. He still works la milpa. Trudi lives too, but she is different now. She rarely comes out of her room. See, over there? The room with the "Feliz 91" painted on the crown of the door, see it? She's ninety-two years old now, you know. A couple of years ago she let go of this place, this beautiful house. She couldn't move around anymore, you know. Na Bolom was taken over by a man that Trudi invited. Armodio, they call him. Then he gave the administration job to a woman who has turned it into a hotel. That's all, a hotel. She doesn't even allow the Lacandones to stay in the Ocosingo Room that Trudi always kept for them. Now they huddle in that old corner room over there, across from Trudi's quarters. It's dirty. They don't get any maid service, no free food at the kitchen like the rest. K'ayum Ma'ax is very mad. That's why he doesn't come anymore. Yo me he envejecido aquí, I have grown old here. Look at me.*

36

Maybe I should have got that job—you know, as the administrator. Things would be different. What can I do? I live in the back, a little farther back than your room. Maybe I could have gotten that job. But the new one . . . she has it. You see the donation box on this desk? People come from all parts of the world and put money in it. "For the Rain Forest," it says. They come from all over the world—Germany, Italy, France. From Los Estados Unidos, from Sweden and England. They put their money here, in this little box, for the rain forest. See how pretty it is painted. The money never gets there. There is no rain forest fund of any kind; it is all a sham. You should talk to the others. Maybe you can meet Cindy and Oscar; they are here as students. They get free room and board as long as they give full credit to Na Bolom and give us their research when they are done. We always have some students staying with us. They study the Indians. Right now Cindy and Oscar are in Nahá. Yesterday they went to visit K'ayum Ma'ax. They'll be back tomorrow. If you want to go into la selva, take a regalito, a pack of cigarettes, they like that there. Cindy and Oscar can help you get there. Maybe they'll go with you too. They're nice kids. You wouldn't believe it, PEMEX came in two years ago and dumped a load of money on the Lacandones. They came to Lake Ocotal. Some of the Lacandones bought TV's, satellite dishes, and radios. This is just a hotel now, that's all it is. I should have received a better post, maybe. The woman that runs this place, ella no tiene visión de algo más allá, she has no vision of what will take this place a little further. When you go to Nahá, you are not going to recognize it. You see these mahogany idols that the Lacandones make, the ones hanging on the wall, by the Zinacanteco shorts—these red bead necklaces? It's not going to last, all of it will go soon. K'ayum got the Chiapas Prize, you know. The mayor in Tuxtla Gutiérrez gave him a diploma and eight million pesos.

I knew Nelly had more to say. She stopped herself when she heard someone coming. She was in hiding in her own house. She folded her hands and looked down. Nelly turned her face to one side to see who was coming. She wrung her hands like rags, but she kept her voice steady, did not allow it to break. I sensed that Trudi was also kept in hiding in her own house. It was true; the walls were gray and had been sealed with a wry smile, a hushed cloth of abandonment—buried frenzy.

There was a deep scream bubbling up from the clean brick floors. Nelly had no reason to disclose so much to a stranger, to me, but she did. Something inside of her was waiting to tell someone a fragment of her story, someone with a mother and an aunt who resembled her.

EATING TORTILLAS 160 KILOMETERS NORTH OF GUATEMALA

At the corner of Calle Vicente Guerrero and Calle Diego Dugelay, a few blocks from the zócalo, an Indian woman sold tortillas from a large basket. She was weaving a thin cloth tied to her waist, bright red strings and electric blue silklike thread. She pulled out from herself, against herself; she unraveled the colors and wove them with her thin hands, looking down at them from time to time.

Something was wrong with her eyes. They were yellow and full of fluid. The small Indian woman said nothing as I approached. Nothing. She wove strings and sold tortillas. ¿Cuánto? I asked. "Two thousand pesos," she said in a weak voice. Gave her three thousand and took the soft stack rolled in a square of old paper.

Walked and chewed the tortillas, tried to push the food down my throat. Even though I was ravenous, even though I chewed hard, I wrestled with the corn paste in my mouth. It went down in clumps. Some of it stuck to the inside my cheeks, some of it dissolved on my tongue and stayed there; the rest knotted itself in the middle of my throat. Even though I had not eaten since leaving Tuxtla (other than a teaspoon of granola from my backpack), something was bruising me and did not allow me to chew and swallow. It was forcing me, against my will, to spit everything out. Most of all it wanted me to spit myself out. The tortillas wanted to turn me over, upside down, with the guts out, with the fluid out too, like the woman kneeling on the curb, pulling strings out of her belly, selling them as ribbons or belts. Something didn't permit me to swallow, to fill myself, to become solid; it wanted me to spit, to drench myself, to scream, to sing, with the head up, with the body open—an unfurled blending into the cobbled street.

39

GATHERING A MAYAN REPERTOIRE

I realized how to gather power in San Cristóbal. In 1970, I didn't know this was possible; could feel it but I could not see it. Now, as I walked into Mexico, as I walked into my Indianness, I gathered aromas from the mercados and plants alongside the road; I gathered phrases and words from the street vendors, I gathered whispers and glances from the Indian women, the shape of the weights held on their backs and bosoms, their quick talk and agile finger language; I gathered their colors, in woven textile patterns of blossomed toads, rabbits, and the Earth Lord stitched into the red-yellow maze of a blouse; the little fragments that entered my dreams from clay gourds and lost spoons on the sidewalk. I gathered silently and I gathered loudly, I gathered high up in the pines among rounded creatures with wise beaks and talkative rivers in their wingspans, down below from the split ground and from busted house walls fading into Chagalls and burnt umber Dalís, I assembled my repertoire; circled my face and chest and stomach and legs with these new figure sticks, given without force, in the sundry instants of walking and being.

FRAY BARTOLOME DE LAS CASAS
Landscape with Graffiti

At the northern entrance to the city, the stone statue of Fray Bartolomé de Las Casas, the Indian protector of the sixteenth century, stood above me.

In 1524, under the leadership of Diego de Mazariegos, the Spanish came in and dismantled the Indian landscape, renaming it Villa Real. In the 1530s they established it as Ciudad Real, and by 1536 about fifty Spaniards had settled in the area and begun to work their encomiendas. Soon enough the encomienda, the institution through which conquistadores won jurisdiction over native populations as a reward for undertaking conquest at their own expense, would be challenged by Bishop Bartolomé de Las Casas. By 1544 Las Casas, a Dominican, had arrived in

Star.

Ciudad Real and together with other jurists had lobbied against the encomienda and succeeded in having the Crown promulgate the New Laws (Leyes Nuevas) of 1542 in order to restrict and eliminate the encomienda. Encomenderos held rights to receive tribute, which they generally exploited in labor and in kind. In 1824, when Chiapas became part of Mexico, Ciudad Real was renamed San Cristóbal de Las Casas in honor of Bartolomé de Las Casas.

I followed along the Pan American highway that leads to Comitán. There were open fields to the west, and children played soccer and basketball on large plots of land. I wanted to get away from the tangled froth of Indians and Ladinos bleeding onto each other, from the thick fur of tourists and social scientists. The concrete foundation of a building that no longer existed opened up before me.

Three columns jutted into the air with bent steel rods breaking out of the stone looking for a lost ceiling, nerve meters without numbers. Wire steles, indecipherable concrete and steel monuments for the winds, lovers, and strangers. The structure bore inscriptions in graffiti red:

Poyín

Poyín

Star

Lobo.

Poyín is a white-skinned Mexican boy who wears a chupón around his neck, a plastic baby teething toy now in high fashion in San Cristóbal. The secundaria kids say that you can buy them at the music store on the corner of the zócalo next to El Faisán, the local high school hangout. They even have a bajo sexto, a Mexican ten-string bass guitar, on sale for 180,000 pesos. Cheap. Poyín is chubby and lets a few of his friends into his innermost intimacies. He prays hard at the Santo Domingo Church on the northern edge of town. He prays for a Walkman and a new bicycle with plastic ribbon around the spokes, and he prays that he doesn't have to walk so far to school. Pretty soon, he says, he'll have a girlfriend just like Star does. Star is lean, and he has a gaunt fawn-colored face and deep black hair. He always wears acid-washed jeans and T-shirts pressed with the names of the latest bands from D.F.—like Bostic, like Maldita Vecindad. Star says he's going to be an accountant; he's not going to slip into the sadness that fills Lobo's eyes. Lobo sells Tzotzil coffee bags to tourists. Most of the time you can find him in the back room of La Delicia, a coffee storefront on the way to the boys' training school, a few miles south of the city by the road to Comitán. Lobo wears gray clothes and an eerie smile that no one understands. He used to sell chicles at the kiosko with the other Indian boys, but now he's moved up to coffee. Once in a while he comes to the soccer fields to see old zócalo buddies, pressures them to come with him so they can all spray their names on the busted palisade in the middle of nowhere, in the center of a city of multiple displacements and conquests.

In the sky, the clouds climbed into frayed ships and explosions of woolly currents. There was a horse behind the soccer players. I stepped into an old school yard. The children swayed easily and weren't bothered. Young lovers leaned with a casual air on whitewashed walls as I passed through and kept going.

TOURIST STOP BY THE CHRISTOPHER COLUMBUS DEPOT

Stop at Avenida Insurgentes: Insurance signs decorated with Batman capes and Catwoman eyes, the sweet burnt-maize grills and rows of Chamula women sitting on the ground, legs sprawled, weaving little things with patience and hard hands. Through an open doorway past the Dulcería Chiapas store, two women in skirts held hands and walked into the back court of the large vivienda. The sign above them reads: "Parafinas. Wax." I don't know if they lived there or if they were buying wax in bulk, for candles or for healing figures. Kept on walking to the northern edge of town. Everything in plastic:

buckets in racing green,
flamingo pink sheets for the roof,
lemon yellow glasses and see-through
light blue bags for clothes and bread

and thin papaya orange boxes for pencils and nails. Everything in plastic so that San Cristóbal can stretch its soul. A goldfish, a marimba diskette, a finely tabulated German entry of travelers checks for the ancient computers of the Banco Serfín where the Indian guards take pride in their fully automatic silver machine guns.

A tilting mercado.

A worn warehouse with nylon bags hanging at its various entrances. Tomato stalls and onion pyramids, squash rivers and romero bushels.

More plastic mixed with sausages, black seeds mixed with radishes, sacks of dry chilis mixed with aged hands and bone knees, zarape stacks mixed with the glare of an army tank in the middle of the street.

Just followed the trail down the sloped street to the north; roads spread into gullies, a few scattered cobblestone houses, an abandoned handball court, and maize fields swished by the wind.

44

ZEN HOUSE FACING TZONTEVITZ

(Sacred Mountain of the Chamula)

Faltered for a moment or two.
I noticed the old colonial house where I had stayed in 1970.

When we were out of money for the hotel, we happened to meet a Jewish rock guitarist named Jeff who loved James Taylor and who had rented the whitewashed ranch house of a Zen Buddhist americano, a local. Jeff let us stay a couple of weeks and offered to drive us back to L.A.

The old James Taylor studio had suffered the weather. Only the road to the mountain remained the same. These were the same mountains settled by people moving up from the jungle lowlands about A.D. 500. They were the same mountains with the same mountain gods.

A beaten road lay ahead: the same road where, every morning, Chamula women come down the mountain into town pinnated with plastic sacks of woolen cloth, garments, tourist ware, baskets and pots, fruits and vegetables. This naked gravel is a painful strip of memories. Until recently Indian women on this road were ransacked by atajadoras, Ladina women who were free to tease them, force them to sell their goods at a low price, or simply to steal their food and crafts. Ladinas stalked them and stole their materials and produce under the terms of the unwritten widow's law, according to which any Ladino widow could pilfer the goods of the Indian women vendors in town. The practice was similar to one prevalent in the 1960s and before when Ladina and Indian women, mostly San Feliperos who ran the market stalls in San Cristóbal, hustled Mayan women and men of their goods at or beyond the outskirts of town. With the growth and influence of the Instituto Nacional Indigenista and the Departamento de Asuntos Indígenas, the atajadora practice has ceased, and Indians have come to dominate the marketplace in the city.

This road was an innocuous reminder of the tight volley of violence between the Ladino and the Tzotzil-Tzeltal *bats'il winik* and *bats'il ants*— "true man" and "true woman." The road was a reminder of how las mujeres, especially the Indian women, the most oppressed sector of Mexican society, turned upon one another for a bundle of corn, a small bag of black wool.

Jeff's colonial house was a bitten box of four half-rooms, weeds, upturned bricks, sad mounds of lime rubble, and shattered Spanish tile. It sheltered crushed boxes and ragged pillows stuffed in bags, brooms, mops, and an inventory of cobwebs and fly-specked windows. But nothing with music. Nothing with sweat or sex or soft hands. Someone lived there long ago. I know, I remember. The Zen man lived well and drank clear water in an earthen jug. He paced his hand-laid Indian floors and rejoiced at his vegetable gardens in the back. His lover lived with him on occasion, when she visited from the United States. She told him that he was too lonely, that he was getting old, but he listened with the tiny ears of the monk-poet, the banker-dreamer. He listened well to her words and her auburn shadows. He found her in the grasses after she was gone, a silvery beetle in his pear tree, a quick phosphor vapor rising from his sunbathing patch.

He was doing well alone. He was writing letters as never before and rereading them at night. He would walk into town and the merchants would salute him, knowing that he was a foreigner. And yet they knew that he was arriving at that point all foreigners must come to; it was a point of loss and renewal; his language was changing. He even took to wearing black most of the time. They called him the Buddhist, they called him el hombre solo. He lived here for years. He spoke Tzotzil to the Chamula women coming down from the sacred mountain. He traded things with them. One time, as he bought eggs and four yards of brown wool, he gave the Indian woman an old Spanish primer. He was that way.

Then one day he rented his house to a New York musician named Jeff. Jeff arrived in a yellowish Volkswagen bus and spoke with an odd accent. Then Jeff brought me to his house and showed me the monk-poet's domain. I slept in the back house admiring the clay figurines on the red clay end tables by the bed. I enjoyed the musk-scented evening by the nestled fires at the foot of the maid's quarters. A month or so later, I left with Jeff and Tomás en route to Los Angeles.

No one knows what became of the monk-poet. No one around here could tell me what happened to him or about the house; did he sell it as he had planned, eight thousand pesos? I didn't know if this was the place where all this might have happened. The road felt the same. One of these four rooms must have been the place where we all told our stories.

Followed the road farther north. Across the way there was a small colonia of new houses for the middle class. The architect had designed this tract as an island city of chalky pastel condos—mauve, ochre yellow, French blue, and adobe. Chamula children, down from the mountain, scurried toward town carrying blue plastic bags of dirty clothes. For the Chamula, things had become worse since 1970. Chamula men would come to me, in San Cristóbal, and ask if I had a job for them; anything would suffice, they gestured. After the 1982 energy crises, much of the land that had formerly been rented for milpa farming had been converted to grassland for cattle raising. Even the Zinacanteco Indians hired fewer Chamulas to work their plots since they were now utilizing chemical herbicides. Who would hire the land-poor Chamulas to work their milpas?

Under a small bridge, the children's mother was slapping clothes on the rocks at the edge of the grass fields. Along with half a dozen other Chamula women, she had transformed the lazy wire fences into clotheslines, into road signs of color without letters. Only blue, red, yellow, white, white—red. Stripes and ragged rectangles of desperation, occasional light and doom.

FROM THE MOUNTAIN FACE

The sacred mountain of Tzontevitz stood before me, stoic and alive. In the forest, the trees were dreaming, swaying to an ancient song that I couldn't decipher; they had no desire to recover the past, no longings or regrets. They were awake as they dreamt, that was all; they swayed and I swayed forward, up the mountain.

The wetness and dryness, the wooden fragrance enveloped me. The elevation pushed the cool air into my lungs. I climbed higher, away from the embroidered carpets of Ladino boutiques and swirls of Chamulas and Zinacantecos swelling and shifting through the mercados. I had entered a different space. At least for the moment, history was hidden. I didn't note its confused hieroglyphics, its anger or wrath. The pine trees thinned out and became sparse as I went up. I turned back to look at San Cristóbal, below, and to the sister mountains on the south side of the city. My head reeled with the climb; I was out of breath and dazed. I gazed across the blue wool of the clouds and sky. Everything was still, nothing revolved; there were no conflicts or accidents from this vantage point— no disembowelments, no crying buildings aching with the stories of their inhabitants through the centuries, no trade, no corn or grains being shoveled by the postindustrial arm, no harnesses or pulleys whirling under the directions of a stern and handsome timekeeping unit. Only a wise wind, an invisible rough-hewn violin being played by a dark child of the green, red, and wet ground of the forest.

The Chamula road unfurled through the city, past the Zen house where James Taylor ruled; Jeff lay on a sofa with the unplugged Fender making rain-drop sounds on the strings. Indian woman leaned on bench rails near the kiosko in the zócalo, by the cathedral in the colonial center of town. I was not in the sky or on the hill. I was not in Mexico or in the United States. I was swaying in the forest. Lacanjá, Nahá were behind me somewhere in the last cinders of the rain forest. Viejo Chan K'in, elder of Nahá, smoked his cigar; he turned to me with an ironic smile, then turned back. My old friend Manuel from Zinacantán stepped up.

Guadalupe Real Street, San Cristóbal de las Casas.

Manuel, a young Zinacanteco I had met earlier at the zócalo, was waving me into his house. This was the first time that I had seen him smile. His wife, Maruch, was smiling too, inviting me into their mud and pine home, a bitten and bushy adobe, wattle and thatch. It was dark inside, no windows; only reddish flames rolled up from the embers in the middle of the dirt floor, maybe a little to the back. I gave Manuel the customary two liters of pox, the hard cane liquor distilled and sold by the Chamulas. I remembered that this was how you must greet the house, the earth, and the people. I offered bags of calabaza, aguacate, panela, chilis, cebollas, and a couple of kilos of tortillas. Maruch smiled again and took them quietly. She placed them on a bluish table by the rounded wall, next to the entrance, then stepped back to tend the fiery three-stone hearth. Manuel asked me to sit on the ground. He sat too and anxiously told me that he had invited his friends Miguel and Pedro to come and drink with us. He said that Pedro had slipped on one of the mountain trails and cut his lower leg.

I was standing at the heights of Tzontevitz, swaying. The muslin pants rode up Pedro's leg. By his right ankle a set of dark red rings flared; they were caked with blood. The surrounding skin was the color of eggplant, cracked, flaked, and in some places shiny. A sparse milpa lay behind him; a water bucket sat by his bare feet. Maruch's mother, Pasquala, stood nearby with Matal, a young woman. Matal's little daughter, Calixta, played at the center of the yard. Matal's face was alluring—smooth, polished, and triumphant. Both women were wearing the same kind of thick wool wrapped skirt, white blouse, and candy-apple-striped rebozo. Pedro played a song with his friend Miguel in the yard. Miguel was more severe than Pedro. He strained as he moved over to lean his guitar on the wall. We both drank and toasted in Tzotzil.

We toasted inside the small thatched-roof house decorated with mesh bags, tumplines, machetes, and dried ears of maize. The mesh bag knew the roads, the tumplines knew the pressures, the machetes knew the wind velocities, and the dried ears of maize knew the exact calibrations of the days of the Tzotzil in Zinacantán and in these highlands. *Kich'ban*, I toasted in a wild voice. *Ich'o*, they responded, holding their little cups in the air. Maruch and Calixta brought tortillas to the table, where I dipped them into a large gourd of soup with cabbage, avocado, cheese, and tomato. Our eyes were crying—I didn't know from what. Didn't know if it was the smoke, didn't know if it was the air. Didn't know if it was the pox or the food or the salt. Maybe it was nothing, maybe it was one of the little rivers from the mountain that continued to sing and slap its green tongue on our sad faces. *Kich'ban*. Miguel saluted me again and slammed his little enamel cup on the table, took salt, and spoke of his milpa and the old days when he had rented the land from the rancheros on the Grijalva River.

Wanted to see the twenty-two thousand Zinacantecos all at once. They were standing in lines. Hot pink lines of Zinacantecos marching to San Cristóbal and back. Hot pink trenches revolving around the produce markets and mercados in San Cristóbal—selling and buying, buying and selling. Scorched pink lines cutting through the cathedral and by the kiosko. Candy-apple red against deep green. The lines became red wires. They felt warm, secure—then tight, trembling with rage. The Ladinos were pressing the lines, the rich Indians too were pushing against the standing men and women. The lines came back like fog into wool and wool into flesh. Lines of cargo and lines of human reproduction. The cargo holders* circled through the hamlet, old and young men preparing for service to the community. They wanted to heal the tattered spirit of the Tzotzil in Zinacantán, incurring great debts at the hands of the Ladino merchants—debts for ceremonial goods, for liquor, for colors and yarns—and then for a year they would serve their village as alcaldes, as bell ringers or church cleaners. And they would have heated up their *ch'ulel*, their soul, their own blood and their own status. And they would come back to stand in line again, to be counted and considered for a higher post. This was the cost, the dream, and the prize of the cargo.

Wanted to see the eighty thousand Chamulas too. The Chamula women had smaller lines. Private lines inside the house. Leaning by a table next to the hearth. Bearing children, all of them. And their mothers were standing beside them, kneading their backs, massaging their stomachs, kneading their backs again. Even the unborn child was standing inside the womb. She was looking down to the floor, to the hands of the midwife, and she stepped down the red ladder of her birth. The unborn child could hear her mother scream, and then she heard the rest of the

---

*Cargo holders are highland Indian men engaged in the ritual and social tasks of serving their local township church for the benefit of the community through a hierarchical system of religious offices.

family scream back through the circle of the blood sweat hut. The unborn child heard a song, a collective scream led by her standing, bleeding mother. When the child stepped down, the mother stayed standing until the afterbirth fell.

The child was washed and then wrapped and given chilis. "This is so you will remember, the hot spice, the seeds, use them, and cook them," someone said from the birth circle.

The child was wrapped tight in a tiny wool blanket. "This is to keep your body sealed so that your soul does not lose its way," the midwife murmured in a deep voice.

Now the child's head was covered with the blanket. "This is to cover your eyes, so that no one, no stranger will give you evil." Then the wet child was given a digging stick, an ax, a billhook, a shred of cloth. And this was so that she remembered and did not forget her lot in the highlands. The Chamulas poured down the sacred mountain into town like wash water; I followed their direction as best as I could.

NA BOLOM
Histories and Fragmentos

Cindy, a tall and rugged Swedish student on a volunteer six-month residency, announced a tour of Na Bolom. She noted that the center usually housed a small number of students and researchers doing work on the indigenous culture and peoples of the area. They spent their time visiting various archival collections in the city, carrying out fieldwork, and assisting at Na Bolom with just such duties as giving tours. She explained that Oscar and Rodolfo, the other volunteers, were studying Chamula patterns of profit making in their mercado economies.

Cindy recounted the story of Frans Blom, the cofounder of Na Bolom. She stood over us tracing Blom's travels from Denmark at the end of the nineteenth century, his partnership with Aguila Oil in Yucatán in the early 1900s, then his association with Harvard, the milestones of his expeditions into the Chiapas rain forests, and his death in 1963. She spoke of Trudi Blom, her boldness and her determination to go with Frans into the selva in the early forties and how she saved him during one such expedition. Cindy raised her voice and leaned over us. Frans had fallen ill with malaria and could not travel, she said, so Trudi rode on horseback for four days, got help, and came back to Frans with supplies and medical assistance. This incident sparked their eventual marriage and dreams of a Mayan research center in San Cristóbal.

There was more to Gertrude Duby Blom. Trudi, as she liked to be called, was a great teacher and critical force in Mexico. She was handsome, tall, a fiery thinker. In Switzerland, in her early twenties, she had worked as a writer for the socialist press; in England she belonged to the Independent Labor Party. Visiting Italy in the early 1920s, she was deported back to Switzerland for reading subversive books. I thought of the Lacandón Maya research at Na Bolom; these materials were her subversive literature now.

Trudi was doing political work in Germany during Hitler's rise to power in the 1930s, and in the late thirties she came to the United States to organize a women's world congress against the war. After a short visit to France, where she was arrested for her political views, she decided in 1940 to come to Mexico. Gertrude Duby Blom was a woman with a consistent focus on social change; I was not surprised to learn that in the fifties she had conducted a photographic study of the women who fought alongside Emiliano Zapata.

Was Trudi a contemporary Zapatista? Along with the memory of Zapata, was she calling for an Indian and campesino revolution? I wanted to consider her a Zapatista; Na Bolom was her revolutionary poem. Yet the poem negated itself. Na Bolom opposed deep changes for the Maya. If it favored la revolución, it was only in the same manner as the PRI did—that is, in its rhetoric and gestures in the name of the indigenous peoples of Chiapas. Na Bolom's daily operations and preoccupations vanquished Blom's "poem" for the Indian; the waves of americano and European tourists were one clue. The dark women huddled on the patio floors, bent over cloth bundles, sewing color patterns for Na Bolom's high-rent residents, were the next obvious sign suggesting dependency rather than liberation. And almost as in a Mayan Dantesque pit, the levels of suffering and exploitation escalated the farther I walked into the hotel of the Jaguar, Na Bolom. The older Indian maids in the back rooms, hidden from the view of the camera-wielding public, stacked and checked out towels, blankets, and hiking equipment for the various tours into the highlands and jungle country. This was their first and last stop in being Indian women. They were servers of a Mayan cultural experience, an experience that could not be sold and that in the final analysis no one would want to document, touch, or feel. This colonial dependence was not part of the Bolom conversation. It was submerged, hidden from view. In an odd way, Na Bolom was a paradox: what was pronounced and featured for open display was simultaneously erased—el indio, la india. All of us in some way denied the Blom poem's honor. The Na Bolom poem was bitten and bitter from indígena usury and the further abandonment of the Maya.

Who listened to Gertrude Blom now?

Was Na Bolom a tourist trap disguised by a politically correct Indianism and facile environmental platitudes? The myriad of Tzotzil-Tzeltal women kneeling on their prismatic tapestries throughout San Cristóbal seemed to speak of Mexico's "indigenismo," the Indianist project launched in Mexico and other Latin American countries after the 1940 meeting at

Patzcuaro establishing the Interamerican Indian Insitutute and charging each nation with the formation of an instituto indigenista, except the United States, the only attending country that did not ratify the treaty. Although in Mexico and other Latin American countries the resulting agencies, such as the INI, the Instituto Nacional Indigenista, established programs to "integrate" the Indian into the national culture, it was largely a paternalistic, top-down relationship where at best the Indian was kept at the margins of mestizo society. Kneeling in Na Bolom was the key symbol of the Indian's position in the social structure and consciousness of the nation.

The walls of Na Bolom were covered with large paintings, watercolors. Fast and intricate strokes—a carved jaguar lit with moon patterns, foliage in star shapes, stone calendars, and jade rivers. Cindy mentioned that Trudi painted these things. I had not thought of Trudi as an artist.

Na Bolom was her artwork; her radio broadcasts, archives, letters, and documented images were her brush strokes. Where was Trudi? And what was in the photographs, the hundreds of reels still kept under lock and key, undeveloped? *Why* were they still kept inaccessible?

I followed Cindy through the open courtyards to the front door of the library, which was closed for repairs. An old Zinacanteco arrived and began to unfold his satchel of embroidery. A couple of Chamula women came in as usual, to display their wares and weavings to the tourist tenants, student residents taking a break from combing through the archives, and social scientists passing through to follow up on informant interviews and field work. This was the place where the Maya were given their due, in stark contrast to the daily aggressive Ladino hustle outside; here they were native objects of desire. In the courtyard the two Chamulas knelt on a bluish mat about four yards opposite the Zinacanteco and began to lay out their wool tapestries and electric-colored rayon belts.

Cindy's voice came back to me in stuttered fragments:

> 11,000 books, donated
> Pottery from Chiapa de Corso
> you can see it in the courts
> The frieze
> on the front of Na Bolom
> a jaguar

adopted from a Oaxacan jaguar figure
Here is a painting
Frida Kahlo done by Diego Rivera
Here is a photograph by Trudi
a sacred Chamula ceremony,
the Fire Run,
taken at the Chamula Carnival
—1960—
with a trick lens so
that the Indians wouldn't notice
Trudi took this other
the Lacandón rain forest
Did you know that only a fifth
of the forest that Trudi and Frans found
in 1940
still remains?
There are
several projects to reforest
but they are almost impossible
We have a law in Chiapas
it doesn't allow for any more tree cutting
but it's only theoretical.

"The Fire Run" (Photo by Trudi Blom)

Chamulas wrapped in black wool capes. The naked legs raised, the bare feet pointed, the sole smoothing the smoke and orange flames weaving through the burning pine road. The man leading the run wears a white chamorro, a scarf, and a hat. His pants are rolled up to the knees. He is gazing forward as he swings his shoulders back and forth. To his right there is a line of Chamula observers with their arms crossed over their chests. A young boy in a white chamorro is looking at the camera lens. His mouth is about to open, his voice is about to sound; he sees the trick lens, something different pushing into the fire road. The Chamulas are running toward us, the viewers.

I couldn't figure how Trudi managed this photograph without standing on the road herself. Perhaps this was the key? Can we stand on the fire road ourselves along with the Chamulas, the Tzotzil-Tzeltals, the Lacandón Mayas? Can we stand on the fire road that cuts across all of the borders in the Americas? What will happen to our bodies as we begin to run? Will we burn? And if we do turn to ashes, blackened and alive, what will we say? Will we speak to the gods? Will our community heal?

"With a Trick Lens So" (Phrase)

This creative subterfuge disturbed me, and yet I was engaged in a similar gesture. I went about the streets of San Cristóbal with my own personal craft of subversions—my notes, my intentions, my quests; this uncanny project of hammering at my own colonized viscera; my trick lens signaled my privileged ground; all looped into the indigenous lives and quandaries of the men and the women on the bottom rung of the American ladder:
el indio,
la india.

What do we call the New Indio
with trucking business investments?

"Did You Know That Only a Fifth" (Fragment)

Numbers. The math of oppression. Statistics for the elite. For professors and social scientists. For students working on their socially relevant projects. What was I going to do with this one-fifth now? In 1970 I began with the number five hundred. Five hundred Lacandón Mayas left in the rain forest, I repeated to myself day in and day out.

There are other numbers. During the oil boom of the early eighties, industry expanded to 27 percent of the Mexican GNP. By this time, in Chiapas, Indian language speakers were dispersed and displaced into the Gulf coastal zones of oil development, looking for work far from their homes. The seeking migrations roared into the rain forests, from the highlands into Mayan lakes and timberlands, leaving a wounded panorama of blackened stumps and gray skies, a slash-and-burn rosary of charred mahogany. In a short time the spreading grasslands for cattle will have fully displaced the last tropical forests of Chiapas. Given the difference between the general population growth—about 7 percent for eastern Chiapas—and the rate attributable to natural birth over death rates (about 3 percent), the population of eastern Chiapas expands approximately 4 percent per year as a result of migration. As we tumble over the millennium, the rate of grassland spread and razed forests is catastrophic.

What was I, a comfortable americano, going to do with these numbers and tables?

1. By 1980, in Chiapas
    11 oil wells pumped juice on a daily basis—
    123 thousand barrels of crude,
    384 million square feet of gas,
    4 percent and 12 percent of the national output.

2. By 1982, in Chiapas
    80 percent of the 198,622 families residing in indigenous areas still
        subsisted on maize and beans
    100 percent of these same families didn't have milk
    10 percent on occasion ate meat and
    25 percent tasted eggs
    8 percent had no potable water
    100 percent were without sewage treatment
    96 percent lacked electricity
    30 percent worked in peonage, bound to semifeudal masters.

3. More than ten years later, by 1993, in all of Chiapas:
    15 percent had septic tanks (what of the Indian communities?)
    30 percent remained without electricity (what of the Indian com-
        munities?)
    50 percent plus were still without access to sewers (what of the In-
        dian communities?).
    (What was I going to do with the unknown numbers on Indian land?)

4. ? percent subject to sexual abuse and servitude or, as they say,
        "derecho de pernada"
    ? percent dead on a "sol a sol" work schedule including labor in the
        master's house, "fajina" work, on Saturdays and Sundays
    ? percent of master-Indian offspring working out their Indian parent's
        plantation debts, pulling at their multitrack of metaphysical guilt.
    What were the real numbers now?

"Several Projects to Reforest" (Phrase)

When I strolled through Las Paletas, as the taxistas called San Cristóbal de las Casas, I was on a project. The project was called "Dirt Floors." It had other names too: "No Electricity, No Sewers"; "Dead Dysentery Babies."

I was on a project: "12 Million Indians in Mexico Are on Fire, Bulldozed into a Mass Grave."

The project invaded me. Tore me to pieces. Tiny half-diamond shapes, almost starry and natural. Almost transcendent. The project broke into my well-mannered gestures of Chicano politeness and equilibrium. This seeing project, this walking-into-myself agenda. The project walked into me more often than I wanted it to. The project drifted into my dreams after a long day and evening of walking around the town zócalo, along the edges of the Pan American highway, and through the well-swept squares perched in the eastern hills by the church of Our Lady of Guadalupe.

Last night, a dream: Somewhere in this city, sitting with a Zinacanteco.

Xun was an old man, well dressed and elegant in his candy-colored cottons. His skin was dark and his hair was white and silky. I was sitting, and he was saying things that I had always wanted to know—about skies and underworlds, the levels of the cosmos, the raging seas of ablution. He was kind and had smart hazel eyes like my father. While he talked and opened his net satchel, I struggled with myself. I was fighting with my joy. How could he reveal so much to me? This must be a dream, I told myself as I fought off my happiness, as I kicked it into a small shape at the end of my feet.

Who was I? Who was Xun, the old man with my name, Juan?

The old Zinacanteco leaned over me gently and waved his right hand forward, as if pointing to a road. He said we would walk together from now on. He resembled Ramón Medina Silva too, the Huichol shaman I had met long ago in Tepic, Nayarit. It was his alert stillness and openness that I recognized. Or was it the old Zinacanteco who had been at Na Bolom for days, selling his servilletas and chamorros? My project followed me everywhere.

The government's project is to reforest: I believe Cindy. They say they are going to reforest. They have to say this. The land has been pillaged and scarred; their own violent actions require them to use the language of healing. I have taken part in this crime scene, so I know this too. Through my inaction, through my smoldering indifference I have propped up this smooth language of renewal and "paradise." Through my collective genetics and religious DNA that drops down its patriarchal helix at every church in Latin America in the name of Indian conversion and servitude, through my maligned Indian spiritual rubble face that cries out for revenge. A malicious and disheveled crime scene snarls at the heart of my project.

"But It's Only Theoretical" (Sentence)

Cindy continued with her musings as we walked into the museo room. It contained a highly organized set of exhibits on Lacandón material culture—arrows, gourds, incense burners, shards, net bags, tree bark, shredded canvas and twine; 16 × 20 color photographs pushed the various ethnographic items into motion.

This is a picture
the Balché ceremony
Balché roots soaked with sugar and honey
five to six days
they ferment, you vomit
and you are purified
the gods are satisfied
smoking is part of their life.
El Viejo Chan K'in,
the elder of the Nahá leads the ceremonia
He is wearing a poncho
made of tree bark
painted with stars,
it is the universe,
with two holes
one for the sun, the other for the moon
the stars
sprinkled over the body
Only he can wear this. The chief
of the forest.

"Chan K'in says that the roots of all living things are tied together. When you cut down a tree, a star in the heavens also falls." Cindy ended with this quote. A movie on the life of Trudi Blom was to follow, she said—*La Reina de la Selva*—and she left.

"When You Cut Down a Tree" (Echo)

In front of us, on the museum wall, was a portrait of Frida Kahlo by Rivera, beaten with fog and dampness, sad-eyed, in auburn and light emeraldine, the hair gentler than it should be, the eyes without their ferocity, the forehead simple and unmarked by the usual flash of her electric and continuous eyebrow.

ADMIRE THE MAID INTO REVOLUTION

Na Bolom frightened me. Everything whirred in the proper, manu-factured motion of "native" admiration and preservation.
The maids scurried
to our quarters after we left. They skittered with rags
        and buckets.
                    With mops and toilet paper rolls.
On occasion they were accompanied by their children eating a bo-lillo. They made their three hundred thousand pesos a month, a little over three dollars a day, like half of the Chiapas workforce, in the company of bad water, loose hair on the bowl, stained linen, and busted pipes. In the mornings, from my Chamula room, I could hear their young husbands, up at six splitting logs and kindling. When the foreigners left their rooms for breakfast, they rushed in to clean the dirty hearths and refill them with wood, neatly stacked. The very old maids remained in the back, sitting on stools, stacking linen over their knees. At night they were in charge of "expedition" supplies for the tourists who wanted to play à la Frans Blom, checking out hooks and army-green-colored equipment, ancient hammocks and sleeping bags bitten with gravel and thorns.

One of the old women in the back quarters was called Doña América. Her face was dark and wise; her aquiline nose and her watery eyes, her nimble fingers, and her rough-cut voice soothed me. She reminded me of my own little mother who had died a few years before.

My mother was a maid in El Paso in the thirties and forties. My aunt Aurelia, my grandmother Juanita—all the women in my family were maids. As a child I listened to my mother's stories of bruised and cal-lused knees, of sponged hands, of bowing her head and her back, squat-ting in perfect houses she could never live in, licking the mixing bowls after the pudding was prepared. I listened to her account of the bad wages, the working sweat of El Paso, the long walks up to Mount Franklin from el segundo barrio, the second ward, carrying small cans to

62

Women downtown, San Cristóbal de las Casas.

be filled with leftovers and taken back down the slope to the brick-floor house, a stone's throw from Juárez. Within that tiny arena, my mother on occasion wore homemade gypsy dresses, bracelets, and fake pearl necklaces; she dreamt of joining Los Pirrines, a popular working-class theater troupe in El Paso. At every edge of San Cristóbal de las Casas I began to recognize my own myth, my own projection of the suffering Indian figure. What could I do with this flesh-and-blood image of the Ladina maid? My own curled-up San Joaquín Valley campesino childhood?

When I talked with Lupe and Fidencia, two of the maids at Na Bolom, I recognized their accents, the pleasing voices, the entertaining conversations. The laughter, carefree and jubilant; the nervousness was familiar too—how it erupted by force as if they were standing in front of a sergeant. Recognized their waiting, their pauses, waiting for me to inflate myself into an americano, as most visitors do, especially the male residents at Na Bolom—an americano who would make easy chatter about Chiapas and its people as artifacts; and as I "grew" during the brief exchange, they in turn would diminish as the sí's sputtered from their mouths. The script for this drama was archaic. Who believed in it? None of us; yet the script seemed to have a life of its own. What were the deeper scripts? This moment alerted me to my secret mission, to undo the Ladino americano schema of numbness toward a genuine América where maids would no longer be Mexican or Indian, where the criada position itself would vanish to sabotage the manifold lines of apathy. These two women, wrapped in spotted scarves, bent over bowls and foam, were the spark. My inner prowl to become complete once again rose up inside me; a billowing spiral of pain heat came up from my belly, my face flushed with the fiery will to speak and crash through the collective crimes wrapped around all of us.

Lupe and Fidencia were my signposts to the Mayan edge, to our lives bound and disheveled under one caoba tree, they were pointing me in the right direction. They were the Ladino bowl cleaners who deserved revolution—nothing short of revolution.

We resembled each other: an ancient mother held in common
our timelessness,
our green-brown color,
our penchant for a religious smile.

THE NATIVE POSITION

One hole for the moon.
Look in and you'll see.
One hole for the sun.
Look in and you will witness the fires.

In San Cristobal de Las Casas, I acted as if everyone was positioned for my spiritual transformation, along the open vistas on the road to Comitán, behind the scientifically ordered mercado fruit stands, walking in the middle of the main street with protest signs, in rebozo or calzón, in wheat-colored straw hats or shredded scarves, everyone was propped for my spectatorship. This was the farce and the miracle. All the while Ladino and Indian maids and their servant husbands and spotted children dangled in the neon neural tube of national political disintegration and cultural exploitation.

Leaning against the kiosk at the zócalo, I recognized Concepción, the Chamula with the Ph.D. in social anthropology. She did not engage in cooperative trucking or in elaborate interstate flower-vending operations, as some of the Zinacantecos did. Concepción gave tours through Zinacantán and San Juan Chamula. Forty thousand pesos, almost half of an upscale maid's monthly salary, and you could stroll with Concepción into her own sphere of peoples and time. You could hear the idioms of erudite Ladino schoolmasters and of the university as she spoke of Tzontevitz mountain with her ethnographic language, with her foreign poetics of self. She was tall, with dark muscular arms and a piercing gaze. Concepción, my other half;
the Indian onto Americanness.
I wanted to join her tour upon my return from K'ayum's country—
the selva.

INDIAN CORRIDOS FOR JUSTICE

A corrido in long-winded chants,
with drums and women's voices, rises proud
with the arc of tarnished trumpets in the background.

The drum was getting louder. Looking to my left, into the street, toward the southern edge of town and the Cristóbal Colón bus depot, I could not believe what I was seeing.

Hundreds of Indian men and women marched on the streets toward the zócalo. Along with the Mexican flag they held up estandartes with the image of La Virgen de Guadalupe and muslin sheets displaying large hand lettering: POR NUESTROS COMPAÑEROS DE TZAJALCHEN Y . . .

The flags and banners whipped and waved with the same force and desire as in their messages and the faces of the people marching. "For our comrades from Tzajalchen and . . . " the sign read; I couldn't make out all the lettering. But it wasn't the flags or the sheets of La Virgen that stopped me; it was the women in the front line. They were young and stoic. They held their arms crossed under their white cotton rebozos dotted with red diamond patches. The rebozos spoke louder than the flags, louder than the men lined behind them. As they crossed the street and passed under the ornate sign of the Hotel Santa Clara, the flags unfurled again:

SIMOJOVEL APOYA.

Simojovel. I repeated the name of this mountain town. Simojovel with defiant numbers—the numbers of semifeudal workers under the control of a few landowners. In Simojovel they had been marching along with the Indians of the neighboring municipios of Huitiupán and Sabanilla. The vast expansion of agrarian reform during the forties had been largely due to the policies of the president, Lázaro Cárdenas. At this time almost one-fourth of the total population had rights to half of Mexico's arable land. These parcels were granted in the form of communal holdings of cultivable land, pasture, and woodland known as *ejidos*. Ejidatarios are those

66

who hold title to land in ejido tracts; usually they are vested in communities and managed by an ejidal committee. Since 1976 Indians under peonage, along with ejidatarios and jornaleros (day laborers and hired hands for the ejidatario or landowner), began a campesino movement for expanded ejido land tracts mostly controlled by a few Ladino plantation families. Since then they had been on a quest for better labor rights for all, especially those under peonage. In 1977, the government responded by sending military personnel into the region, burning houses, pillaging villages, and jailing 250 men, women, and children. Three children drowned as they crossed the Río Portugal trying to escape.

Run toward a river and you will be shot in the water.

The Mayan maxim of Indian and campesino freedom.

This was the deep meaning of being a "wetback." The meaning involved considerations regarding spirit, being, body, and powerlessness. It required me to think about the metaphysics of being Indian, of betrayal, and how rivers carry the dead.

As of 1980, campesinos from Simojovel and adjacent municipios formed the Central Independiente de Obreros y Agrícolas Campesinos (Independent Confederation of Agricultural Workers and Peasants) in order to augment their demands for labor and human rights—eight-hour days, payment of the minimum wage, the end to "derecho de pernada."

They coordinated strikes in thirty-four coffee plantations, and again they were met with violence and false accusations of invading the master's house without permission. To this day, the municipios of Simojovel, Venustiano Carranza, Las Margaritas, and Ocosingo march for their lives, meeting violence and repression face to face. These conditions were aggravated with the privatization and commercialization of campesino and Indian-held land. Salinas de Gortari's 1992 reform of Article 27 of the Mexican Constitution and of the Agrarian Code undermined the hard-fought struggle for land that had gone on since the Plan de Ayala was declared in 1911. In a single grand stroke Gortari had dismantled President Lázaro Cardenas's agrarian reform of 1934–40 in which 20 million hectares of land were distributed to over 776,000 campesinos in Mexico. It is no surprise that the Zapatistas gained widespread campesino and Indian support together with considerable sympathy at the national level.

During the late 1960s and early 1970s, Emiliano Zapata's old revolutionary call for "tierra y libertad" was taken up by the Chicano movement, particularly by members of my generation. My own response

came through the investigation, production, and performance of poetry
and teatro. In Los Angeles and at UCLA, I had been working with various student "resistance" organizations demonstrating against the policy,
role, and involvement of the United States in Viet Nam, such as Students
for a Democratic Society and the Movimiento Estudiantil Chicano en
Aztlán. Inspired by the millions who had marched against the war on the
East Coast the previous year, I had given much energy to the upcoming
Chicano Moratorium slated to take place in the streets of East Los Angeles on August 29, 1970. Chicanas and Chicanos from every corner of
the nation were making similar plans to attend and speak up, to mark a
key moment in the making of Chicana and Chicano consciousness. However, my tasks and dreams pulled me in another direction; I headed
south to Chiapas in search of my ancestors' ways of doing art and using
language as ritual. Political theater and poetry were complex and powerful weapons, and they needed to be investigated and tuned, and most of
all their internal structures and social connections needed to be on Indian
terms, on the cultural and conceptual foundations of the Américas. As
the Black Panthers had clearly said, it was about self-determination. I
had already been with the Huichol Indians of Nayarit and the Totonacs
of northern Veracruz; the Maya were the missing link.

As it happened, I arrived in San Cristóbal de las Casas via Villahermosa, Tabasco, a few days after the twenty-ninth of August. That day I
purchased the Mexican daily, *El Excelsior,* and inadvertently opened the
page that read "Mueren Varios en Manifestación en Los Angeles" ("Several Killed in Los Angeles Demonstration"). I was reading about a mas-
sacre on my own home turf, East Los Angeles.

The Los Angeles sheriff's department had penetrated into the midst
of the Chicano demonstration against the Viet Nam war and fired at the
crowd, killing innocent victims. Rubén Salazar, a *Los Angeles Times* journalist, had been attacked point blank with a gas canister at the Silver Dollar Tavern, not far from the demonstration site. In the summer of 1970,
after a wild three-year mix of hard-core Chicano nationalism, Jimi Hendrix, Janis Joplin concerts, acid trips, spontaneous poetry, and jazz teatro
experiments, I wanted to ignore the headlines. I wanted to go about my
indio euphoria. But it was impossible. I had been involved in too many
walkouts, police street attacks against students, community members,
and children. The political realities of mexicanos in "el Norte" punished
me as much as those in "el Sur," in those evident in the Mayan Indian

and campesino stumbling figures on the narrow and broken pathways of San Cristóbal de las Casas. Now, once again, I was split—

between the squalor and abuse of Mexican Indians and the on-slaughts against working class mexicanos in California. "In-between people" appeared before me: Indians with trucking cooperatives and Indians with new-fangled tourist ware—twisted clay dolls wrapped in coarse black wool patches. The fractures between my own Amerindian utopias, the socioeconomic wedges of class between Zinacantecos and Chamulas, and the cruel sniper work in urban America gnawed at me.

Twenty-three years later, in the first month of 1993, in "Las Paletas," another set of reversals punished me with irony and pernicious continuity: At the center of an Indian march against injustice, rape, and tyranny I was caught with questions having to do with Indian political organization and how these groups wielded their interests in relationship to other Indian groups and most of all to the Ladino centers of power. The call for Indian unity startled me. This is what the PRI relished—the rhetoric of Indian unity. This is what Chicanos in the States fantasized. How could I measure the call for a "united front"? A thick and complex system of power networks within the campesino and Indian municipios pulled me in different directions while on a search for myself and the thin trail back to the Lacandón lowlands.

I wanted to hear a collective echo rumble with every shout by the protest marchers: East Los, Simojovel, Las Margaritas, Chiapas, the Southwest, Tzotziles, Chicanos, Tzeltales, mexicanos, students, campesinos, do-gooder Ladinos. Could the symbols mesh? Virgen de Guadalupe flags, United Farmworker eagle motifs, Tzotzil corridos, and Chicano power chants, mexicanos, Ladinos, brown-skin americanos in between brown skins—fused and fissioned on a giant concentric wheel of connected systems, cycles, and faces of oppression.

This is what approached me, chilled me

and floated

toward the main square on a late afternoon.

The frocked Indian women in red diamond patches, the men with dark coats and white shirts, the musicians with requintos and guitarras pasted with religious estampas—I heard them roaring in unison. I ran and kept to their beats as they curved through Avenida Urilla. A few of the men and women passed out flyers:

Somos un grupo de campesinos que estamos luchando por la LI-
BERTAD de nuestros compañeros que están INJUSTAMENTE ENCAR-
CELADOS por problemas de tierra que las autoridades y reforma
agraria no han querido resolver en las comunidades de Tzajalch'en
y Tzanembolom, Municipio de Che'enalho, y ahora los VER-
DADEROS CULPABLES de homicidio, tentativa de homicidio, robo y
violación están libres, mientras que los injustamente encarcelados
tienen Auto de Formal Prision.

We are group of campesinos who are fighting for the
LIBERTY of our friends who are UNJUSTLY INCARCERATED due
to problems related to the land that the authorities and the
agrarian reform program have not wanted to resolve in the
communities of Tzajalch'en and Tzanembolom,
municipality of Chenalhó, and now the ONES TRULY GUILTY
of homicide, intent to commit homicide, theft, and rape are
free, while those unjustly incarcerated are held under the
Formal Prison Act.

TE AGRADECEMOS TU AYUDA, TU APOYO Y TU PRESENCIA EN EL
PLANTON QUE HACEMOS EN SAN CRISTOBAL FRENTE A LA
CATEDRAL.
INDIGENAS TZOTILES DE CH'ENALHO.

WE APPRECIATE YOUR HELP, YOUR SUPPORT AND YOUR
PRESENCE AT THE
VIGIL IN SAN CRISTOBAL IN FRONT OF THE CATHEDRAL.

TZOTZIL INDIANS OF CHENALHO

Young Ladino students on the street followed the march with seeking eyes and half-open mouths. The locals had seen these demonstra-
tions day in day out, for years. The majority of the Ladinos and tourists
stood by for a moment and snapped back into their own rhythms of indifference and numbness. An older Indian woman gave me another
flyer. Xeroxed letterhead from the Fray Bartolomé de Las Casas Human
Rights Office, a month-old communiqué to all women's groups:

CENTRO DE DERECHOS HUMANOS
Fray Bartolomé de Las Casas December 17, 1992

COMMUNIQUÉ TO ALL WOMEN'S GROUPS

Fray Bartolomé de Las Casas Human Rights Office asks all women's groups and all people who are conscious to the impunity with which women are made to suffer violence to react with demands for justice in the following cases:

1. On December 9, 1992, three native women were savagely attacked and raped by a group of native men from the village of Tzanembolom of Ch'enalo county in the state of Chiapas, Mexico. The attackers had previously shot at the husbands of these women leaving all wounded. One of the three men died several hours later.

2. After raping the wives, the attackers proceeded to rob them of their few poor belongings. The attackers then proceeded to celebrate their victories by having a party at which they ate some of the animals they had stolen.

3. A Presbyterian elder, Manuel Pérez Gutiérrez, together with three other men of the same denomination: Sebastián Pérez Vásquez, Felipe Hernández Pérez and Antonio Pérez Gutiérrez, together with Mariano Pérez Vásquez, a Catholic lay preacher of the village of Tzajalch'en, were asked to attend the wounded and provide them with spiritual assistance.

The above mentioned Presbyterians and a Catholic lay preacher were maliciously accused and detained by police when they arrived at the office of the county authorities in the town of Ch'enalo where they went to accompany the wounded. Those who ordered their detention are the county authorities of Ch'enalo, who because of interpersonal problems took advantage of the situation to accuse the five men of good will thus leaving the real culprits off Scott free.

Because of all of the above mentioned, we believe it to be urgent necessity that all women's defense organizations and other honest people who are struggling for the end to impunity in such cases, speak up loud and clear for justice to be done in Chiapas.

In your letters request that a thorough investigation of this case be carried out, that the real authors of these crimes be punished and that the "scape goats" being used to calm political interests of the area in question be set free.

We wish to remind solidarity groups of the impunity which assassins of homosexuals enjoy in our state and that which serious violators of our state laws enjoy. We know that the native peoples in the villages of Tzanembolom and Tzajalch'en know perfectly well who the criminals are in these sad cases. Let us exercise all the pressure possible in the above mentioned cases of the native women and men in question, so that impunity will not be given free reign.

Yours truly,

5 de Febrero No. 6 San Cristóbal de las Casas, C.P. 29200, Chiapas, Mexico. Apartado Postal 178. Tel. (91-967) 8-35-48 FAX: (91-967)8-35-51

The Centro de Derechos Humanos had translated their communiqué into English. Maybe, they thought, every year, out of all the thousands of European and American tourists and Mexican nationals parading through the streets, riding Mayan tour buses across the forests, just maybe someone would listen, turn, and take action. Just maybe the government's human rights organization, the Comisión Nacional de Derechos Humanos (CNDH), a national agency with local offices in Chiapas, would move forward. And if not, then the Centro—as an independent branch of the Catholic Church and parallel organization to CNDH—would have to do it alone.

The issue of homosexuality jumped up from the page. Was this march of Indian pueblos also a march for gay rights, however cloaked and indented at the end of the communiqué?

Was this march an ongoing drum of rebellion about to explode from the highlands and humid lowlands, how long would it play, how loud would it resound, could it be heard by the Ladino, by the United States, was the Mayan and campesino edge about to break off?

RED REBOZOS FOR RIGOBERTA MENCHU

This is a multitrack of unknown numbers,
realities, red rebozos and violence
in a raging semifeudal continuum.

The women from Chenalhó leaned forward in the protest march around the city zócalo. Their dark foreheads led them to the cathedral square and their scarves flurried in the late afternoon winds.

They multiplied. Their bodies and arms spread and dispersed into each one of our souls and memories. They were Rigoberta Menchú with crossed arms and staunch hearts. They were young and barefoot, combed and stern, full of compassion and terrible pictures held tight in their

Mayan protesters at the zócalo, San Cristóbal de las Casas.

73

braided hair. They were the braided spirits of Doña Petrona Chona, whose body was machete-cut into twenty-five pieces by the bodyguard of a landowner in Guatemala, pieces that Rigoberta Menchu's father placed in a basket.

> Petrona,
>   shredded
>   into pieces
>   congealed
flesh

because she didn't permit Carlos García, the landowner's son, to rape her. Petrona, in pieces, came back to us this afternoon. Her head, her arms and hands. Her legs and thighs. Her belly and her breasts. She was woven back, through stone, through national borders and border-guard time; she had come back through the valley of machetes, broken galeras and fincas and was present in this sudden multitude, calling out for justice. Petrona was leading the march with her Mayan sisters and brothers; this is why people stared. This is why we stopped breathing. The Indian women here knew Petrona Chona did not die in vain. They knew the women of Chenalhó were not raped and wounded in vain.

What about us? I thought:
the onlookers, the note takers, the accountants, bookkeepers, and anthropological shadows? What did we know? What taste burned in our mouths, who was hidden inside the tufts and bright locks of our hair? What pictures fell from our heads onto the public square in such a loud and loving fashion?

The Indian women and men gathered at the open square facing the entrance of the cathedral. I remained at the back, sat down and smoked. A few of the men sat by me—young men burned by the sun, looking ahead at the archaic and sealed doors of the cathedral where the leaders raised los estandartes of la Virgen de Guadalupe, the Mexican flag and their own red and gold cloth on sticks.

Those in front stood in silence, about a hundred or so; around us pressed another two hundred. Children ran about, dodging each other; the mother's brought out foodstuffs from their satchels and handed them out. A voice in Tzotzil came through the speakers. Ahead I could see the speaker, a young man kneeling at the foot of La Virgen de Guadalupe. His voice carried a cavernous tenderness; slow, then quick. He was singing, almost, but he was beseeching the pueblos of Mayan Indians before him. He was naming the raped, the innocent; he was crying out, and his voice was shaking. He was crying out with one arm holding the estandarte of la virgen and the other arm down, still, close to his chest. I didn't know the words but I could hear the pain.

Walked up closer. Everyone's head was bowed down as they listened, crying out with their brother for their families, stricken once again. The other two estandartes were held up by women who lifted their rebozos to their faces with their free arms so they could cry into themselves. The whole plaza was mourning the dead; all the men and women, all the children were in tears. I let my crying take me to their crying and envelop me in their weeping; this was one thing I could do. It came up without question or analysis, without notes or reflections; I was singing with my Indian sisters and brothers, I was singing for the dead and wounded and for their transformation into fullness and freedom. An Indian woman took the microphone after the man's voice faltered. Her voice was determined, clear. In Spanish she announced that later there would be a gathering for the Indian pueblos inside the church quarters. She spoke with her head up and her shoulders bright.

The thick doors of the church never opened. The bishop never came out. It was as if the Indians had come to seek solace at the foot of an ancient shrine. All I saw were Indians standing at the gate of the church, crying, singing, and holding up their own faith and community. Something had been buried under the church, under San Cristóbal de las Casas, that lay there with its eyes awake and its heart ready to fly. They gathered their strength here. They knew, I knew, that the onlookers would go home with a different taste in their mouths, with something that they had kept hidden from themselves in their mercado baskets.

Sat down again and offered a cigarette to the Tzotzil-Tzeltal men next to me. They were surprised and thanked me. We sat and smoked and listened to the demands in Tzotzil, to the names of the lost and the names of the determined.

A tight group of tourists swiveled behind us. They asked questions. I could hear them speaking in English. It was Concepción and her tour. I recognized her from the folded cloth on her head, a Chamula woman's attire mixed in with her Ladino dress.

Night drifted over the cathedral. The streets emptied; only a few people remained. In San Cristóbal there are no visible party palaces, as there are in Veracruz, D.F., or Guadalajara. Here the night wrapped the streets and left a few lingerers idly smoking cigarettes or listening to a small box radio inside some hole-in-the-wall tienda de abarrotes where they sold stacked kilos of tortillas, hard pan dulce, bolillos, tall bottles of Coke, eggs, dry chorizo on a wire vine, and Raleighs and Mexican Winstons.

Made another round through the kiosko so as not to appear awkward. I was the only Ladino man out in the plaza next to the church. The Tzotzils were huddled inside the back quarters of Bishop Samuel Ruiz's rectory. They had nailed two effigies on the wooden beams that held up the veranda. A small light bulb shone on ragged and ashen figures murmuring night words and unknown languages of ascensions. They gathered in the back, some forming a line against the wall. They had come about rape and a larger vat of venom, genocide.

Step inside:

I receive you like the Chamula cloth dolls at birth, this draped night, this second half of the sky dome; I clutch you without language, without a text for my transformation. You are changing before my eyes and my skin; you with the same burrs and loud scarves and scars as my mother, with the same crooked elbow as my father. I receive you as I received those that gave me birth, I take you with your severities and assassinations, with your new flower business routes from Mexico City, with your meager landscapes of torture, cornslush, incense, and woven faces. I receive you with your night-stringed innocence, with your oppressor's nailed knife in wooden slats, as effigies, as practices to sweep the evils from your soul, from your village of blue navels, from the iris of your mountainous village waters. You are transforming before my walking, before me. In my absence and in my presence you have transformed; I would have stayed and remained alone, inside the city bank, inside the fashion fair prowls of my metropolitan euphorias, in my escape-ladder suits worn with melancholy and ice intelligence. I would have stayed in that balsa, that crumbled American pocket of losses and tiny furies at the feet of the beggar boy; I would have stayed back there, in my comfort and in my high-rise grape-picking valley, in California, or in my open desert floodwater volcanic Midwest stone, in the land of Lincoln, next door to Dorothy's flight to Oz; I would have kept all my fine flared writing pens, my self-made quills, and tall proud movimiento notebooks and have looked elsewhere for my rain. I would have looked elsewhere, somewhere between fanciful Americanness and brown-skinned oblivion; instead, a tiny step, for a few seconds back, then forward, through persistence and memory, through timelessness and ripped-out sidewalk trails, rock & roll moss, city steam, and Indian town fungi taxis. I took a second or two and ran into you, by mistake; I was looking for a tour and an interpreter, but my suit had grown too thin and I was freezing. I needed your smoke, your boiled woolliness, your fawn-colored warmth, your eternal half-smoke ferocity face and your warrior prayer hands pointing to the effigy on the bishop's veranda. I receive you without any words; I am still unformed, I am changing with you as you go to your uncombed triumph, gilded with your names up in the sky flares, held up by the women of the villages, to continue to remember that you continue; I go on through this street of a thousand flayed hearts asking for your name, but all I hear in the distance, on this cobbled ribbon of Calle Diego Dugelay, is music.

LATE SHADOW AT THE MONASTERY

At Na Bolom the office light was still on.

The clock on the wall read 10:14 P.M. Nelly Maldonado was at the door with one of the office assistants. They were holding up another woman.

The night shielded her face. She was barely walking with her jagged cane. They carried her gently and quietly almost as if conducting a nocturnal ritual of closure for the research center; a ghostly queen in a long blackish gown was going back into the realm of dream and void. Nelly motioned to me to come closer.

The three women were floating toward me. I was tiptoeing to my room in the back side of Na Bolom, a little cabin behind the palatial ancient monastery. I was halfway through the patio where the vases released the perfume of their thick jasmine fronds.

Come, Juan Felipe, come, Nelly signaled me again.

White powder makeup smeared on her face, rouge slipping from her mouth, sharp line pencil marks for eyebrows, and a shocked gaze; I walked up and recognized the woman in their arms.

"Buenas noches, Señora Trudi," I said. "I came to visit here about twenty-three years ago."

Flung my hands in the air, made a sour attempt at laughing at the amount of time that had elapsed. Then I turned to Nelly and her assistant for a word to break the silence. Quiet. Their eyes moved from side to side. They nodded as if to answer for Trudi.

"¿Cómo está?" I asked.

Trudi lifted her head, looked at me, and tried to speak. Guttural sounds. Her eyes brightened and her forehead arched. She began speaking in German; her demeanor changed and she gave out commands in the old language. A conversation with someone else on another plane, or was she warning me about something?

Nelly and her friend walked Trudi to her room a few feet behind me. Buenas noches, I said, out of rhythm; the words turned into a whisper as I stepped back to the Chamula room.

78

Open-air tomb, San Cristóbal de las Casas.

Thought of my aunt Aurelia, who had a series of strokes and then died in the hospital two years earlier. Her face was in shock too. Her eyes were alert, and every part of her wanted to make the words bounce from her soul into the open air. When she managed to expel the words they would emerge in a shriek or a series of stuttered vowels, and I would kiss her gently on the forehead.

Na Bolom was made of sadness; I could hear it escape with the winds through the crevices of the tall, powerful wooden doors.

II

Welcome to El Próspero

THE DESOLATIONS OF OCOSINGO

Welcome to the nightmare.
—Subcomandante Marcos of the EZLN
in an address to Mexican President Zedillo

Mist and a bluish road to the northeast.

After packing and seeing Doña América at Na Bolom for a mosquito-net hammock in the wee hours of the morning, I came upon Antonio, the combi chofer, next to the Cristóbal Colón depot on the outskirts of San Cristóbal calling on customers to join him on his daily passage to Ocosingo.

Antonio is a tall and alert young man who drinks coffee at the same time that he runs to the middle of the highway to see if he can convince a couple of campesinos to take his early-seventies, still-running Volkswagen bus, the combi, instead of the microbús, a larger vehicle parked a few yards behind us. He manages to snag them and brings them over.

"When do we leave?" one of the men asks.

"Ten minutes," Antonio says.

They climb in and greet me, buenos días. A woman hunched by the awkward tarp slung over her back scurries to the combi. She unwraps her bundle and sets up a table. In minutes she is blowing onto charcoal to spark up a flame under a tin template, where she arranges a coffeepot and a bucket of fresh pork tamales. The men step out, look at their watches, and order coffee. I realized that we wouldn't leave until the van was nearly full. A half hour later we were bound eastward, passing the city tangled in smoke and streaks of darkness and bluish light.

Green hills and icy shacks, steep slopes and winding curves. I wondered if this was the road that Trudi and Frans Blom followed in 1943 on their trek to the selva. "A mule pack and nine days to Ocosingo," Trudi had written in her journal on la Selva Lacandona.

We passed the Tzotzil pueblos of Huixtan, Abasolo, and Oxchuk. The towns were at the mountainous edge of the road, stacked in awkward

83

mazes of boards, laminated roofing, and brick shanties; archipelagos, tectonic accidents, floating in the rough sea of the brown-green jungle desert.
The chofer packed another six men into the van, eleven of us altogether. After three hours we arrived in Ocosingo, the old outpost between the world
of the Ladino and the realm of los Caribes, the Lacandón Mayas. In
Ocosingo, I sensed the tilt between the fincas and the city, between el monte
and seekers of profit and questions. Ocosingo stood high with mountainous peaks and low with studded rows of small sundry goods; it stood
crossed and crossed over with ancient roads of Indian tribute and labor.

By the time Trudi and Frans passed through here in '43, the selva was
lost to the encroachment of landless campesinos, loggers, chicleros, disease, and missionaries. In 1970, I didn't pass through the land; instead I
was transported to the Lacandón villages in a prop plane flown by Luis
Carlos, a dare-devil Cessna pilot. I gave Antonio, the chofer, his eight
thousand pesos and asked for directions to la selva.

Antonio and I were maneuvering on the land base where the Mayas
practiced elaborate agricultural techniques in direct harmony with the
environment. What was it like during the Classic period of the Mayas—
A.D. 250 to 900? This once was the home of the Chol-speaking Mayas, the
green-leafed slate where the ancient Mayas drew out their complex systems of astronomy, commerce, writing, and religion. Not far from these
raw streets the first murals of this continent were created, inside cities of
stone and plaster. The jungle undulated as far as the eye could see.

Waves of woven trees and vines meshed to the horizon. What made
the Mayas leave their green paradise between A.D. 700 and 900? I peered
at the Maya families crossing the street, hunched under immense nylon
sacks. Did they know?

Farther down the slopes of Ocosingo and into the lowlands were
Lake Miramar, Lake Ocotal, and Río Jataté, the village epicenters where
the early Mayas flourished with the trade of feathers, dyes, wild cacao,
and copal incense. Then Cortés's shadow of European diseases crawled
into the jungles decimating the peoples, followed by the Spanish soldiers. Alonzo Dávila, searching in 1530 for the path that Hernán Cortés
had taken in 1525 from Mexico to Honduras, occupied the island of Lacam Tun on Lake Miramar. The island was the root point of the Lacandón, a Spanish derivation of Lacam Tun, "Great Rock." I was headed in
this direction, en route to the people of the Great Rock.

"Tumbo," Antonio said abruptly and smiled as he walked away to hustle passengers on their way back to San Cristóbal. I thanked him in a confused fashion, hoping that Tumbo was the name of a bus line. By noon the Tumbo will arrive, he said as I slowly paced to the edge of the curb and sat down with my bags and turquoise-colored backpack.

On the sidewalk. Smoked a Delicado. I felt the journey had just begun. I was sitting at the crossroads of buses, Indians on horses or packed into tiny Ford pickups with tarps, tin booths selling Fantas and onion-flavored chips. A policeman across the street stepped into a barbershop and shouted out the beginnings of a conversation. Men and machetes, sombreros and dirt roads. Tzotzil women walking up the hills with buckets of bundled tortillas. Four of five combis parked with their motors running. Some heading north to Indian towns like Chilón and Bachajón, others going back to "Las Paletas."

A chofer wearing a diesel cap, tight polyester brown pants, and a sleeveless T-shirt stood in the middle of the dirt road a few feet in front of me. He cocked one leg over a stone, threw his head back, and guzzled a dark soda. With his free hand he popped a plastic bag of Ganzito sugar wafers, then stuffed them into his mouth as soon as he stopped drinking. Inflated his cheeks and jammed the bottle back into his mouth. Sweating and chewing. After he washed the pastries down, he taunted my chofer about his empty van and laughed. Antonio replied that at least he'd already made one trip and was filling his van for another.

"Just taking a break," Antonio explained. "Yo la sé trabajar," he added to the Ganzitos man.

"Mira, trabájame esta," the Ganzitos man retorted, rubbing his crotch with the half-empty soda bottle.*

In a protracted campaign to bring the Lacandón Maya under colonial control, the Spanish conducted a series of military and missionary onslaughts against them from 1559 to 1712. Tzeltal and Chol-speaking families were forced to work on sugar plantations and cattle haciendas in towns outside the selva proper. During the seventeenth and eighteenth centuries Mayan refugees from occupied territories in the Yucatán peninsula filled the vacuum. These people were also called Lacandones, a term the Spanish applied to all non-Christian Indians of the jungle. I was headed in the direction of buried and remembered usurpations.

---

*"I know how to work."
"Hey, work on this."

I was getting worried about the Tumbo. I didn't know what it was or how I was going to get on it or where it left from. A man sitting next to me, on the sidewalk, sensed my frustration and asked me about my destination. La selva, I told him. He nodded and studied my bags and my brand-new black Wranglers.

See back there, by that blue sign, he said pointing to a beaten garage to our left. Yes? Well, pretty soon they are going to open. You can buy your tickets there. I thanked him and offered him a cigarette.

"I'll watch your bags if you want," he said. "I'll buy the tickets for you too."

"I'll wait a while," I said.

Tight and wired. My pants were too thick and clean. I was feeling distrustful and nervous. I realized that my Americanness was spilling, and everyone could sense it. Even though Ocosingo was an in-between realm of seekers, choferes, indios, and campesinos, I was rigid and hadn't let myself go. How did Trudi do it? The first white woman in the selva—how did she cross through Ocosingo? How did she speak to the Tojolabal men and women, how did she commune with the Tzotzil campesinos as she walked through these roads?

It wasn't my Americanness.

It was my Indianness that was feeling cornered. It had been buried so long it had forgotten to move its limbs and arch its back, stretch its earthen sky soul. It had forgotten to trust its own reflections. Instead it recoiled and twitched inside my throat.

By two o'clock in the afternoon, a large broken bus in its fifties regalia, wide mouthed and rust grilled, rumbled into the intersection and pressed through to a makeshift depot half a block up the hill to my left. The display window read in large tattered letters: TUMBO.

Tumbo was the last village on the route through the selva, one of the choferes said. I remembered Trudi's 1940s travel journal into the selva. Tumbo was also an old Spanish term for the station where mahogany and cedar are felled, limbed, and dropped whole into the river en route to the logging mill. In her travel journals, Trudi Blom had kept detailed notes on the logging operations of the region and made ample notes on the Tumbo. Tumbo, I said to myself: the proper language for the scattered and severed colonias (settler villages) and peoples drifting in and out of the scarred landscape; the term was the master key to my passage through this gateway into the lowlands.

Picked up my hammock and bags and waddled halfway down the block to the back open court. The station resembled a busted handball court with a small table by the wall where a man wrote numbers in pencil on a stamp-size ticket book. Handed him twenty-two thousand pesos. Seat number two, the ticket read. Leaves in five minutes, he said.

I stepped in, stuffed the sleeping bag and one bag into the wire net compartment above me, then sat down and shoved the hammock under my seat.

Inside a rounded steel canopy: Indians and one Chicano with an American face, loose Coleman sneakers, jeans from Wrangler. Tumbling down to what the early 1600s explorer Diego de Vera Ordóñez de Villaquirán called "El Próspero," a Spanish version of a Mayan Cibola, a Lacandón Maya paradise.

I was about to head southeast near the route to the archaeological sites of Toniná, down the winding slopes and rings of powerlessness with sixty to seventy Tzotzil-Tzeltal Indians and campesinos; over the rutted trails, swerving and stopping every twenty minutes for new passengers from the fincas. I was about to slide down the truncated ridges of rancherías and colonias at the edge of the gravel tongue; spinning down the new road built in 1983, la Ruta Maya, connecting la selva to the commercial centers of Palenqué and Ocosingo and farther east to Tenosique, Tabasco. I was entering the Great Mexican Last Chance for refugees from Guatemala, for Protestant Indian families driven out of their hamlets following their conversion from Catholicism or from their native religion, for campesinos and Indians on the run from squalor. Since the sixties Mexico's agrarian reform policies had welcomed the nation's poor campesinos into the uncolonized land in the South. In the 1980s officials specifically encouraged settlement along the Mexico-Guatemala borderlands in order to arrest the refugee flow from Central America. This was the Last Paradise Inn.

El Próspero lay in front of me, in its swollen child bellies, in its hard paradise wind tunneling through the upper slopes of the jade-colored mountains, over the isolated, politically abandoned, and economically devastated pueblos and colonias and past the tattered forests where the sacred lakes of the Lacandón reflected the ruling sun. Somewhere near those last lakes, at the heart of this greenish and dry yellow inferno maze, I wanted to find an old friend—K'ayum.

LA RUTA MAYA

What used to take a day's walking from la selva to Palenque now takes the Lacandón a few hours on the bus or a combi. La Ruta Maya— new roads, new products for the Lacandón villages, and new profits for the city centers.
Cassette players, bicycles,
                     televisions, and more wristwatches
for the villages; this is the exchange rate for oil, tropical hardwoods, xate palm leaf, and cultural siphoning in the name of a new Indian America.

Rolling down the winding path seated next to a middle-aged man, about my age. He carried a long steely machete as a mark of his education; I carried a nylon bag of high-grade color film as a sign of my eye-

Anonymous colonia along la Ruta Maya.

lessness and thirst, as a sign of my hunger for meaning, ferocity, and spirit. There was no language to break the boundaries between us outside of a few stiff and casual greetings and accommodations.

Out my side window: open landscapes of patched green mounds and bitten hills, signposts of old and new upheavals, onslaughts for economic and cultural refuge, colonias of the dispossessed. Three hundred colonias. Indian and mestizo campesino settlements, thickened by the loss and furies of the metropolis where they float without names and familiar terrain to sleep on at night. They came here for land to slash and burn into corn, to slash and burn into fríjol, banana, and squash; to slash and burn against the multiple onslaughts of cattle ranches handling about 3 million head of cattle throughout the state and the concentrated power of the super-landowners; to slash and burn their lives into El Próspero:

Nueva Morelia
  Santa Tierra
    Santa Isabel
they came in tercets;
Agua Dulce
La Península
Plácido Flores

      Chultetik
      Monte Libano
      Yaxoquintela
the villagers sat or stood or hung on the dust, on the spliced logs, inside the steaming adobe and tin shrapnel blankets, alongside the pet dog with a malicious eye;
Tecoja
La Victoria
La Sultana

Pichucalco
Calvario
Villa las Rosas

        El Limonar
        Africa
        Nuevo Palestina

the tercets fall apart and the colonias sprawled as the wheezing tires of
the Tumbo squealed and stumbled;
Plan de Ayutla
    San Javier
        Benemérito de las Americas
            Zamora Pico de Oro

Taniperla
Nuevo Galilea
    Colonias near and far; in sediment green heat, braided ribbons on
young women, rebozos and machetes, muslin suits and dark reddish-
brown faces with alert eyes and intelligence, with harnessed Belgian
bulls grazing in the ripped yards, uprooted and naked tree roots, with
Japanese and Czechoslovakian beads around the breasts, shrunken huts
and open-air kitchens made with laminated sheets, thorn-leaf fondas,
greenish chasms with naked men swimming in the waters, howling se-
cretly to a water deity or was it simply for water? Tilted wooden teen
brides, chalkdust bridges, and slumped women carrying water up the
hills, rusted steering wheels up from the dirt, girls carrying ocote with
one arm and their pure backs of strength and endurance; through this
window, they gazed back, peered into me—the brown man with a weak
face and his mouth pressed against the glass.

    The Summer Linguistics Institute transplanted Protestant churches
into the jungles in the early fifties, a decade or so after they had introduced their brand of religion in the highland communities surrounding
San Cristóbal de las Casas. Waves of jungle growth and waves of religious interventions. One replaced the other. The myriad of Indian and
campesino settlements and villages wove their prayers and decorated
their shelves with ancient gods and the gods of the Spanish, with the
gods of the South and the gods from El Norte—where I came from.
    Welcome to El Próspero it whispered, this road.

TUMBO
(Meditations en Route)

I pass through you and you pass through me.

I pass your rivers of two hundred thousand mouths speaking through the sod, in the sculpted roadways of la Ruta Maya seeking your own bones, seeking your soul, what I left behind, many lives ago, in fullness and amusement with a green sea of leaves and tree trunks, wise turtles and furious night bats, without the rumble and rubble of colonists, missionaries, without monteros and chicleros, without PEMEX, Mexican techno-billionaires and their petrochemical jaws.

Do you remember that time?

Before they called the people from Lacam Tun, the large island of Miramar, the Lacandón?

Before Bernal Diaz del Castillo, Cortés's soldier and chronicler, spoke of the Lacandón in Acalán, Campeche, saying that they were destroyers and fire wielders.

Before 1553 when Fray Tomás Casillas, the bishop of Ciudad Real de Chiapas, wrote to the King of Spain about the savage Lacandones.

Before la Real Audiencia in Guatemala joined him in accusing these Mayan rebels of killing christianized Indians?

Who remembers now, who has kept account, wisely, patiently, through the ages? You are wondering too.

You are collecting your own ferocity, your own trueness in shards and thimble-size saucers, by la Ruta Maya, by the petro smoke, by this lineage of incursions and invasions.

This bus must be the tracing tin, so that we can meet and sing for our lost soul, our intrepid pelt with riverine eyes and feline brows. Who has them? Where have they roamed? Are they up there behind those mountains, behind the primary school shacks named after Emiliano Zapata, by the weathered stacks of empty soda bottles, detoured from their crying body, from you and me, are they riding, with their little arms banging against this window, banging somewhere behind me,

in seat number 16
or 49,
are you back there,
is that the cry I am hearing?

Or am I on another track now, is the water from your eyes coming at
me in a torrent of glass slivers, am I listening to a young campesina
mother slowly standing up reaching for seat number one, walking up to
the chofer? Or is she laughing at my romantic seriousness?
"Drop me off at La Península."
That is all she says, and "thank you," she says, "buenas tardes." Is
she speaking to me?

> This is your curandera multitrack mind. Tear through
> your ancient fingers. Pass the busted bus walls, candle lights
> into the healing skin—on one windshield you place El Santo
> Niño de Atocha, the little boy dressed in a ballerina suit,
> furled and olive colored, on another, a Charlie Chaplin hat,
> Gortari with a Buddha face, you place him there
> next to La Ruta.
>
> Is he your Capitalist father? Will you take
> the old man dressed next to you in student khakis?
> Lay him down on the bench,
> this shrunken diner; bend his shoulders with ruda oils,
> copal smoke where he moans and drowns and seeks
> his earthly escape from this last version of Mayan Being
> into Nothingness. What are you saying to him?
> Are you whispering in Choltí, are you caressing
> him with a jaguar song? Will he awaken?
>
> Welcome to this nerve meter path biting my waist,
> knotted with an Army blanket, to wonder again
> and scratch the bottom slate of this dreaming wheel.
> You must ask for a vision from the colonia shells,
> for the true road to América.
> Begin with your healing. Begin again.
> It is you lying on the demolished bench—
> on the other windshield, Mayan and bloodied,

this porous landing, crooked from El Norte, tiny
Americas, splinters and viruses, hollowness and
wakefulness, the kind that keeps you awake forever.
In river wash water, petroleum, diesel oil,
shredded psychic mist and jade ocean droplets.

Lean with the lost ones, young women, studious
and alert, aboard this ragged bus, a boy
with a Michael Jordan shirt descends
into the subterranean seas of this Indian Metro,
200,000 Indians, refugees, wary campesinos
against the cables and glass, cheering
against the cattle ranchers, landlords of Chiapas,
the PRI police and the Mexican Army:
Welcome to El Próspero.

Welcome to this tropical lowland paint on the skin:
15,300 kilometers of green sweat, human fronds, lakes,
valleys, and canyons shaped and bitten by the river basins.
Alto Usumacinta, the Lacantún, in the archaeological stone
dust of more than 250 Mayan ruins,
sacred cities—Bonampak, Yaxchilán, and Toniná.

A Zapatista glyph forms
as the campesinos face the rubble.

My sternum bends: this greenish mantle water reed
with bulldozers and mechanical digging chains, under
stone, in this odd mass of humid existence, called Selva.

The Indian woman steps down, and the heavy chromed doors snap
at her skirt, the wheels churn, and we dive deeper into la selva, the most
densely populated region of Chiapas.

This was my midpoint; I wanted to look up and see a little Cessna flying, carrying me across the skyways to Lacanjá. Only the rough heavens
appeared, whitish with a thin blue water color, only ruffled heat ahead,
in dust clouds and neatly dressed campesinos and campesinas waiting
for a ride to the next finca a few miles farther down and another somewhere in the maze of scorched forest plots, on this new route toward the
possibility of staying alive for one more decade, for one more day.

THE MAN WITH A MACHETE

After two more hours, the chofer stopped the bus and told us that we could take a break.

A line of men and children ran out. I followed them toward the side of the road to relieve myself. The women stepped out and ambled over to a makeshift restaurant at the side of the road, the whole thing the size of a small California living room.

Walked over too and ordered a hot orange soda. Inside the kitchen, I could see the backs of the choferes as they moved their heads over a large bowl of menudo. They squeezed lemon and poured salt over their bowls and rolled tortillas with one sweep of their hands.

Back on La Ruta, the light brown gravel road swam ahead of me, a snake of rubble and white powder from the crushed stones. The man next to me was sitting very still, his machete resting at his right side. The colonias blurred in whitish and green colors:

La Sultana
Pichucalco
Calvario
Villa Las Rosas
El Limonar
Africa
Nuevo Palestina
Plan de Ayutla
San Javier
Benemérito de las Americas

Didn't write or feel like pulling out my camera, fully loaded with in-frared black and white. The ride and the riders, the campesinos, had given me something already, without any questions or conditions. Something inside of me wanted to unfold and lay down its sundry machinations of caution, boundary, and bogus inner talk.

The Tumbo tossed itself down the scraped lane of small stones. I fiddled with the lime green net bag that I bought in D.F. and pulled out a couple of bolillos.

"This is for you," I said, handing one of the bread rolls to the machete man next to me, who seemed to be deep in meditation. He relaxed a little and bit slowly into the roll, savoring it as if he was eating beef. He curled the rawhide string of his machete handle around his wrist. Both of us ate and tasted what was inside of our mouths.

Another hour: San Xavier, the chofer shouted, adding that Nahá was the next stop. The man with the machete was a husband and a father. I had seen him alone, next to me. I had forgotten that I had a father once, a campesino who jumped the train north to the Unites States in the early nineteen hundreds. Felipe Emilio Herrera: I had forgotten him so many times in my feverish escapes into art and youthful searches. At sixteen, I had let go of him too soon upon his death at the age of eighty-two. We rarely spoke, yet I knew his smile and his humor, his gait, and the kindness in his hazel eyes and soft voice. We planted corn together in the outskirts of small towns in California, makeshift gardens at the edge of the city. I listened to his stories about life as a Mexican campesino from Chihuahua, and on occasion we would trade conversations. He would tell about being born in a horse carriage in 1886, and often he would speak about being orphaned. He would cry when he mentioned the name of Benita, who was his mother. I was an orphan too, but I rarely thought about this. Maybe I was running from my orphanhood, maybe I was seeking my unborn language; I carried a puzzle of figures inside of me. I looked over to my right, to the dark man next to me.

My father was still there, inside the shirt I was wearing, next to me with hands coarse from digging ditches, planting corn, driving tractors, and pulling rakes and hoes. I had come to the Mayan edge, ground down by the motion and weight of colonias and abandoned souls in descending scales.

VISITATIONS

On a bed, huge as a life raft, floating
fire visited me with dreams of sweats
and spongings.

—Víctor Martínez, from "Fever"

Standing alone on la Ruta Maya.
The prowl was over. Or had it just begun?
El Tumbo swerved and rumbled and swelled its cylinders; it crushed the soft rocks by the side of the road and disappeared in a ball of black and white smoke to the north toward Palenque.

K'ayum Ma'ax's house.

Chan K'in José at the edge of la Ruta Maya.

I was in the same position as I was in 1970 with Tomás when the Cessna dropped us off in the middle of the selva green. Something was very familiar, yet everything fell back from me the more I squinted and pulled at my face. A Lacandón woman walked onto the road about fifty yards north.

I thought about coming to the Mayan edge of Mexico. Why was I doing this? What desperation had driven me this far again? No one was waiting for me. The road was flaccid, nebulous, and resigned. What once had been a hidden Lacandón outpost now was another colonia pitstop along la Ruta Maya.

The woman stood still at the edge of La Ruta, in full Ladino dress, worn and whitish. Her hair was long and her skin was brown, dark. This is all I could distinguish.

"I am looking for K'ayum," I shouted. "I am looking for K'ayum Ma'ax," I called again. Nelly Maldonado had said K'ayum's full name was K'ayum Ma'ax.

The Lacandón woman pointed with a long arm stroke to the house a few feet in front of me. I pointed to it too, and she nodded her head.

I shuffled forward. Music poured from the laminated-roof house, a high-pitched rocanrol that boomed. Red slabs of mahogany, sawed and rough hewn, framed the small home. It could easily have been a four-bedroom house in Fresno or Chicago, except the roof was a silvery steel and the patio was a rough square of concrete with grass eating at its borders.

Nelly was right, I told myself as I peered at the satellite dish in the open patio. She said that things had changed; she had smiled at me when she said that. Maybe this was a colonia, and I had gotten off too early. Maybe Nahá was a few miles farther on and the chofer pulled a fast one on me. Three young boys in white tunics came out of the house and greeted me.

"I am looking for K'ayum Ma'ax," I said. The sun was coming down hard on my face and on their white tunics. They inspected me gently.

"K'ayum Ma'ax is my father," one of the boys responded. "He'll be back soon. My name is K'ayum Mario. And this is Chan K'in José," he added as he looked at the tallest boy with a pouting face and steady eyes. Chan K'in Francisco was the smallest, about twelve years old with a wide smile. We shook hands as if holding feathers, the same easy way you shake hands in the Huichol mountains of Nayarit.

"If you know my father you are welcome," K'ayum Mario assured me. "He'll be back. He's out with a couple of students from Mexico City."

"Students?"

"Yes, they have been here for a couple of weeks. See over there, that's their tent," K'ayum Mario said. I took a few steps around a small one-room building next to the satellite dish and noticed a modern fold-up tent dome. Students in Nahá?

Sat down on the bench, letting the rocanrol hit me from all sides, letting the thick green leaves from the hills come at me in waves, mixed with the heat and the questions of my young buddies. Pulled out some Mexican Winstons and smoked. Gave each of them a pack. Then I pulled out a handful of cassettes that I brought as gifts for K'ayum. I had read somewhere that he was a radio disc jockey, a selva D.J. Nelly also mentioned it.

"Try these," I told K'ayum Mario: a collection of Viva El Tirado, classic Chicano movement pieces from the late sixties, Arrested Development, a cassette single from the soundtrack to *Malcolm X*, Spike Lee's film, and another cassette single by TLC, a new women's rock group.

Chan K'in José's eyes lit up. "We'll be right back," Chan K'in Francisco said, running and sliding on his white rubber thongs over the smooth concrete floor.

Music blasted from the caoba house. The boys turned up the stereo and came back with plastic cups and a tall clear bottle full of hard liquor. "It's cañabrava," Chan K'in Francisco said scientifically.

"But I just got here," I told them as I tasted the distilled cane liquor. "What will your parents say?"

"No problem, they let me do what I want to do. Sometimes we all drink together," K'ayum Mario assured me.

Laughed as the sweet liquid went down my throat and began to burn a cavity of its own; a minty fire shot up from my liver area. Viva El Tirado blended into Arrested Development and then into the smooth teen funk of TLC.

The American music was bothering me; the drink burned in my belly. K'ayum Ma'ax was not here, and I was getting loaded on white fire juice with his son and the boys from next door. Now the older boy, the sullen one, was asking me personal questions.

"Do you have dreams?" Chan K'in José asked.

"Yes, I do."

"Yes I do," I repeated.

"What do you dream?" he said quietly.

"My mother," I told Chan K'in José. "She comes to me often in my dreams. The day after she died I dreamt of a giant rolling tidal wave. I was at the edge of the shore stepping down a scaffold. The wave was rolling toward me, in a slow and kind fashion. But she is gone now," I said as the others crossed their legs and laughed on the grass.

Chan K'in José looked at me directly. Came close. "Are you sad?"

I nodded and shifted my eyes.

"When you dream of her," he said, "she is with you, there at that moment, in the dream, with you." Chan K'in José smiled a bit and tilted his head to one side to see if I understood what he was telling me.

"She is with you when you dream," he repeated and bowed his head toward the concrete floor.

"You were sad for a long time, weren't you?"

"Tranquilo," he said in a genuine manner. "Relax."

Sitting on the grayish wooden bench next to the satellite dish with Chan K'in José. In a matter of minutes, in a quick and sudden exchange, I was falling into a whirlpool.

In a matter of a few strokes, Chan K'in José had slammed my psyche with a simple truth about my mother. "How she visits," he said. He used that word, "visit."

She visits you in your dream.

He was pulling at my sadness—a sadness that I thought I had cajoled and talked my way out of; a raw blueness that I thought I had boiled away during the last seven years, walking and jogging through innumerable urban parks across the States: San Jose, San Francisco, Iowa City, Fresno, Carbondale, Illinois. Chan K'in José had touched the sadness pools inside of me and with one thought had turned me around. It wasn't the cañabrava. It wasn't the juxtaposition of the redwood house with laminated roofing and the wide silver satellite dish propped up to the skies behind me next to the rushing heat.

It was Chan K'in José and his young voice that had broken something inside. In a few strokes, the ground had given way to the buried waters. I was speechless in the center of this caribal, this small Lacandón settlement of houses with walls of bajareque, crossed thin sticks and limbs pasted together with mud and grass and roofs of guatapil palm leaves. I was frozen in the late afternoon minutes of the sun, under the small slope shadows and the flashing tree branches above us.

The boy at the bottom of the whirlpool began to uncurl.

I have been writing my dreams into a journal since my mother's death. Maybe one day you can work your dreams into your poetry, a therapist friend had said. The idea didn't make sense to me. It was painful enough to go over the dreams of the morning after she passed away:

> My mother disintegrating,
> my mother swollen in a whitish room,
> my mother asleep in an old Victorian house wearing
> a dark colonial dress
> my mother in the night gathering water from a spigot in the
> garden by the side of the apartment offering me a drink
>   from her
> tiny cupped hands
> My mother in half-light
> My mother with the same blouses I had seen her wear
> when I was a child,
> then, my mother without a head
> My mother's ashes on a dresser while the house burns
> I am saving the ashes
> from what?
> My mother feeding baked salmon to ex-cons,
> leaves me none
> My mother tells me she has guided me far enough:
> "It is your turn now," she says.

I prefer to look away and write about things outside of me; it is more comfortable. Poems about refugees, about Chicano borderlands, about lovers in aviaries, footloose exiles on the march to a new country, hungry musicians, poems wrapped in memories of childhood or in stride with the political machinations of apartheid, homophobia, poems about the Americas and the theft of language, about Mexicans caught inside the metropolis without bread or names or memories, about psychic metros screwed with desire and magic poems severed from the stuff of my personal deaths, my mother's last day; her last ride in a taxi to the San Jose hospital where she would sleep her last sleep and step into another world, far away from me. I do not mix this pain with my ink. No one reads these lines that I scribble for myself.

In a matter of a few seconds, Chan K'in José, a fifteen-year-old Lacandón boy with long black hair and a taciturn air, told me that there was
someone in my dreams, my mother—Lucha. She came to me in a true
form, in the same form as I entered the selva.

NOTHING IS TAKEN THAT IS NOT GIVEN
Ode to the Traveling Men

The rap beat of Arrested Development flared through the reddish walls of K'ayum Mario's house. We drank and saluted each other. More Mexican Winstons, one after another, out of their shiny red package. I didn't think of the boys' ages or whether they smoked. The thought that the Lacandón harvest tobacco and use it for ceremonial occasions, where it cuts across status and generations, or that even smoking a cigarette could have many meanings, did not cross my mind. I had no rationale. I offered them a smoke out of a crazy exhilaration and separateness that I felt. I had arrived at K'ayum's house; would I be welcomed?

K'ayum Mario's lightness made me think of my son Joaquín, the boy I had known briefly in Venice, California, before his mother and I separated in 1970, a year after our marriage. She was a Jewish girl from Queens whom I met during my first year of college at UCLA. I didn't see Joaquín again for nineteen years, until I received a letter from his mother in 1989 asking forgiveness for banishing me from him and inviting me to visit them in upstate New York. I hadn't mentioned all this to myself for a while. This was buried too, along with my mother and father.

Following my divorce in the early seventies, I had remarried twice in California. The second marriage was a turbulent affair with a woman with whom I had had a daughter, Alma. In time we divorced as well, and—still not knowing how to communicate or what it was I wanted in a partner—I married a woman from the Pacific Northwest. This liaison ended with my predictable three-year quandaries and foibles. Finally, in 1983, I met Margarita Luna Robles and fought out and cried out my pain. I learned to let myself love and be loved. By the late eighties, I met Joaquín again, now twenty-one years old, and my second son, Joshua, also from my first marriage, whom I had never seen.

I thought of my distant sons and daughter as I listened to K'ayum Mario's laughter. I thought of my stepchildren, Marlene and Robert. I could see all my children at ease in Nahá, running down La Ruta or

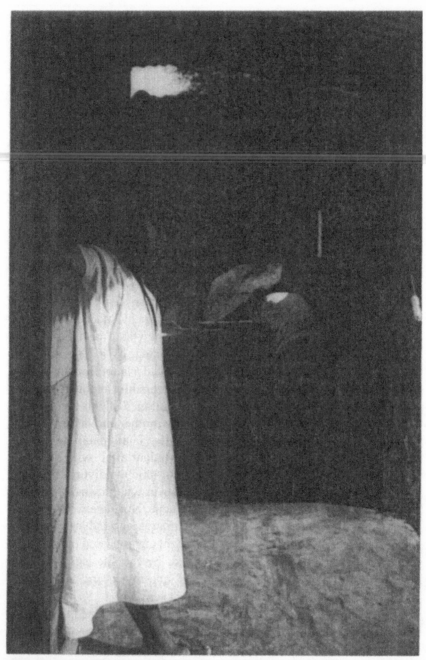

Chan K'in José and Carlos Enrique.

carving a face out of a chunk of caoba. I could see them in their true form. Another romantic illusion punished me.

Just got off the Tumbo from Ocosingo.

I was retracing Trudi Blom's trail that she laid down with Frans in the forties, I was going over the conquest routes to El Próspero. I wanted to excavate into their motives and fascinations; their own dreaming and jottings. I was asking for their lost pages of the shriveled colonias propped up on stilts and swollen vines. I came off the bus, waving good-bye to the machete man, the one I broke a bolillo with. I fell out and ran to the edge of La Ruta with my bags and the ancient hammock Doña América let me borrow back at Na Bolom. I found three young boys full of smiles and lost resemblances. I found my mother drifting by me and the children that I had yanked out of my bones many years ago. Pain and desire in the mix of an unfettered smooth selva heat.

"My father will be here pretty soon," K'ayum Mario said. "Don't worry." K'ayum Mario took a deep drag, turned his head up to the sky, blew the smoke out. The rap soundtrack to *Malcolm X* bounced through the giant satellite ear and played itself in the hot vegetation curled around us.

Another drink of cañabrava. K'ayum Mario told me he had been to Los Angeles with his father. "They invite us every now and then," he said. "My father just won the Chiapas Prize. They gave him eight million pesos."

Chan K'in José and Chan K'in Francisco fiddled with their cigarettes as K'ayum Mario provided me with an informal résumé. I noticed his Spanish. He rolled his R's and used the Castillian zeta. I wanted to ask him about his facility with the language. In 1970 only a few of the elders spoke in Spanish. I stopped myself.

Stopped

asking
the native questions
about his progress. I caught myself acting out an old colonial gesture, following the hardened tradition of anthropologists, archeologists, and "native" seekers:

traveling men with swords, bibles, machetes and notes, traveling men with satchels and journals and blurred maps, hammers, and mosquito nets between themselves and their project, their sturdy objects of study; their language thefts for the sake of an enlightened Europe and "High" America.

Grand Excavators,
High Voiced Speakers-for-the-Object,
Commanders of the New Colony,
Tomb-Gatherers,
Shard Experts,
Ink Drinkers of the New World,
Civilizer-Surgeons,
Indian Carnival Cartographers,
Journalists of the Sacred Drinking Gourd,
Filmmakers for the Archaeology of Usurpation,
Oil Vampire Drillers with a Holy Book of Salvation
and a mask of Ecological Harmony.

No more questions.
No more cameras.
No more film.

No more recordings or picking up the latest net bag from the shelf. I sickened myself with my own grand quests. I caught myself in my own seeker thirst and seeker suction. Chan K'in José's words about my mother resounded through me.

Visit, he had said.

She *visits* you often.

She *visits* you.

I realized the beauty of my dreams, the follies of my self-made utopias. There was no need for my bag of equipment.

After twenty-three years of going over my memory notes on Nahá, I dropped my nylon bag of intentions. I dropped the archaic grammar of conquest. There was nothing to translate, nothing to take back. How could I take back what Chan K'in José has given me? How could I take back the cropped greenness of the caoba trees or the stillness of the lakes, the deepness of the oil drills?

Here were the initial questions:

Who will read?
Is reading enough?
Take back and leave what?
Take what from whom?

Take back to what?
What did the Mayan Takers cull from la selva?
Whom did they represent
in the last five centuries?
How do we listen?
What satellite dish has received the news?

I thought of the Traveling Men who had passed through these Mayan regions:

Don Diego de Vera Ordóñez de Villaquirán, visionary of El Próspero
Fray Diego de Landa of the Franciscan Order
John Lloyd Stephens, the American traveler
Frederick Catherwood, Stephens's English artist companion
Alfred Maudsley, the English explorer
Sylvanus Griswold Morley, the American archaeologist
Alfred Tozzer, the Harvard archaeologist
Charles Olson, the American Black Mountain poet
John Teeple, the American astronomer
Frans Blom, the Swiss mapmaker and selva stepper
Allen Ginsberg, the Beat Sutra singer
Hermann Beyer, the American Mayan hieroglyphic reader
Sir Eric Thompson, the British New World archaeologist
Heinrich Berlin, the German epigraphist, expert of Palenque
Yurii Knorosov, the Soviet linguist
William Coe, the American archaeologist
Ian Graham, Coe's American colleague
Roberto D. Bruce, the American Lacandón anthropologist
Victor Perera, the Jewish American journalist
Juan Felipe Herrera, the Chicano poet with a funny face

How can we unearth the Mayan language from four thousand years of drift outside the epicenter, in the highlands of Guatemala, from its split into thirty-one distinct tongues, from its channels into Yucatecan and Cholan, subgroups that spread northeast of the highlands into what is now sectored as the tiny northern village of Nahá and its southern neighbor, Lacanjá Chan Sayab?
How did these Traveling Men leave these sites, these tombs, these

burial mounds, these loud stone mouth slabs and stele, how did they leave the broken villages of chapay, guatapil, and sival?

What was the cost?

What New World language did these Traveling Men edify, reconstruct, and translate?

What Travelers New World Brittanica did they contribute to? In what museums and culture boxes is it housed?

What is the shape of this revered monument given to us by these New World Traveling Men?

To what unleashed codex do the ones left behind run to?

Could the Lacandones, the ones we quickly see as the "silent subjects" of Mesoamerican research, also be the "speaking subjects"? Speakers for themselves—across cultural boundaries in time and space? And the 999,500 non-Lacandón Maya of Chiapas?

Nothing can be taken, only given.

Nothing was taken that was not given.

IN A FIELD OF ARROWS

The wry cylinders of another Tumbo rumble
and fade through La Ruta.

K'ayum Ma'ax walks up from the road, three young Mexican students following behind. Is this the K'ayum I remember? What will he say?

K'ayum Ma'ax walked up to us on the patio. His solid hair, long to the shoulder, clean bangs falling over his forehead and his clear dark eyes—came forward. He stepped lightly and firmly, then waited a moment to hear what his son was telling him about the newcomer.

K'ayum Ma'ax leaned over his light-skinned son and smelled his breath. Turning to me, he excused himself. I heard the music being switched off and the scolding begin. The other boys ran back into the greenness. I was left standing with Carlos Enrique, Luz María, and José, the students from Mexico City. José seemed out of place.

"He just got here from D.F.," said Carlos Enrique in a casual voice. "He's constantly rubbing mosquito ointment on his neck," Luz María joked. She laughed about their trek from the Universidad Autónoma de México (UNAM) and explained that they had been in Nahá for a couple of weeks and were collecting data for their masters' theses.

They were the kind of serious, well read, and articulate Mexican students I had met on other treks into their country—students whose gravity and discipline always stood out in contrast to the educational tomfoolery in the States. Mexican students always intimidated me. They knew their subject. They stood up in class to respond to the professor's queries. Their voices were loud and clear; they allowed their solar plexus to swing with their theories.

"It's José's turn to make rice. We'll see you at dinner," Carlos Enrique said.

Nelly had given me a note of introduction for K'ayum Ma'ax. Fiddling through my backpack, I found it at the bottom of the granola bag. What will I say to K'ayum Ma'ax? I had been in Chiapas about eight days and two weeks in Mexico. Plus twenty-three years of prowling through photos, old poems and notes, maps, magazines, and memory fragments.

I took out the 5 × 7 black-and-white photo of K'ayum that I had been carrying in a crumpled red folder in the backpack. Maybe this would bring us together. K'ayum Ma'ax left the house and came up to me, attentive. He apologized about his flurry with his son. My drinking didn't appear to bother him; his formal manner was familiar to me from my last visit in 1970. Jorge Paniagua, whom I had met at that time, at first conversed little, made few gestures, remained at a distance. Yet I wasn't sure; nothing was truly familiar anymore.

Gave him Nelly's note, showed him the photo. I was still standing in the same spot, outside on the patio. Frozen by the bench, under the shadows of the satellite dish, at the pit of the slanted hills that climbed above us, behind the mahogany dwelling where K'ayum Ma'ax lived.

"This is not me," he said, examining the photo. "This K'ayum is from Lacanjá Chan Sayab." He read the letter and looked up at me. Speechless.

I didn't know what to say.

I realized that I was in the wrong village.

Somehow I had been intent on coming to Nahá instead of Lacanjá Chan Sayab, a few miles to the south. That's where K'ayum lived, the K'ayum in my photo. I was intent on coming to Nahá thinking that it was Lacanjá. Now what was I going to do? Maybe stay at one of Trudi's campamentos, local tenting grounds that Trudi Blom set up for visitors to la selva.

"Maybe we did meet," K'ayum said, his eyes softening. "I was a young boy twenty-three years ago," he said.

"Around twelve," I told him.

"Yes."

I went on: "I met your father, Viejo Chan K'in, at the milpa on the other side of the lake. Jorge Paniagua and his little daughter brought me and my friend Tomás to see him in a cayuco. He was sitting down in the milpa smoking a cigar. The rest were stacking cane, threading it in bundles in the middle of the field, a few yards from where your father and Jorge Paniagua talked while we took photos. There was a little boy in the milpa too, with a machete. He kept on falling down at the end when the group got up and went back to the lake. Your father sat back with Jorge, smoked and laughed."

K'ayum Ma'ax's air had changed. I could hear a few trucks rumble nearby. Two Lacandón women walked the shoulder of La Ruta to our right, chatting. The small village entered into the evening with warmer light and gossip.

K'ayum Ma'ax sat down next to me. "If you know my father, then we must have met. I was young. But I think I met you when you came. If you know my father, that's all you need. You can stay here, with us. Or if you want you can stay in the campamento. I'll fix up this old house behind you. Our old house. There's a bed in there. I'll fix it up for you. You'll dream very nice in there. You can stay as long as you want. My father isn't feeling well. I'll take you to see him in a few days when he's better. And you can talk with him."

The connections of the past and disconnections of the present startled me. It was true: the K'ayum in the photo was another young boy with the same name. I had met him during my visit to Lacanjá Chan Sayab, the southern village that I visited after going to the milpa with Jorge Paniagua in Nahá. K'ayum Ma'ax cut cane with his older brothers; I had also met him in 1970, if only while he worked. This was the right place. I was in Nahá, where Viejo Chan K'in lived, in the northern village. My minute exchange with his father more than two decades ago was sufficient for K'ayum's cordial welcome.

Worries and a rush of mixed feelings came over me. In 1970, Jorge Paniagua told us that Viejo Chan K'in was about eighty years old, which would make him over a hundred by now. How ill was he? Would I see him? My stumbling was typical of the tourist—landcapes, villages, social relations, and people collapsed in my city mind; it was a familiar jumble in the folly of Chicano "ancestor" searches. Everything had fallen, and yet I remained standing in the same position.

I thanked K'ayum, swallowed my ineptitude, and managed to say that I had brought some gifts for him and his father, Viejo Chan K'in. He replied that he could not accept anything, but I began to pull things out of my backpack.

See, this tape recorder. Voice activated, here take it. More cassettes. Batteries for the recorder. A engraved pencil with a monkey head. Pulled out a plastic bag of longaniza, Mexican sausage that I bought in San Cristóbal. K'ayum Ma'ax smelled the sausages and mentioned the name of the San Cristóbal carnicería that made better longaniza. I took out a small box of Lifesaver Holes rolled in plastic cylinders with pop-up spouts and one of the rumcakes that my brother-in-law Jesse gave me for Christmas. These are for your father, I told him.

"You give it to him when we go," he said.

He walked back into the house with an armful of small gifts. I could tell that he liked the recorder. K'ayum Ma'ax didn't know that I had not planned to give it to him. He didn't know that it was the last thing that I would have expected to give away at this point, after so many years moving from city to city with a cardboard box full of reel-to-reel tapes of Huichol and Totonaca village talk, with a couple of reels from Lacanjá Chan Sayab, in Mayan, conversations that I never transcribed into English. The tape recorder was supposed to be my memory maker, my voice taker, my history recorder. I could have recorded stories, myths and tellings, family histories and tales of the village, of the mahogany cutters and slime makers dressed in their corporate-owned bulldozers. But in a matter of a few hours, Nahá had changed all this; Chan K'in José jarred me off my project. I gave the little self-activated machine to K'ayum Ma'ax; the voice box from the States was his now. I let go of my "ethnographic intentions."

Still, I managed to fall into an old colonial relationship; I was one more visitor dumping guilt and technology, proffering an exchange between the Modern and the Savage. Without realizing it, I had replayed the dependence drama that the Bloms and Na Bolom had set off in the forties.

I thought back to the early fall of 1970 when I came to Nahá with Tomás and remembered the cayuco ride with Jorge Paniagua. Water lilies shooting up from the green waters, tiny ring figures shaped by the water currents, the caoba oars cutting into the waters and the stillness around us, the blackness beneath the immense trees circling the edge of the lake. I walk up again to the milpa behind Tomás, behind Paniagua. Slouch up the thick trail of leaves and swollen roots. Enter the sharp greenness of the milpa and the cane shoots. The young Lacandón men lean against the cane bundles, and Viejo Chan K'in sits with his knees up against his chest, his black hair curled at the tips. His eighty years are not apparent; he is youthful, dark, and alert. He points to the young boy falling. The air is cool and the wind shifts. The boy pulls himself back up on his knees and uses his machete to push himself upright again. It is K'ayum Ma'ax.

I had never known the boy's name. He was an unknown figure in my pasted video collage. K'ayum Ma'ax, Viejo Chan K'in's third son. K'ayum was right; we did meet, for a moment, in the small field where he was gathering cane for the making of hunting arrows.

HALF CONCRETE, HALF CAOBA

I dropped my bags and Teenage Mutant Ninja Turtle backpack on the floor of K'ayum's old one-room house. Because he was now in middle school in Fresno, my stepson Robert had discarded this pack for a more sober one.

The concrete room contained a double bed with clean sheets and a loose blue blanket on top. A few plastic bags of clothes and vinyl luggage lay on the smooth concrete floor; otherwise it was empty. K'ayum had mentioned that Roberto Bruce visited on occasion. Bruce was an American anthropologist living in Mexico City, a pioneer in the study of Lacandón Mayan language and culture and a friend of the Lacandones since the fifties. I couldn't believe I had made it to Nahá.

Later K'ayum Mario came over with Chan K'in José. K'ayum Mario had been busy doing family chores and was probably grounded for drinking. Chan K'in Francisco was nowhere in sight. Chan K'in José asked me for a cigarette and startled me again:

"Maybe tomorrow we can drink balché."

"Balché?"

"Yes. K'ayum Ma'ax makes it."

"I don't think I can drink it."

"Yes you can—tranquilo."

"It is a sacred drink."

"Maybe we can drink it."

"I don't know."

"You are a Hach Winik."

I stop again. Chan K'in José had called me "Hach Winik," a true person, the term that the Lacandón Mayas use for themselves; but maybe he just wanted to drink and get intoxicated. Maybe things had gotten to the point where the sacred balché ceremony had become a party favor.

Outside José stumbled over the concrete step to K'ayum Ma'ax's house. Dressed in green fatigues, tennis shoes, a checkered shirt, he entered the empty dining area, then shuffled to the adjacent kitchen with a

113

plastic rice bag in one hand. The night covered Nahá with a thick blanket of humidity, a velvety screen of thin winds and mosquitos. Carlos
Enrique and Luz followed José, inviting me to join them. They said I was
next on kitchen duty. I walked in after them and met Nuk, K'ayum
Ma'ax's wife, who was standing by José, surprised that he was making
rice on her new Campesino stove, which was an industrial version of an
American Coleman camping stove. She smiled a bit and shook my hand
lightly. Her dress was different from the men's tunics. She reminded me
of my stepdaughter, Marlene. Dark, round eyes and a small lithe body.

Nuk hovered among the men. She had her own position, yet I didn't
know what it was. It was secure, watchful, and profound. She laughed
as José struggled with the rice, batting and swishing it with a long metal
spoon, poking at his thick black Clark Kent glasses.

In Nahá dresses are something recent for women. I noticed it when I
first arrived. The women wear Ladino dresses, pastel blouses, and even
plastic pumps, although most of the time they still walk barefoot. When
I first came in 1970, everyone wore tunics; now the women stand apart
in a Ladino frame.

I knew there were deeper differences taking place, deeper than attire
and plastic navy blue pumps; in a few hours I had seen men boarding
the Tumbo toward Ocosingo, toward ancient colonialism, en route to the
PEMEX plants. I had seen Tzeltal Indians headed to their colonias a few
miles north, Indians who had been displaced, as most settlers in la selva
had been displaced, and now followed an awkward search, carving out
crooked strips of forest for milpas and vegetable patches.

"The rice looks pretty good," I told José as he waved the spoon over
the rice, sprinkling into it tomato paste powder with chicken bouillon
from a Knoor box. K'ayum Mario handed plastic plates to each of us. My
chair was an old portable tree stump, and Nuk sat on a tiny wooden baby
chair; the rest found places on the floor. As K'ayum Ma'ax mentioned
his ongoing project to finish building his new house, I looked at the
Campesino stove, the brand-new refrigerator, and the tiny chair. Windows were cut into the red mahogany walls, unfinished; the room was
open to the elements, the entrance half made with concrete mix still in
bags. A giant water heater lay on its side on the concrete floor waiting to
be assembled and connected to the new sockets and plumbing. The
sweet night fragrance came in and carried the rice flavors back out to the
trees.

We talked and made jokes. Carlos Enrique jabbed at K'ayum Ma'ax for getting him "bolo" a few nights before my arrival. "You even brought out a case of Modelo beer from your stash," he said to K'ayum Ma'ax. K'ayum nodded and smiled curtly.

After more banter and smokes, K'ayum Ma'ax slipped into his living room and lay down on a white hammock. I gawked at the thirty-inch color television and brand-new sound system; the stack of cassettes that I had given to K'ayum Mario sat on top of one of the speakers. K'ayum Ma'ax's little granddaughter, Margarita, sat on a tiny chair next to him. The room was a spacious red wood studio with nothing but the television, the sound system, and the hammock. Its concrete floor was clean and shiny.

I felt awkward about the silences. Everyone seemed to walk within a large bubble of free space, each in their own. At times we would connect, at others we would float to our own quarters. I was used to a continuous jabber, a heavy exchange of verbal action. Here the words had to come from the gut or they did not come at all. The foliage intervened, the thickness of the colors, the gravel by the ruta, the ebb and flow of the passers-by. The electric hum of the refrigerator, the hoarse whispers of the Coleman-like stove, the children that hung on to the unfinished caoba window frame of the living room watching TV along with K'ayum Ma'ax; these gestures and village sounds provided a language in their own terms.

Back on the patio, I could hear Carlos Enrique, Luz, and José in their tiny tarp behind my little house. They were doing what good anthropology students must do. They were going over their notes, their taped interviews, checking their schedules for the rest for the week. Supplies, batteries, cameras, film. It was as if I was looking at myself twenty-three years ago in Lacanjá with canvas bags of appropriate ethnographic paraphernalia.

Seated on the bench, under a starry patch of open sky, I gazed over K'ayum Ma'ax's new mahogany house, half concrete and half red tree skin from the caoba. Blue light from the thirty inch spilled out of the empty window rectangles. The kitchen light was still on. José came out of the tent with a toothbrush and a tube of paste, ambled to the large concrete sink at the entrance to K'ayum's place. The toilet and the shower were back there too, enclosed by caoba doors, built on a small rectangle of concrete. Half concrete, half caoba, the strongest wood on the face of the earth. Three Mexicans, one Chicano, and a village of Hach Winik. José brushed his teeth, I smoked.

DREAM PROWL

Lean back and rest a little before going to sleep. Chan K'in José, Chan K'in Francisco, and K'ayum Mario—whisper the names. Settled, nudged against this caoba bench, I groped for the spirit child in me—how it had walked me back to this new starting point, to this seeing and being, to my own inner worlds, to this slaughtered vastness where there are True People, where there are dream tracks, alive, silvery and untouched, where the dead converse and chatter and continue eating and standing by the fires, telling us stories. Even if in half concrete and half laminated roof, the other half still lives. Lives fully; the embossed side of the spirit tree roots. Lacandones go and they come on these dream tracks, the dream tracks of Nahá.

My prowl is a dream prowl, it is a spirit child prowl, a mother prowl; a prowl for the lost ones, the dead ones, the hurt ones; it is a healer prowl, a singer prowl, a father womb prowl, a prowl of soul pauses and psychic forest silences. I had to uncover the landscape, the campesino-Indian political mesh, the air of national disinheritance—I had to begin to scrape off my city skin tunics. My prowl was my prayer.

LAST SONG OF THE WHITE TURTLE

A couple of days later, K'ayum Mario invited me to go to Lake Nahá, a quarter of a mile north, alongside La Ruta. After brushing my teeth over the bottomless sink, I joined K'ayum Mario, Chan K'in José, and Chan K'in Francisco. Carlos Enrique and his comrades came along too. K'ayum Mario ran to a distant figure on the edge of La Ruta and came back with Viona, an americana from a commune in northern California who arrived in the Tumbo a few days after I did, without an agenda. Chan K'in Francisco, the smallest, hurried to fetch the cayucos through the sword grass mud.

In a matter of a few hours we reassembled ourselves: Mexican students with cameras, a young white woman with a glazy gaze, myself with my odd wondering, and the young boys, dedicated and intent on a visit to the sacred lake.

"I'll patch up the holes with mud and we'll be ready," K'ayum Mario told Carlos Enrique as he worked on the cayuco. The dugout canoes were about twelve feet long and three feet wide. We stepped gently on the soft earth so as not to slip in the muddy edge of the lake.

Chan K'in José stood at the front of my cayuco, pulling the water with a caoba oar. K'ayum Mario worked at the back, also on his feet, following the strokes of Chan K'in José. Lined up in the middle were Carlos Enrique and Viona and me. Behind our cayuco Chan K'in Francisco led a second one bearing José and Luz. Pancho Villa, another small Lacandón boy, steered at the back of that cayuco, gently directing it into the heart of the lake.

Two cayucos.

The waters full with secrets.

Water lilies with light red ink veins behind their petals, large snails sucking the leaves, tiny fish skittering through the vines underwater, a few inches below the surface. They were showing me how to behave. I resisted them. I was frozen. They were beckoning me to spread myself over this infinite sacred pool, to turn red with them, to show the backside of my dreams, the flesh dream, the bone-marrow dream.

The fallen boy in the well dream:

His face turns to me. One leg is curled back. He was looking for a short-cut across a neighbor's yard at night, in a village a few miles north of Mexico City, but he fell. He almost glided across the hidden village well, except he tumbled and was swallowed deep. His eyes and cheeks are wet. Only his head moves, down there in the small dark round circle of moist stone and reddish roots. The boy has my face; he fell without anyone knowing it. He fell while he was playing. Into sudden darkness, into sudden inner exiles and awakenings, into his lost and forgotten self, doubled up at the bottom of a warm and watery pit. He is rising now. His left leg is curling back to its original position. His whitish feet are muddy and his toenails are long, curved at the ends. The belly breathes; the face—my face—wants to howl.

I ran my right hand through the sweetness of the lake. Cool to the touch, then immediately warm. Tangled webs of plant growth, light golden nets of leaf and green bristles. The water, speckled with moss and flecks of plant life. Chan K'in José looked away into the blue greenness as he pushed the oars; he smiled at Chan K'in Francisco as he struggled with his cayuco behind us. K'ayum Mario's mud patches smeared our pants as we sat on the curved floor of the cayuco.

Carlos Enrique took off his pants and shirt and jumped into the waters. I stayed in the swishing cayuco with Chan K'in José leading the way through the vines. In the distance, José splashed into the lake too. We were all going with the inner motions of Lake Nahá, the ancient water that Villaquirán wanted to taste so he could heal. I looked for water creatures and wondered about them.

Chan K'in José began to speak:

> Viejo Chan K'in says that we used to have many river turtles, many tortugas blancas, years ago. The rivers were full with them. I've seen them in the Tumbo bus, tied up with nylon rope, sliced and bleeding from the spears of the poachers. They come to the lakes with their equipment. They come to la selva when the turtles lay their eggs, between September and May. They drown them in their nets. They drag them all the way to San Cristóbal, Tabasco, and Veracruz. Fifteen hundred pesos per kilo, if they are alive still and in their shell. Then the big city merchants sell them for ten times more. I see them sometimes, in the Tumbo, in

pick-ups on the way to San Cristóbal, in green nets, with
fins tied, bleeding. I don't know what's going to happen.
The trees seem to be getting smaller. Viejo Chan K'in says
that many years ago they used to grow seventy to ninety
meters, all of them. Some still grow like that, they still watch
over the lake. Right now they are watching over us too.

The selva occupied 4 percent of the Chiapas terrain yet contained
about half of country's mammals. I had read this in a recent report. I
asked about my favorites, the monkeys.

Viejo Chan K'in tells us that the sarahuato, the black howler
monkey, and the mono araña, the spider monkey, are hunted
down by the new colonists. The little ones. The little ones are
hunted down by the comerciantes and sold as mascots
throughout the country. He says that the new colonists are
pushing the monkeys out of the forests. He says the foreigners
eat our peccaries and hunt the tapir. There are very few tapirs
now. When the xateros come to take xate palm leaf, they hunt
the peccary, the monkey, all the animals they can find while
they set up their camps. Sometimes they even catch a jaguar
or a puma and sell them in Tuxtla Gutiérrez and San Cristóbal
for a couple of million pesos. K'ayum Ma'ax says that it is
against the law now, but they come anyway and take what
they can, they sell it and make millions of pesos, and they sell
the xate too. He says that when he was a child the Ladino
xateros came to Lacanjá Chan Sayab with exclusive rights to
harvest the palm leaf. Everybody cut the xate, sold the xate,
stocked the xate for the businessmen, who allowed the Lacandones to act as bookkeepers and managers. Soon the young
ones were drinking with their new salaries, and a cantina was
set up in Lacanjá Chan Sayab; then everything turned sour.
They had to go farther out to find xate. They didn't want to go
to their milpas anymore. They wanted to cut and sell xate.

About xate, I only had a few notes and statistics gathered from the
Reserva de la Biosfera de los Montes Azules study conducted by the
CIES center in San Cristóbal as well as from conversations with the peo-

ple there. In 1986, 300 million xate leaves had been exported to the United States for use in the florist industry, particularly in California. After they are harvested in the Lacandón jungle, they are hauled to Tenosique, Tabasco, where they are packed in "freezer trailers" and shipped to distributors in San Antonio, Texas. An article in the Reserva report written by Ignacio March, a lead investigator, mentioned that in 1992 a bushel of xate (two hundred leaves) in perfect condition brought about fifteen hundred pesos. Chan K'in José's cayuco stories literally hit home. The florist commerce for Valentines, weddings, birthdays, the circus of sundry celebrations in parlors and restaurants, and of course the drone of funerals, all profited from the xateros' daily summer grind of gathering, at best, four bushels a day for no more than the equivalent of four U.S. dollars. Xate production by itself pointed to our middle-class collusion with lethal forces in Mayan terrain. I didn't want to interrupt Chan K'in José as he looked into the distance with the oar in motion and the water answering to every stroke.

> Viejo Chan K'in tells of the colibrí tzacatl, of the zopilote de cabeza amarilla. He says that not too long ago there were guacamayos rojos everywhere, just a few miles from here in Lago Ocotal. What do you see? I can remember since I was about five years old many people coming to la selva. As they have come, the animals, the birds, the monkeys, and the turtles have hidden.

I stayed in the cayuco with K'ayum Mario. The rest were swimming in the lake. José came up again pinching his nose in the distance. Pancho Villa and Chan K'in Francisco had abandoned their cayuko. They screamed from afar that the water had broken through the mud packs and was flooding their cayuko. Viona asked K'ayum Mario and Chan K'in José if it was all right if she removed her blouse and pants and swam half naked, with only her underpants on. They looked at each other for a moment and said yes, surprised that she had asked for permission. I was caught between staring at her or going along with the boys, telling stories. K'ayum Mario and Chan K'in José were perplexed and amused with her request; then they went about their paddling.

I saw the horizon ahead of us, the wild smoke in the trees, greenish, connecting the forest surrounding us as if a pulsating ring with a liquid eye at the center peering on another eye, an infinite one—the sky above, that second eye focused on Chan K'in José's white tunic. With its pure light it washed the cloth, made it lighter, feathery, glowing. A young man on fire, his face hidden by his long hair, sat before me, his rhythm going with the lake, the cayuco, with us and the rest of the village. We were alone in Nahá, meditations and flames over the Lake of the Great Water.

As we walked up on the shore, a tall Lacandón drove up in a Travel-All station wagon with two children in tunics. His jeans and tennis shoes stuck out under the tunic. There was something odd about him. Dark-rimmed glasses and an unshaven face, and yet his easy conversation with the boys made me feel he had been here a long time. Later, as we walked La Ruta back to Nahá, Luz told me that his name was Leo and that he was from the United States. He came a few years ago and stayed. He married a Lacandón woman and on occasion gave the Tzeltales rides to Palenque, made good cash.

We passed by fields of papaya, bananas, and sugarcane and open stretches of cut trees and thick forest. Chan K'in Francisco tickled me with his smile and spontaneous energy. He sat down in the middle of La Ruta and pulled a thorn out of his foot, jumped up, and ran into the center of the village. We walked freely. K'ayum Mario looked silly with his rubber boots, tunic, and short hair. The forest was cut into large sections for planting, others for cattle grazing. A few Lacandones in the distance of the woven hills waved as we passed. The shadows cut through our sand road as we trotted and laughed. The sun burned on my skin. Water, oars, vines and found stones, laughter, play and nakedness.

For years I had remained aloof and tangled in my own machinations. Something was catching up to me, but I didn't know what it was. I knew it had to do with this land, this Mayan chunk of greenness at the southern edge of Mexico's starvations and huddled Indian seekers of survival. I knew it had to do with my own resurrection, with a tiny soul link to the Lacandón, a lost loop, a continuous gathering of healing stories. The bloody xate leaves, the poacher's hands, the new colonial Ladino trapping machine—they were here too, to point me back across the illusory borderlands between our cultures, countries, and desires.

KASSANDRA AND THE DESCRAMBLER

At K'ayum Ma'ax's house, the TV blasted out a telenovela imported from D.F. featuring the dilemmas of Kassandra, an upscale Ladina caught between two lovers. She lived in a middle-class studio and dressed in a violet miniskirt and pink ruffled top. Silver bracelets jangled as she moved her painted figure across the screen. The voice—an exaggerated purr of posh D.F. smoke-filled "intellectual" cafés in the Zona Rosa, the "pink space" of middle-class Mexican teeny-boppers, latex-skirt sex workers, and flatulent americanos on a loose salsa stroll. Kassandra filled the Lacandón entertainment center. Cut to mixed images of MTV on another channel. The strip

wavered and shut down.

Leaning through the unglassed window I popped my head deeper into the room. K'ayum Mario on the hammock. I told him that in the U.S. we had little machines called descramblers that altered the channels so that we could view any program we wished.

D E S C R AM BLER.

He repeated in a mouthful of tongue. We had television in common instead of a fire at the center of our rooms.

Descram   bler.

"How many channels do you get?" he asked me. "At what time do you get to see Kassandra? How come you know so much about descramblers?"

Later K'ayum Ma'ax came in, eased onto the hammock, changed channels with the remote. Clinton and Salinas de Gortari were on CNN, appearing in an open plenary with journalists from both countries. Salinas de Gortari and his attendants waited at the microphone for Clinton to walk out and join them in announcing the new trade agreement between their nations.

"Salinas de Gortari looks worried, looks like he is about cry. Clinton isn't coming out. That's bad. Wait, there he comes!" K'ayum Ma'ax said.

"Something is wrong," I said to K'ayum Ma'ax. Something had gone awry in Clinton's address to the public. Something about Mexico's indebtedness. Something that he should have kept under covers. Salinas came back at Clinton in a forceful manner. As the program closed one of the reporters from Mexico asked them if they were in agreement with the basic premises of the plan for the trade agreement. Clinton responded in a rehearsed and polished accent that everything was going at its optimum pace. Salinas de Gortari made a strong case for accord as well.

"Obviously something is wrong here," the reporter noted. "Both of you show signs of anxiety. You do not look like there is much agreement between you at this time."

"Did you see that?" I asked K'ayum Ma'ax.

"Yes, Clinton blew it. And look at Salinas de Gortari. He's mad as a bald badger. That reporter sure got Clinton. He nailed both of them," K'ayum Ma'ax said as he exploded into laughter.

Later in the afternoon we reenacted the presidential address with its oddities; K'ayum Ma'ax started it, and I joined him. Nuk laughed at my clown work as I swiveled my head like Elvis and coughed in my hand, imitating Señor Clinton.

"Can you believe it? The reporter said that there was something wrong. He told them that he could tell by the way they were talking to each other," K'ayum Ma'ax reported to our little audience in the kitchen hovering over the Campesino stove.

Carlos Enrique had been listening to our pantomime. "What does this mean then, Juan Felipe? What does it mean?" He was serious.

"I don't know," I told him.

I wanted to elaborate on various political matters: on the dependent status of Mexico, on the few options Mexico has to gain economic stability without closer ties and concessions to the United States. On Salinas de Gortari's undermining of land reform and the dire consequences of colonization in the lowlands; I wanted to summarize the last two hundred years of U.S. domination over Latin American peoples, their labor, their spirit. I wanted to talk about this TV in the living room, K'ayum Mario's perfect Castillian Spanish, the satellite dish in the patio, the shape of this Lacandón house, the concrete squares of floor, and the expensive water heater still boxed in the front yard because no one knew how to install it.

Carlos Enrique studied me, waiting for my answer. I mumbled something unintelligible, generalities. Bad news, that's all I could say. Another sham, one more deal down the good old bottomless Mexican throat. One more intravenous cable at the boundary between American capitalist enterprise and Latin American servitude.

The NAFTA project paralleled the colonial and corporate encroachment on the Lacandón Maya and the Lacandón Mayan rain forest—all in the name of mutual expansion, mutual economic growth, mutual energy development programs.

NAFTA seemed to legitimize the United States' economic and cultural suction on Mexico soon after World War II. With its explosive postwar population increase, Mexico was set up as economic fodder for major American conglomerates:

Uniroyal with rubber.

Firestone with more rubber.

Goodyear with endless forests of rubber.

General Electric with toasters, with irons and blow dryers, with refrigerators, and with innumerable forests of televisions.

Then feed the Mexican Indian mouth with Kellogg's corn flakes, with a Campbell soup can on the kitchen altar in Atizapán de Zaragoza and H. J. Heinz's tomato sauce boiling over Popocatepetl and Ixtacihuatl, and Coca Cola with its obsidian baritone voice syrup.

Colgate Palmolive to bathe and scratch off the color of being Mexican and Indian.

Johnson & Johnson and Bristol-Myers to soothe the stripped skin.

Eastman Kodak to process and disperse the new image.

Sherwin Williams to paint the new thatch-roof hut.

ITT & IBM to make sure everybody knows.

After the sixties Nissan, Volkswagen, and Renault provided more elaborate locomotion for the Nuevo Hombre and Nueva Mujer of this booming ragged middle class.

And the de la Madrid–Gortari–Zedillo party technocrats? The new class of Mexican billionaire families? They ask for the bull's ear at the bullrings, they speak of the Olmec mother culture, of Quetzalcoatl's symbolic influence in present-day student Pan-Indian revivalist cults; they even discuss theories of the disappearance of the Classic Maya; they pay homage in front of the camera. See them visit El Tajín, Tulum, Palenque, and Bonampak. Note how they kneel at the foot of the temples. "Let us honor our indigenous culture," they say. They say this the way they say "oil, power, and profit" when they promote NAFTA—with the erotic power fix of a rapist.

The Mayan edge spoke of another factor:
This factor is not mutual: human exploitation.
This factor is not mutual: resource exploitation.
This factor is not mutual: cultural oppression.
This factor is not mutual: tribal powerlessness.
This factor is not mutual: forest and soil destruction.
This factor is not mutual: floral and faunal extinction.
This factor is not mutual: the end of green winds.
This factor is not mutual: bleeding caoba and cedar stumps.
This factor is not mutual: suited men with bulldozer faces.
This factor is not mutual:
                    tourists with mechanical extensions.
This factor is not mutual:
a national American ID card issued to all Mexicans participating in this NAFTA presidential project. Those outside of it shall remain in the Anonymous Colony of Servitude (ACS) pronounced AXE.

Is a descrambler needed? DE S CRAM BLA.

American arrogance, Mexican technocratic rape—that's what I wanted to tell Carlos Enrique. Mexican dependency cloaked in presidential machismo. That's close to what I wanted to say. But I thought of it too late and the night had come down again. And the new Indian arrogance, the ones with VCRs, with high-tech agronomy and eighteen-wheeler trucks. The invitation to cook rice on the Campesino stove had gone unheeded once again; the predator in the dark greenness was silent yet present.

EL EMPERADOR

Outside, under the dark trees by the bench, K'ayum Ma'ax talked about his favorite movie: *El Emperador*. I tried to think about a movie from the States with this name. *The Emperor?* There were a couple with that title.

"The movie was filmed around here, not too long ago," K'ayum Ma'ax said. "I love it because the jungle fights back. The jungle takes over. You can see the tree's blood. The blood glows when it's spilled on the leaves. All of a sudden the jungle becomes solid and jumps on the backs of the invaders. They can't see it, but it is there. Right in front of them. In plain sight. It is always there, high up. Or down below. They have to run from it. But they don't know what they're running from. One by one they die. Until one is left. He must meet the jungle face to face, if he can.

"They filmed it nearby, not too far from here," K'ayum Ma'ax repeated. Then he mentioned Arnold Schwarzenegger—El Grandote.

"Predator. Yes, yes. The jungle fights back," I said. Yes, yes, *El Emperador*. This must have been the translation, I thought.

Was this jungle fighting back? I couldn't tell.

We walked in, had rice with a few words. With the boys coming in for Coke from a liter-size glass bottle in the refrigerator. Pancho Villa called me to come outside. "He wants you to buy him a Coke," said Carlos Enrique. "We are all out of money and Pancho Villa is still thirsty."

Outside, by the door, smoked another Mexican Winston. Luz chatted with Angélica, K'ayum and Nuk's teen daughter. This was the first time that I had seen her.

Luz asked Angélica

an ethnographic question:

Do you know a story about the moon or about women in relationship to the moon?

Angélica nodded her head.

It was a good anthropological topic; I could see Evans-Pritchard, the English anthropologist, asking the African tribal groups, the Nuer or the

126

Dinka, something similar about their spirit worlds. Levi-Strauss, the French anthropologist, came to mind with his own pursuits in Brazil, figuring out a system of wife exchange. The moon. Lacandón Mayan women. Folktales, belief systems, symbols. Gender rituals of initiation, taboos. A new feminist model. There must be something to all that.

The only problem was that it was a question, one that created the answer: an arrow-shaped incision into the native. The only problem is that the question was in Spanish, an unfortunate mishap. This clouds the air. The only problem was that a female missionary worker already had asked that in the name of Fray Diego de Landa. The only problem was that Angélica did not answer the question.

Perhaps the other problem was that Luz had to find this out by herself after many more hours and weeks and years. After she had learned Maya and blended into the landscape. After the question had left behind its predator-shaped voice.

NUK OF LA TIENDITA

Strolled with Pancho Villa to the little store at the edge of La Ruta where the road wound up into the hills and disappeared into San Xavier a few miles south on the long trek back to Ocosingo.

The tiendita was housed in a tiny broken cabin made from old, gray slices of caoba lumber. The upper half of the front wall facing La Ruta was open, supported by a stick propped on the ground as if it was the hood of a giant forties truck. The front half of the cabin offered the village and passers-by a sundry selection of goods from headache pills to rolls of cookies wrapped in bright red and silver paper. The back half was dark and screened by a rough blanket, a private family dwelling. One of the family members would emerge through this curtain when someone called for a purchase. Bayer aspirins in plastic wrappers were tacked on the front wall. On one of two shelves were a couple of cans of Embasa stewed tomatoes. On the other slab, a few tiny boxes of Knorr tomato paste. Pancho Villa and I leaned on the open frame and called out for service.

Nuk, a young Lacandón Mayan girl, walked through a torn blanket from the back and stood facing us.

"We'll have a large bottle of Coke," I said with village savvy.

"Hot or cold?"

"Uh, cold."

"None of that."

"Well, uh, hot then."

"Galletas," cried Pancho Villa.

"Oh, and, uh, cookies. Make that two galletas."

Nuk reached under the counter and brought out two large rolls of Gamesa sugar wafers. "Anything else?"

"Nothing else," I said, and Pancho Villa smiled a toothy and guilty smile. He was a small Lacandón boy, about nine or ten years old, who called me as often as he could so I would treat him to galletas and large liters of warm Coke. I gave Nuk five thousand pesos, and we jaunted back to K'ayum's house. We ran over to K'ayum's TV window, a village theater of sorts, and stuffed ourselves with Gamesas.

Nuk had the same name as K'ayum Ma'ax's wife. I realized that Lacandón Mayas share a few names: Nuk, Chan K'in, K'ayum, Bor, and a handful of others.

Nuk of la tiendita.

She reminded me of Maruch, the Chamula Indian girl that I met in San Cristóbal in 1970. Was it her age? Was it her leaning to one side, coming from behind a ragged curtain? Was it her small smile, her elegance? It was her Mayan self intersected with the ever-expanding encroachment of americano corporate interests, Mexican campesino cultural fractures, wave upon wave of Tumbo colonia passengers from all points of southern Mexico and the Guatemalan border. She was the young figure of doomed passage, of the last stop before unmitigated dependence or revolution flooded the region.

I never found Maruch again. A few days before I left Na Bolom, I thought I saw Pasquala, Maruch's mother, at the mercado by the Santo Domingo church, at the northern edge of San Cristóbal. For a moment I thought I recognized her among the Chamula women speckling the ground, on their knees, busy with their wares: Guatemalan jackets, chamorros, woven bracelets, and hair bonnets. When I caught up with the Chamula woman, she was poised. I stayed and asked her if she knew Maruch, daughter of Pasquala. I pulled out my photographs. Do you know her? I asked. Have you seen her? She looked up at me and nodded her head, businesslike.

Who was I looking for? Generations of Indian children grow to the age of thirteen and then they seem to disappear. They turn into sharp-angled work paraphernalia, into vendor vines that grow at the Ladino corners, next to the supermarkets, or they become markets themselves, tienditas. Little Nuk was a sign that the children of the most remote region of Chiapas had joined in the short and arduous march toward servitude and oblivion.

LAKE WATERS OF THE WHITE JAGUAR

Seven in the morning. Stepped outside in my black jeans and a white cotton T-shirt; brushed my teeth at the awkward sink in the yard. The sweat, dust, and mud of the lake still clung to me. A brisk shower outside K'ayum Ma'ax's new-fangled house. Ice cold. Shivers and jitters. No one in sight. As I dressed in the caoba shower cubicle something startled me—the dream of the night before:

Preparing the cayuco. Left to right: Pancho Villa, Chan K'in José, K'ayum Mario, and Chan K'in Francisco.

I am walking with my mother along a ledge, or is it a fence? She is at my left side, inching sideways. I follow with my hands on the fence. Inch by inch. It must be about three or four in the afternoon. There is still plenty of light. We are on the beach. I can tell by the sand under us and the waves beginning to crawl after us. My mother jumps off the ledge; I follow. Now both of us are walking on the sand, carefree and unencumbered. We walk on the gray sand. All I can see is her side, then her body from the back. I know it is my mother by the way she walks, by her long cotton dress, a violet color, and her sweater, an avocado green.

I finished dressing, tying on my old brown high-top tennis shoes. A light feeling came to me from my dream. My mother and I were both on the same trail, walking more openly. Neither of us clung to the fence anymore, even though the waters were beginning to roll toward us. I thought of what Chan K'in José had told me about visits, about sadness and joy, about entering into another world, about receiving visits and gifts from afar, about dreams and mothers and lost sons. Water, waves, and tides have been a recurring theme in my dreams.

A walk down La Ruta toward the lake felt like the right thing to do.

At the lake I gazed over the cool waters and went over my dream, my reasons for being here. I realized I didn't know how to return to the States. What would I do with these meager landscapes? How would I carry myself?

The lake was the same one that Villaquirán wanted to reach with his outstretched hands before he died in the early 1600s. Lago Nahá was the same lake that carried the native people whom the Spanish called Lacandón, Indians from a tribal center in Lake Miramar called Lacam Tun, Great Stone. Later, in the nineteenth century, the lumber-mill workers, the monteros, cut caoba and mahogany and called the entire area, *the Ocosingo Desert—the Desert of Solitude.*

The recent designation of this area as the Lacandón rain forest was based on biological, botanical, and political considerations. This was the same forest and cultural space that occupied the Petén in Guatemala, on both sides of the Usumacinta River, Mayan mirror of border conquests and spiritual rebirths.

I imagined the onslaughts of invasion and the ecstasies of rebellion.

The limestone and the foliage-laden mountains tossed up by tectonic blasts in the Tertiary and the Quaternary periods remembered the conquering business. Concentric rings in the trees still circled and re-

flected the conquest voyages, the arrogant usurpations since 1525, when
Bernal Díaz del Castillo warned Cortés and his soldiers of the Lacandón
"enemy."

The lake was the inkwell of each intervention; the waters contained
the letters of each pronouncement. What was left of the forest still carried the language of the one thousand Lacandones living at the time of
the conquest in this northeastern forest patch of Chiapas.

The waters, somewhere in their depths, held maps on the Lacandón relocations into reducciones in 1560 by the Dominican friars; they noted Fray
Pedro Lorenzo de la Nada, who founded the colonial pueblo of Palenque,
grand collaborator of relocating the Indians to the exile-pueblos of Tila,
Yajalón,

   Ocosingo,

      Bachajón,

         Chilón,

Tumbala. This small round water mirror still held these images, even
if silvery and wound in algae.

The last lake of Nahá knew the language of the conquerors and of the
exiled; it knew the Spanish verbs—to save, to safeguard. The stories
of invasion and protectionist verbiage had been carried for centuries,
in cayuco and milpa conversations by the lake; the lake remembered
Cortés's dictum to Spain: Cumplo pero no obedezco (I'll accomplish but
I won't obey). In the name of the Crown, Cortés indeed established a settlement in Veracruz, where he and his men landed, but he also expanded
his powers and appointed himself governor of New Spain—forces that
ultimately ravaged the Mayan peoples and landscape. The lake remembered Chol, Choltí Maya, the language of the hard-backed milperos.

I thought of the Lacandón insurgence against the relocation centers
and their attacks on Bachajón and its Tzeltal colony in 1552, the Battle of
the Lacandón in 1559. All this was still here, in some form. Due to the
urgings of the Bishop of Ciudad Real and the Dominican friars, the government of Guatemala organized a military invasion into the area to capture, deport, and kill all those at Lacam Tun Lake. The lake contained
this, as an earthen jar must keep all the sighs and whispers of its owner.
I thought of how the Lacandones came back once again to fight against
the Christian project keepers, how the Spanish colonists returned too, in
1586, and how they burnt down Lacam Tun with a twenty-league radius

of fire around the lake and how many of the Lacandón rebels fled and formed a secret pueblo,

Sac-bahlan-te, White Jaguar.

Sac-bahlan-te had stood for more than a hundred years when the Franciscan missionary Antonio Margil de Jesús came upon it in 1694. Margil de Jesús called upon the Audiencia of Guatemala to begin a series of attacks on Sac-bahlan-te, and within a year the new colonists—in three simultaneous invasions from Chiapas, Huehuetenango, and Verapaz—quelled the White Jaguar and baptized it, calling it Nuestra Señora de los Dolores, a new mission and presidio in the tropics.

Diseases, deportations, and relocations followed. By 1769, in the ruins of a Guatemalan barrio called Santa Catarina Retalhuleu, all that remained of the White Jaguar Lacandón rebels were three old people, wasted and immobile, two men and a woman.

The waters knew the histories: the sad end of the White Jaguar rebels and subsequent exile and rebel Indians fleeing bloodbaths in El Petén of Guatemala during the seventeenth and eighteenth centuries. This latter group of Maya-Yucateco speakers are the ancestors of the contemporary Lacandones of Nahá. Since then they have tilled their milpas of maize, beans, chilis, squash, and a variety of tropical vegetables and fruits.

The call of Captain Cayetano Ramón Robles still rippled in the lower sheaths of the lake. In 1821, the same year that the state of Chiapas shrugged off its Spanish yoke and became independent, Captain Robles, a member of one of Ciudad Real's wealthy families, arrived in the Lacandón rain forest along with business associates to exploit its tropical hardwoods, caoba and cedar, which could be sold for half the price offered by the American market; the finest hardwoods in the Americas were deftly severed from the land. Using the rivers to float them to transportation centers, Robles garnered the bounty.

Others soon followed Captain Robles. In 1859, Felipe Martín, an outstanding student of the captain's early example, launched seventy-two caoba and cedar sections into the Lacantún River and later gathered them in Tenosique. These were the initial trials at cutting the forest down, the beginnings of the montería industry, which established transport routes at the mouths of key jungle rivers such as the Lacantún, Pasión, and Usumacinta. By 1880 individual timber projects were overshadowed by three major lumber enterprises from Tabasco that had moved into the region:

Bulnes Hermanos
Valenzuela e Hijos
Jamet y Sastré

The Trinity of Tropical Hardwood Blood Inquisitions.
The waters remembered the floating wood en route to London

to New York
to Liverpool—they called it "madera de Tabasco."

The year 1892 marked the beginning of the Golden Age of Extraction,
the liberal policies of the federal government. The trinity of companies
expanded to an octet of jungle hex:

Casa Romano
Casa Schindler
Maximiliano Doremburg
Troncoso-Cilveti
Ramos, Ocampo y Martín.

By the end of the nineteenth century the Selva Lacandona had been
branded with a death mask of monterías, leveling trees with an army of
axes and oxen to drag the cedars and caobas, and half-naked monteros
to kick them into the tragic hum of tributaries and rivers.

Although the lumber companies momentarily asserted greater control in the early 1900s by expanding their boundaries of proprietorship,
after World War I they withered with the distancing of the European
market after 1918. A respite in the extraction of precious woods lasted
into the early fifties, when the waters trembled with a new foreign wind
from the north, the United States: the Vancouver Plywood Company
(VPC).

The VPC took advantage of the northern areas of the selva, the ones
closest to the Usumacinta and, perhaps most significantly, to the railroad
system of Ferrocarriles Sureste.

In the guise of a Mexican company, Maderera Maya, the VPC raised
its gargoyle head by 1954 as commander of a latifundio stretching over
420,262 hectares of rain forest. These were the years when Frans and
Trudi Blom inaugurated Na Bolom in San Cristóbal de las Casas.

Pressure from landless Indians and Ladinos followed. They were searching for a chunk of free selva in which to locate their thatched-roof chozas and their scattered plots of maize, corn, chili, and squash and pasture for their cattle. New Chol and Tzeltal colonias charged into the green. Ladino ranchers came in clouds from nearby areas such as Salto de Agua and Palenque.

The Department of Agrarian and Colonial Affairs nullified land grants and titles doled during the Porfiriato and sponsored ranchers and new settlers, opening the selva for further exploitation.

Indians and ranchers came regardless of laws; they came with flood force from Ocosingo, from the withered coffee plantations, and the unbearable labor of the fincas in the highlands, from misery, from suffering. This is how they came—in terrible bundles of pain and desire, and by 1964 they came as a stampede of slash-and-burn invaders.

The clinching levers of Aserraderos Bonapak, a subsidiary of Maderera Maya, broke into the ground with new machinery, opened the roads, and created brechas de camino into inaccessible regions of the selva. The federal government, in nervous tics and shudders, rumbled through the rubble and parceled land in an attempt to control and shape the remains of the forest. In 1971 the government declared a reserve of 401,959 hectares in the municipios of Ocosingo, Trinitaria, La Independencia, La Libertad and Margaritas.

The waters contained this, after all these hundreds of years. These were the antecedents of what is now the governmental creation of
La Zona Lacandona
614,321 hectares of communal land
in the name of
the Lacandón Maya.

Two years later, in 1973, the government decreed the formation of the Lacandón Forestry Company, another attempt to control the unbridled colonization of the territories. Once again, in 1978, the government intervened and formed la Reserva de la Biosfera Montes Azules, a rainforest reserve covering 331,200 hectares.

In the last forty-three years: they have come in tidal waves:

lumber monterías
ranchers, Indian and Ladino
campesinos

refugees and exiles from Guatemala with the exodus of forty thousand
jungle steppers in 1981.

All this travels through the lake. Lago Nahá—

the bones and gold teeth of the Spanish drag at the bottom of the waters. A rust metal crucifix—Dominican in its luster, Franciscan in its
steadfastness, Protestant in its distance—goes down through the mud,
below the crushed shells of the white turtle, below the debris of language
and Spanish scrolls, to the king and queen. The lake remembers and
passes on its knowledge to its allies in its surround.

The waters blink. They know destruction is on the way, newcomers
in hard hats—engineer conquistadores, petrochemical planners, construction workers—slicing the road flesh, making wider incisions for
larger invasions of exiles, refugees and bulldozer men with cabled eyebrows and winch noses.

The sun burned my face. I could feel my skin redden on its own. The
lake was vast in its blue greenness, and quiet—tranquilo, as Chan K'in
José liked to say.

The Lacandones walked by the shoulders of La Ruta. They knew this
lake; the lake in their souls was the same shape. It coursed in the same
channels and was filled with the same creatures, voices, and adversaries.
Yet they went about their sundry motions with their heads up, with their
eyes deep and steady.

Not far from where I stood, K'ayum Ma'ax was building a table in
the backyard behind my little house, under the trees that slope down
from the hill and arch up to the sky at a steep angle. He was busy shav-
ing red mahogany slats into even and smooth boards. The wood was
propped over a couple of old chairs. The trees cut sharp light over his tunic, his smooth and fast strokes. At his feet the reddish curls of precious
tropical wood formed a still life of amber-colored fire.

YOUNG HUSBANDS

A few days later Viona came to the open gate; she had been staying at the campamento a couple hundred yards down the Ruta. Said she was leaving, in a little voice. She came up to K'ayum Ma'ax and me, shook his hand and then mine, and walked out to the edge of La Ruta to wait for the Tumbo—back to Ocosingo, San Cristóbal, then northern California. I realized she had the right approach to things.

The Tumbo came within an hour with its gargantuan tires and feverish engines; she was gone, up the winding and boisterous road.

By mid-afternoon K'ayum Mario joined me at the famous bench by the satellite dish. Playing, sketching cartoons on one of my noteless notebooks.

"Have you seen an Aburbahn?"

"A what?"

"Aburbahn. They are big trucks. Can haul anything. Roberto Bruce has one. We go round the village in it."

"You mean a TravelAll like Leo has?"

"No, Aburbahn. Wait, I'll draw it for you."

K'ayum Mario bit the end of the pencil and studied the blank sheet before laying down an image. He started to draw a hard-line station wagon of sorts. Extra-large bed.

"Saburbahn," he said. "Suburbahn."

"Suburban," I mimicked. "Suburban. Never heard of it," I tell him.

"When you go back to the States send me a picture of a Suburban."

Juan Carlos came out from the back of K'ayum Ma'ax's house. He was one of the Lacandón teens whom I had seen once or twice. He was darker than K'ayum Mario, a bit older, maybe eighteen. A serious air enveloped him, and yet he seemed to be aloof to the world around him.

"Tengo flechas," he said—I have some arrows for sale. "I make the arrows in my house, back there, behind K'ayum Ma'ax. I smoke the wax, then I pull string through it. I take this black string and tie the feathers to the end of the cane shoot. I use the black smoked string to secure the

137

K'ayum Mario drawing a Suburban truck.

arrowheads. Cedar for parts of the arrow. I make them small, less expensive and more affordable. Arrowheads made of chipped stone—for jabalí. Made of cedar for guacamayo and saraguato. Tonight I am leaving for Palenque where I'll market them. Leo will give us a ride. Do you want to come?"

I looked into his large round eyes and told him that I wouldn't be going with him. Too little time left, I said, and thanked him.

Had almost forgotten about these arrows; they are much shorter now. In 1970, when I met Viejo Chan K'in at the milpa with Jorge Paniagua, the bamboo was over six feet tall. They cut it down to about four feet, perfectly straight, in bundles. Later, at Na Bolom, I saw the arrows and bows stamped on the museum wall of the research center. I took a set with me that year, and for years I carried it from town to town—Santa Monica, San Diego, San Francisco. One day I looked for them and they were gone. Now they came back to me in the strong dark hands of Juan Carlos, the young husband of Angélica, daughter of K'ayum Ma'ax.

Juan Carlos took me back to his house: a single room broken, dark, and slanted with the weight of years, tropical heat, and rainstorms. A large rumpled bed took most of the space. Angélica lay on the bed, wearing an old pink wrinkled Ladina dress and breastfeeding their little baby girl. I greeted her quickly and attended to Juan Carlos's business concerns. On the loose gray caoba shelves were a number of ready-made flecha sets, a ball of black wax and waxed string, a little pile of flint points and flecked chipping stones. I bought a small set and paid him fifteen thousand pesos, about three dollars.

"We leave at one in the morning," he reminded me as I stepped out. Juan Carlos's old one-room palmita tilted in stark contrast to his father-in-law's fresh redwood-walled and laminated-roof house. The new economic cleavages between the Zinacanteco and the Chamula in San Cristóbal echoed at a lower scale in Nahá. Yet not all Lacandones have thrived as K'ayum Ma'ax has. Many lived like Juan Carlos. Not all Zinacantecos were wealthy, not all Chamulas were destitute. Juan Carlos's tiny arrows pointed the way. I thought of the Santo Domingo Church in San Cristóbal and its intricate rows of Chamula women selling jackets sewn in Guatemala and Zinacantecos diversifying their wares for tourists. I could see the women from Tenejapa unfolding their textiles on the brick passages. Mayas throughout the highlands and lowlands were creatively responding to economic and cultural pressures.

I examined the set of small arrows, shorter than my forearm. Would a day arrive when the Lacandones would fight back again? The jungle fights back, K'ayum Ma'ax had said. He liked Schwarzenegger's movie because it was filmed in the Chiapas rain forest. What arrows would the young husbands make? The arrow sets were shrinking. Something was eating away at them. They were penetrating into another source, one that I couldn't see. Or were they simply shrinking, dying, deafening, going up to Palenque, to the museums and vendor stalls next to the embossed leather wallets engraved with blurred hieroglyphics?

Carlos Enrique, the anthropology student, had told me about the night jaunts the young Lacandón husbands made to Palenque.

"When these kids come back from Palenque with a wad of money from selling arrows and polished mahogany necklaces, they rent a taxi, drink cañabrava all night, spin around the village in circles until dawn, until they are limp, hanging over the door. A day later they start over. More arrows. Another drive to Palenque. Then one more taxi spin with cañabrava juice."

Carlos Enrique mentioned that this was the kind of stuff for a novel.

Yes, I told him, it would make a good story, a novel. But I was not interested in writing a story. Or a novel. I was not interested in any story. All I wanted to do was to get a little closer to the truth, to the day-to-day reality of the people in these southern regions. All I wanted was to get back to a ripped-out portion of myself, left flayed and buried among the caoba many years before—that bad day when I had come into being, a feverish rape scene where a criollo man captured a Mayan woman and years later the mixed-blood boy drifted away from the papaya vines and left for the fabled cities of Cíbola, far up in the north country, on the edges of Anahuak, where he floated up through years of migrations into the aloof territories of the Separated Land—the United States of America.

I was fooling myself. In Nahá my own father's separations from me, my isolation as a child in the small farmworker towns of the San Joaquín Valley of California, bubbled up inside of me. The deeper I stepped into la selva, the more I delved into my own pain—I was letting myself get carried away by my language. I was not letting the young husbands of Nahá tell me their truths.

CULOS EN LA PIEDRA

Late evening inside K'ayum Ma'ax's kitchen—rice again. Tortillas again. A liter of hot Coke again. Knorr tomato powder on the rice again. We sat at odd angles and chatted. K'ayum Ma'ax spoke of Palenque, a bit more serious than usual.

Culos en la piedra, that's what they are.

That's what we are. Asses on stone. They sit there, by the ruins. With their arrows in neat little packs, in plastic bags. Selling and buying. Selling and buying. The tourists come and finger the arrows. They want longer ones. They want shorter ones. We give it to them. We make it for them. With wax, string. We smoke the wax. We tell them how we make it. How we shoot it. Buying and selling. They mention the jabalí, the saraguato. They want little wooden idols that we make from mahogany and cedar. They tie them to a leather strap. Culos en la piedra. The museums come to us, the galleries. They even call me from Spain. I took K'ayum Mario to Spain recently. Madrid. They treated me and my family very nice there. I bought a guitar. They wanted to know about the Lacandón Maya. Palenque. Now it's just a few hours by truck. And we sit there. They sit there, with their tunics, dirty and tired. With their hands full of arrows, with bags of bows. Big and small. With their ass on stone. Culos en la piedra.

We ate with mere gestures. K'ayum Ma'ax bit hard into the large handmade corn tortillas. I bit hard too. Carlos Enrique, Luz, and José chewed without words. The boys outside played and ran down La Ruta, laughing and screaming. The night was black, solid black. Juan Carlos strolled in and mumbled something to K'ayum Ma'ax and fixed himself

141

a plate of rice. Carlos, the anthropology student, began to joke about how drunk, how "bolos" they all had gotten before I arrived.

Nothing from K'ayum Ma'ax. He stood up and walked over to the front room with his plate and kicked the boxed water heater on the floor. If Roberto Bruce was here he would help me put this up. Tomorrow, K'ayum Mario, you go to Ocotal and see about this. This is all K'ayum Ma'ax said.

EL HOMBRE DE LA SELVA

The next day, in the kitchen again, Carlos asked K'ayum Ma'ax to clarify something. "How many days did you say you could last with the tejón, the badger?"

"Five days," K'ayum responded with a ball of laughter and maize in his mouth.

"Five days?"

"That's right. You hunt the badger, strip the meat. Then you take the penis bone."

"The badger has a bone there?"

"Yes, about the size of your little finger. You take the little bone and you grind it, let it dry into a fine powder. Then you drink it into a tea."

"A tea?"

"Yes, you drink it like tea. Then you better have many lovers to give you sex because you won't be able to stop. Five days, five nights. You will be raw."

"Do you take that tea?"

"No, no, I am good, I am good still. The tejón tea is for the older ones."

"What if a young boy takes it?"

"He's in trouble. But it probably won't work on him."

"What if I take it?"

"You'll be hard, mighty hard."

K'ayum Ma'ax made a gesture with his hand in front of his crotch. "You'll be hard way out here," he said. We were falling apart with the idea of drinking badger tea.

"What if a woman drinks it?"

"Nothing happens."

"What about Viejo Chan K'in, does he drink tejón tea?"

"No, he doesn't need to."

"He doesn't need to?"

Chan K'in José.

He knows the words, the words that come from the trees. That is all you need, if you know the words. You pronounce them. They are secretos. He knows the secrets. Doesn't need the tea. He doesn't need to hunt the badger. Nuk's father, Antonio, knows the secrets too, He doesn't need the tea either. Viejo Chan K'in, my father, is the t'o'ohil of the village, the one who knows the secrets. He knows

> 'U K'ay Tumben Läk, the Song of the New Incense Burners
> Mensäbäk, the Lord of the Rain, how to sing
> Kisin, Lord of Death, how he was born
> Hachakyüm, the Creator of the Lacandones, of Stars, the Flood
> Xtabay Goddesses, their red faces, their red vaginas, their red
> thighs the color of Brazil tree flesh.

"He knows about el hombre de la selva, the Jungle Man."
"¿El hombre de la selva?"
"Yes. I cannot tell you about this," K'ayum Ma'ax said. "Last year a foreigner was here. He was asking questions, taking photographs, I think his name was Christopher. Maybe. He was recording los secretos. He stayed quite a while with us. My father told him many things. Then one day he told him about el hombre de la selva. Christopher recorded what my father was telling him, he took many notes. A day later he fell into spasms on the ground, not too far from my house here. I went over to him, but I couldn't wake him. He was stiff and getting cold. I called my father, Viejo Chan K'in, to come. My father pronounced words. My father prayed for him for hours. Later this man Christopher woke up and was well. But he continued to ask the questions, to take the story down. That day he came to my house. I could tell something was wrong, but I didn't know what it was. Something was off, though. I could tell. So I offered him a cup of coffee. 'No, I don't drink that,' he told me. This startled me because I knew he loved coffee. Then later he came back asking for some tools. 'Why didn't you ask me earlier, when I invited you to a cup of coffee?' I asked him. 'What coffee?' he said to me. 'When you came a short while ago.' 'I just got here,' he said. I knew then that the man who had come earlier was not him. It was a double. Something terribly wrong was happening to this foreigner. In a few hours he fell on the ground again. Once more my father came and prayed for him. And again he awoke from a deadly sleep. He left after that. He never finished recording the story about el hombre de la selva.

"You know what, I am going to write my own book," K'ayum Ma'ax told us. "All the people who come here have it wrong, even those who have stayed with us for many years. I must write it. I will tell about all these things one day, in a book. I am going to work on it. The secrets come from the air, from up there, where the trees are. Every tree has a heart. They come from that heart, on the wind."

Carlos interjected again, out of context, "How do you say heart in Maya, nose, beard?" He jotted down K'ayum Ma'ax's responses and went on asking about as many body parts as possible. K'ayum Ma'ax, Nuk, and K'ayum Mario shouted out the terms in Maya as if they were sergeants. Carlos was doing his research on the Lacandón notions of the body. He was intent on learning Maya; he bent his bushy head and scribbled frantically in a tiny hand-size notebook. The rest of us listened and finished our cold plates of rice.

All our conversations were going astray into their own tracks of separate reality, it seemed. Could the wind carry language? In the selva, on Lacandón ground, can dreams be one of the most potent forms of knowledge and awareness? How could Carlos Enrique and his cohorts investigate the meaning systems of the people at Nahá by jotting down terms in Spanish and without knowing Maya? And K'ayum Ma'ax, owner of a satellite dish, businessman, and knower of the deep truths of the T'o'o-hil? Was there such a thing as an "objective" and culturally "pure" viewpoint? From whose stance—K'ayum Ma'ax, Carlos Enrique, Viejo Chan K'in, mine? Having been in Nahá just a few days, I could see the people and their lives were connected almost at every breath to the trees, the terrain, the ecology, as much as they were to new and radical invasions of outsider colonists, tourists, and corporate petroleum hardware—this was the Lacandón place. Being in Nahá was a particular way of knowing Nahá. Fracture was onmipresent; but was it fracture for K'ayum Ma'ax? Maybe the dream-wind of knowledge would only register as an interesting "concept" for me and Carlos Enrique and company. Our dreams would be void, our learning would be slow and excruciating.

K'ayum Mario stopped the vocabulary drill and ordered us to follow his example:
Say
yit,

    yat,   yet,
                yot, you know,
                yit, yat and so on. Like that.

K'ayum Mario smothered the laughter from his mouth with both hands. Carlos and I followed his instructions:

"Yat, Yet, Yit, Yot, Yut!"

K'ayum Mario split with hilarity.

"You know 'yit' means 'ass' in Maya," K'ayum Ma'ax said. "You can learn Maya," he told us. "Very easy. Very easy. In a month. Very easy, Carlos. One month? That is all you need?"

"You're crazy, K'ayum. You think it so easy for us," Carlos snapped back.

"Just let the words come to you from the trees. Let the words come down from the mountains back here. When you go to sleep, they will visit your dreams. They come with the winds, like this, easy. No writing is necessary. Just relax, lie back; as you sleep you will learn."

K'ayum Ma'ax went to a back room and carried out a twelve-pack of warm Modelo beer and watched me closely to see if I was going to lose my head with the first few swigs. We drank and laughed. We made fun of Carlos, who was deeply interested in making badger tea, the where-abouts of badgers, how to package the stuff. K'ayum Ma'ax said that if he didn't catch a badger maybe he could catch a bobcat.

"The tea from the gato montés only lasts one day and you cannot re-peat it," K'ayum said.

Even Luz poked fun at Carlos. "You look like a badger. Your hair gives you away," she said.

I had come to like this crew from D.F. They were part of my trek to the Mayan edge. We were all related to each other in an odd fractured cinema strip of abandonments, separations, and refuge and wonderings for each other's body. Carlos Enrique's focus on the Lacandón notions of body was on the right track. Yet it wasn't an issue of symbolism, belief systems, or the complexities that have to do with how environment and colonization shaped Lacandón cognition and perception. The subject was eluding all of us.

What notion of body was I after?

What were we all looking for in this green- and sand-colored spot on the la Ruta Maya? Was it the body of powerlessness, of spiritual resur-rection, of petrochemical encroachment, of genocide, revolution?

THE COMING OF THE
BLACK OCEAN LINER

On a high ledge. Made of blue-brown slime, oil fudge, earth sod. Barely hanging on at the top. On the right side of my dream.

The other side of the ledge is made of stone. There is a woman on this side. She slips, then hangs on. We both look to our right and see a colossal dark ocean liner floating by us on the bay. A thin chicken-wire fence separates us from the bay and the ship. The ship breaks through a curtain of mist. I can see the tanker's white deck. A deep energy overtakes me. My body is frightened. I have never seen anything so powerful. The ship is immense, pointed, silent, intent, steady, weathered, closed, and dark—a great force coming home to anchor. Only the chicken wire separates me and my companion on the other side of the ledge from the ship.

In the neat one-bedroom house, the dream left me in a state of alarm and wonder.

The ship, its darkness and heavy posture, its lightness and focus. The wires between me and the ship, the woman on the other side; the boundaries, the force of the water—the elevation and the depth. What could I do with these senses and images, with this inner story given to me in Nahá, in the guest house by la Ruta Maya, where things come from the hearts of mountain trees? I was in every one of these dream puzzle pieces. The wire separated me from la selva. Could I snip through its border-making edge?

Was I the ship?

Deep colors and tiny confetti windows. Was the ship made of sadnesses? Was it made from a collection of hidden figures, the ones I had gathered on this journey? Was this the weight of my own inner visitors that I had been calling for, the voices of my ancestors, the voices of my dead mother and father? Was it an inner call to continue? The woman—why were we hanging on the ledge, one side sweet slime and the other gray stone?

A few nights ago, in another dream, I was walking away from the ledge with my mother, and the water was to my left. I let go of the ledge that night and let my feet touch the sand.

These dreams attracted me. They repelled me as well. I wasn't interested in falling into the easy paradise-talk of indigenous exaltation journeys—how the lost Ladino boy finds his soul in the jungle. This line of thinking was my enemy. And yet I dreamed and noted the dreams down. I could let them go as usual. I could also be open to them, to their landscapes.

The black ocean liner was an ominous sign. Could there be something in la selva that would soon arrive? Could there be a ship about to land and deploy its inhabitants throughout the region? I was close to this awareness, that is all I could tell. The dream slipped back into the moss-covered stones and ancient leaves where it had come from.

PEMEX BOULEVARD

One morning K'ayum Mario invited me to Ocotal Lake, a few miles south of young Nuk's tiendita. We jumped into the Tumbo and got off about five minutes later. K'ayum Ma'ax had asked him if he could locate Jacinto, a PEMEX plumber, so that he would come over to assemble the water heater.

The PEMEX campamento was a shaved forest expanse, an open field of about three acres with five or six rows of cubicle-like worker housing. Each row consisted of about ten tiny gray one-room houses with squeezed porches and clean patches of roofing. At the back of the petrochemical complex, I could see several large oil tanks painted in brilliant white and green. The glow was deific; I stood before the new Spirit of the Forest, the Techno-Petro-Gods of Nahá.

To one side of the gated entrance we read:

PEMEX
Petróleos Mexicanos
Región Sur / Distrito Ocosingo

Está prohibido la caza y tráfico
de especies silvestres, acuáticas y
forestales, la persona que sea sorprendida
realizando estas actividades
será acreedor a:
por parte de PEMEX: rescisión de contrato
por parte de SEDUE: multa por el equivalente
de 10 a 20000 días de salario mínimo y cárcel*

---

*PEMEX, Mexican Petroleum, Southern Region / District of Ocosingo

Hunting of and trafficking in aquatic and forest wildlife species are prohibited, [and] any individual apprehended in these activities will be subject to:
PEMEX: cancellation of contract
SEDUE: a fine equivalent to 10 to 20,000 days of minimum wage and imprisonment.

We stepped into the campamento. I noticed the PEMEX sign propped up over a sculptured rock garden: "PEMEX campamento." A red eagle was profiled against a pyramid; the colors of the Mexican flag were well integrated into the design. And yet I wasn't convinced.

The warning against poaching didn't convince anyone. The only travelers were Lacandones and worn-out campesinos slouching on mules or bumping along in dilapidated fifties-era buses. They knew how much land had to be razed and how many ancient trees had to be felled for the construction of this petro plant. This was the land of the jaguar, not the eagle.

A small group of Lacandones waited at the information office and checkpoint. A Ladino man wearing a blue-gray jumpsuit and a steel blue baseball cap sat inside the booth, reading a paper and listening to a mariachi song on his box radio. A small fan whirled at the desk.

"Is Jacinto here? I need to see him," K'ayum Mario asked.

"He's still sleeping. He's sleeping in the lobby, in the back," the blue-gray guard said.

The exchange was casual and seemed characteristic of the set-up that PEMEX engendered. The campamento was a perfect cultural vortex for the fission of the "savage" and the Robo-Ladino—hard-hat mestizos who seemed to identify more with the technological façade of energy processors than with the people of Nahá, whose lives and dream worlds were cast in the shape of the caoba forests and the earth that sustained them. The Lacandones, two men and a woman with a baby, are waiting for the campamento clinic to open.

In the lobby with its adjoining cafeteria, K'ayum Mario asked two suited men on a red couch about Jacinto. Who knows? One guy shrugged his shoulders and jerked his head back to the television mounted on the wall.

"Who's winning?" I asked.

"Los Buffalo Bills," he said curtly.

Silently we left the campamento, passing the woman with her baby still waiting in the booth. We crossed La Ruta in the direction of Lake Ocotal, a hundred yards distant.

We ran through the weeds and followed an old muddy trail under branches and thick foliage; we stooped through the green leaf cave almost as if cutting through time, almost as if running for shelter and salvation.

K'ayum Mario found two large cayucos at the edge of the marsh. They belonged to Mateo, one of the elders of Nahá. I hadn't stopped to see him and only would if invited. Later I would see Viejo Chan K'in if

K'ayum Ma'ax remembered to invite me. These were things that had to happen on their own. K'ayum Mario checked for holes and patched one of the cayucos with mud. I boarded holding my camera to one side. With K'ayum Mario at the helm, we slid off into the water lilies, into the center of the green liquid world.

I let my hands trail in the water as K'ayum Mario worked the oar. This time there were are no words, no urge to swim. This time we fell silently into the sacred waters. We flowed as if PEMEX was a dream and the lake was all encompassing, as if its waters could heal us. The light played on the water lilies. In the distance the forest sang with its creatures. I heard whistles and a deeper voice from the foliage and branches. The voice was unformed—a perfumed and watery presence, that was all; I could feel it fan out of the dark strands within the trees.

K'ayum Mario pulled out a handful of fishline from a little plastic bag and tied a hook to it. Then he brought out a Clemente Jacques can, the small kind. I recognized the brand. When I was a kid in third grade, in San Francisco, my mother would send me to buy Clemente Jacques. "They have the best pickled chilis," she would say. This can held worms. K'ayum Mario pinned one to the hook and threw out the line.

"What do you think you are going to catch with that little line?"

"Mojarrita."

"Keep on dreaming," I chided him.

"La mojarrita likes these worms."

"La mojarrita is on vacation," I said as I took out my camera.

"Tonight we'll have tacos de mojarrita. Just wait." He looked up at me.

"Tonight we'll have rice tacos," I told him.

An hour later the bag was full and I ate my words. I was beginning to look forward to the tacos de mojarrita à la Lacandón. We went deeper into the lake.

The camera was a habit more than a project. I took it out to mark a twenty-three-year cycle. In 1970 I had crossed Lake Nahá with Jorge Paniagua and his little daughter carrying a 16 mm camera. I remembered the waterlilies and the darkness of the lake, the cayuco and its wide mouth. I remembered the little girl rowing with determined eyes. This time K'ayum held the oars; this time the light was abundant, and to my left I could see La Ruta curl around the mountains. I could see the PEMEX temple and its white capsule gods without a face or a name.

K'ayum Mario held up the thin mojarrita; I adjusted the lens and snapped the shutter.

On the way back to Nahá, K'ayum Mario wanted to give me a taste of the mountain treks. Leaving the road we entered the forest and ran up the inclines and down the slopes, with our heads down and our shoulders in tune with the hanging vines and sharp branches. I was out of breath and my head was pounding, but somehow my legs still shot out from under me as I rolled into the clearing behind K'ayum Ma'ax's mahogany house.

The Elmer's glue table was still on stilts, wound with rope; PEMEX was behind us, on the other side of the mountain. We were back in the village, in a shriveling oasis of casas de palma and a few with laminated roofs. Lake Ocotal was behind us also, still reflecting the sun blaze. The cayucos were tied to her with sword grass and vines. For a moment each world was still intact, but the borders between them were as tenuous as the drifts of wind in the trees; as I snapped the shutters, the tropical forest village landscape stood out in bold outline for a second or two and then dissolved into a phantasmagoria of faceless dynamo installations.

BOR WITH HAND SIGNS

Bor, one of the young sons of Viejo Chan K'in, about sixteen years old and wearing black rubber boots and a tunic, stopped by for a moment in the middle of La Ruta, the front yard of the Lacandones. He was deaf and communicated with a self-invented repertoire of hand signs.

Raised his right hand. Thumb and forefingers fashioned an invisible box. He slapped this sign on his tunic sleeve. An insignia of some sort, on someone's shirt, I thought. Then he spread his left arm, smoothing an upward arc through the air. His hands grasped a steering wheel made out of air. Was he driving? We both laughed as I watched his language.

I liked Bor—his piercing eyes and lithe frame, his finely tapered fingers and his quick smile, his aloneness. He followed the other young boys and played with them. K'ayum Mario, his nephew, spoke to him with a few signs and invited him on several of our jaunts. Bor carried something that the others lacked; maybe it was his inner intensities, maybe it was an extra dose of intimacy with his father and mother, with their day and night worlds. He had cut out the landscape of Nahá in a different manner. I could sense Bor's unique position and way of seeing.

What was the story that he kept repeating—the one about the square box, the imprint on the shirt, and the upward swerve in the sky?

The story came to me: A sergeant's stripes on the sleeve; he came in a plane one day. He drove. They came. Military men with wings and machines. They drove with their badges on their bodies. They went into the villages, into the chozas. They swung their shoulders, their air was metal-like, they came down from the sky. Another sky. The striped badge on their shirts was heavy; it was red and stood out. Everyone in the village saw them, they saw the stripes, the metal on their strong arms. They noticed how they came driving in one day, how they stood tall. How they came and left. Or was this being told to me in a future tense?

Would there be men with stripes on their attire, with machines in the air, with strange jackets on their bodies? How will they hover over Nahá? What will their mission be? Who will live, who will die?

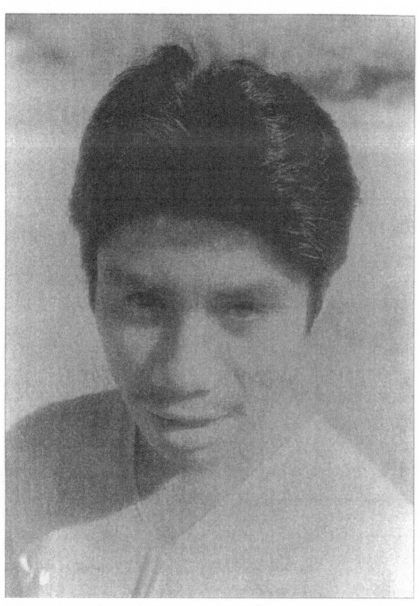

Bor.

I invented the story as Bor repeated the movements over and over, as he moved his hands over his body and through the space around him. This reminded me of Spielberg's early film, *Close Encounters of the Third Kind*, and how the lead character played by Richard Dreyfuss kept on sculpting towers with his hands, out of mud, and no one understood him; clay towers and mashed-potato towers, until the day came when the tower appeared before him and the rest of the world.

One year later, to the day—American jets owned by the Mexican military fired missiles over la Ruta Maya.

ANTONIO, SEVENTY YEARS OLD

Late one afternoon, Antonio, K'ayum Ma'ax's father-in-law, ambled by to talk to K'ayum Ma'ax, who was still working on the caoba table, preparing more boards with commercial glue.

Antonio stood tall, barefoot, with long black hair and a tattered tunic. He spoke with few motions. I had seen Antonio on my visit in 1970. He was huddled next to Viejo Chan K'in in the small milpa. I couldn't explain it, but he hadn't aged. Antonio was ashen colored—almost as if he was made of something other than flesh and tunic, some other substance like vine meshed with stony minerals. I recognized him from many years of poring over a video copy of haphazard clips pieced together by my buddy Tomás—our first attempt to edit the film we shot in 1970. All the original film was lost in East Los Angeles where Tomás lived, except that video sample. I also recognized Antonio from several monographs on Lacandón culture in *Geomundo*, as well as Trudi Blom's photos and several studies from Europe. I felt awed—not because he was one of the last of a long line of elders in the village but more because of the way he carried himself, how he talked to K'ayum Ma'ax, and the way he looked at me from a distance. Antonio was very still and yet swayed inside, it seemed, like Lake Ocotal and Lake Nahá, like the trees. I wasn't interested in his knowledge of Lacandón religious matters or even his memories of life in Nahá for the larger portion of this century; nor was I going to inquire into the ways of tropical rain forest agriculture, strategies of thinning that enable a relatively small plot of Lacandón land to yield over seventy different crops. I had made up my mind on the first day that I was here that I wasn't going to butt into anyone's business. I had given up that project. I wasn't here on a "field" query. I was merely here, without much reason other than to visit at best.

Antonio attracted me because I recognized in him something deeper than information and Indian talk—he reminded me of my mother. His softness and his steadiness. His ease and his erect posture. His disregard for sharpness in his attire and in his reflective manner—and yet he pos-

157

sessed something brimming with power that came from years of being aware of what is true. I didn't have the words for this then and I still don't.

K'ayum Ma'ax was different. Even though he kept to himself and had a keen sense of who he was, he was busy, at task, articulate; he was on a mission of sorts. One day he would retaliate, it seemed to me; one day K'ayum Ma'ax would rise up and have the final say about Nahá and its intruders. He would write it and he would carve it as obstinately as he had welded the caoba table with white glue; he would paint it as he had painted for galleries in Palenque and Spain. I sensed this in him and through the various stunted conversations we had. The glued table symbolized this in a way. He was busy mixing opposite and complementary elements, commercial glue and native mahogany; he was improvising a device for the molding of these materials. His house was another example, concrete against grass, cylinder heaters, stoves, stereos, multitrack television against the secrets of the forest; a satellite dish against a hidden shack of arrows behind his house. Antonio was of another order; he walked deeper on the earth.

They both came up to me. K'ayum Ma'ax reminded Antonio about my visit more than two decades ago. Antonio nodded.

"I think I remember you," he told me. "Yes, I remember," he said.

"How have you been?"

"Good. I have the flu."

"The flu? Are you going to be all right?"

Antonio pointed to the small mountain behind K'ayum Ma'ax's house. "Just the flu. I am on my way back to the milpa," he said in a small voice.

"How have things been since I was here last time?"

"Good. Colder."

"Colder?"

"Colder. The tobacco won't even grow anymore. The flower blossoms but it gives no seed. A cold wind."

Antonio rubbed his upper arms with his hands. Almost shivering. Dark face, dark lips. He stood a few feet from me.

"And Chan K'in, how is he these days?"

"Good. One hundred twenty years old."

"One hundred and twenty years old?"

"Yes. Me, seventy. Bueno, I will be leaving now."

Back to his milpa in the mountains. He'd come back later in the afternoon. Come back to his house behind the trees where K'ayum Ma'ax whittled wood. I asked him to wait a moment.

"I have something for your flu. Here, take these. Two Theraflu packs. Pour these into hot water and stir, then drink it down. Good for headaches."

Antonio nodded and took the plastic pouches. It was an awkward attempt on my part, maybe because I wanted him to stay a few more minutes, maybe the powder could help. Antonio knew many ways to take care of himself, ways that called upon the sources of the forest, yet he thanked me and waved slightly and left softly, past K'ayum Ma'ax in the backyard, bent with a saw and two long mahogany boards.

MALARIA, PNEUMONIA, TUBERCULOSIS

Was it the flu?

I remembered Luz María telling me about the clínica down the road. When I had walked by, it was closed. No one was in the tiny laminated house. What was the government doing about the malaria? Since they had come in with bulldozers and drills, cattle ranches, what were they doing about pneumonia, tuberculosis, parasites, malnutrition—the body, the skin, about living and dying in Nahá?

I wanted to forget about these things. I was powerless. All I had were questions, desires, and the uncanny fever of the do-good poet. There was only one question: How long will this Lacandón body last . . .

if 52 percent of the Lacandón population is under fourteen;

if 70 percent of these suffer from malnutrition;

if 45 percent of the surface area in Chiapas is for cattle carrying more parasites, in the meat and on the hide, heading toward the selva;

if Chiapas is the third-ranking state in the nation in beef production—eighty thousand tons a year;

if every new migration of workers and colonists brings new migrations of disease;

if campesinos cut trees for their own survival and for PEMEX to plunder;

if malaria in the selva increases at ten times the state's rate;

if children in the selva grow weaker from the commerce of rice milk powder;

if the new roads bring increasing tonnage of refined foodstuffs lacking in essential nutrients;

if tuberculosis is the second-highest cause of death;

if the animals have tuberculosis;

if the introduction of DDT pesticides is not accompanied by careful instruction;

if fish, animals, and wildlife die from pesticide exposure;

if this exposure leads to more cases of gastric cancer;

if the roads increase their tonnage of alcohol deliveries;

if only 30 percent of the selva communities have clinics and health care services;

if the clinics remain closed and sparse and Ladino;

if the PEMEX plants suck out ninety-two thousand barrels of petroleum a day and leave ecological decay, alcoholism, prostitution, and hyperinflation;

if AIDS is on a fast track, wearing a fancy hat, en route from Ocosingo, from Los Angeles, from all points east, west, north, and south;

if flu erupts into squalor, pestilence, and death in the face of "Mayan Splendor" posters at the next-door PEMEX plant cafeteria?

I want to add to the tally of the selva colonial tribute: oil, electric energy, cattle, coffee, bananas, honey, corn, sorghum, cocoa, tobacco, soy, mamey . . .

The list is formless—an unending shadow of dynamite and virus blast.

What do you do with these figures?

MOJARRITA

"K'ayum Mario burned the mojarra on the skillet," K'ayum Ma'ax's wife, Nuk, chimed in. "He was so excited watching something on the TV that he burned the mojarra."

"Juan! Juan? Come here!" K'ayum Mario called to me from the kitchen. "The mojarrita is ready," he said with a sad and eager face, his expression between pouting and smiling.

"He burned the mojarra on the skillet," Nuk chimed in again. "K'ayum was so excited watching the TV that he burned the tacos."

Nuk was warming tortillas on one of the available grills. K'ayum Mario swished the skillet looking for a medium-cooked mojarra as if panning for gold. Then he made me a taco of blackened sardine skeletons.

"Just great, delicious," I told him as I chewed and swallowed the fishy gravel. "They are sweet, I must admit," I said. Then I paused. "I'll be leaving soon. I'll be leaving in the morning."

K'ayum Mario listened, objected, and made me one more taco de mojarrita. Later, as we stood outside in the brisk air, I gave him my red and black checkered wool work shirt, the one my brothers-in-law, Harold and George, gave me before I left San Francisco. K'ayum Mario sported his new shirt, pursing his lips and parading underneath the kitchen light.

I exchanged notes with Carlos and Luz, addresses. They were out of film so I gave them my last two rolls of Kodachrome. They said they were staying until the end of January—more interviews, more data. Yes, I understand, I said.

K'ayum Ma'ax came out of the house. He knew what I was saying to the others and asked me to stay a bit longer. This was the first time he came close to me with a personal request.

He talked about building himself a palmita on the hill next to Antonio's milpa, overlooking his house and La Ruta. Awkwardly, I pulled out a fifty dollar bill neatly folded in my wallet. Here, I told him, this is for you, for the house. He insisted that he didn't want the money. I gave it to him anyway. I knew I would spend it for more rent at Na Bolom; I just needed enough to get on the Tumbo, for the colectivo from Ocosingo to Las Paletas, then for the Colón bus to Tuxtla. In the meantime, I would work something out at Na Bolom so I could stay a couple more days and tie up loose ends.

K'ayum Ma'ax took the fifty and thanked me. I knew I had forced the money on him; it was another one of my awkward gestures; I knew that I could be feeding into something that I didn't believe in, but it wasn't the money, it was simply giving as much as I could. Maybe it was a twitch of compensation for Ladino greed. I washed my face in the sink and went back to my house.

K'ayum Mario and Chan K'in Francisco asked me to send them a pair of audífonos, headphones. "Maybe I'll send you a photo of a Suburbahn," I said to K'ayum Mario, joking.

My last night in Nahá was approaching. Burnt sweet mojarra, red-black rice, a solid black sky, and the laughter of the teen boys.

LA ULTIMA VISITA
(Farewell to the T'o'ohil)

Last day.

Going up the La Ruta with K'ayum Ma'ax.

I've been afraid all along to come and visit the T'o'ohil, the Great One who knows the words and secrets and stories, the elder teacher of Nahá. I have thought of him for over twenty years, wondering who he is, what he knows, how he has lived. I have wondered about his ways with the earth, the milpas, how he has taken to the logging companies tearing through his village and his lakes. What has he said to his children, what will protect him and his village, who has come to his side? How did he cure the foreigner who fell ill after inquiring about el hombre de la selva?

K'ayum Ma'ax by the side of La Ruta on the last day.

At Na Bolom Trudi Blom's suffering, and the way her words and mind had been snipped back into stumbling syllables, caused me to wonder about el Viejo Chan K'in. When she dies will he die? Are they on a soul track written in by Hachakyüm, the creator of the Lacandones? If the roots of all the trees are tied to the destinies of the stars, how are Viejo Chan K'in and Trudi Blom related?

On one end of the spiral track: Trudi moves into the selva with hands in the mud, with maps and mapmakers, campamentos, clinics, with the magnifying lens of restoration and world alarm, with a self-made fountain for ecological sustenance, for endangered species and peoples, with a tourist museum and dependence trinkets, with capitalism dressed in "progressive" trousers and do-gooder boots. At the other end of the silvery line: Viejo Chan K'in walks. He walks with centuries of conquests and cultural realignments. The traveling men with anteater-noses fall into the milpas with their blue notebooks frozen in their throats. Viejo Chan K'in ambles toward San Cristóbal de las Casas and points to his incense burners and his star cape behind the Na Bolom display case; he offers balché for the new years ahead.

What dreams does he have as the encroaching orb of Tzeltales and cattle grazers, oil engineers and loggers, missionaries and university students stalk his thatched roof and satellite-dish village? I wanted to go through these reflections and dreams with the t'o'ohil. But I didn't have the words.

K'ayum Ma'ax led me up La Ruta in the morning. Behind la tiendita we scaled the forested slope, turned to the right, and followed a dirt trail. Barking dogs. Sweet smoke in the cool air, moistness under my feet. Outside a large palmita.

"Wait here," K'ayum Ma'ax instructed me.

I was at the entrance to the house made with bajareque walls. My destination: a wide mud, straw, and tree-branch house topped with a column of smoke where a pair of thin, sharp dogs stood at the gate. Soon Koh II, one of Viejo Chan K'in's wives, came out, smiled, and with a large gesture of her arms announced that I could enter.

As with Antonio, I had seen her in photographs on Lacandón culture in French, Spanish, and German publications. It was as if I had to tear through an elaborate screen of pilfered images and histories that had nothing to do with these people other than to record a vanishing face; they represented a knee-jerk historicism, what global powers do in their spare time—chart explorations and excursions into the wild. Then they pause to take stock of the "primitive," to measure the raw figures against their "advanced" selves. I knew this gesture well; as an American, I was on the verge of becoming an expert at seeking people on the edge of extinction—except in this case I was part of what I was seeking.

For a split second I enjoyed Koh II's welcome, her stern and gallant face, her worn red-striped Ladina dress against the speckled adobe. Her severity and her quick kindness.

As I stepped into the darkness of the house, past the little fire near the entrance where a younger woman and a child turned the embers, as I went forward to the center where K'ayum Ma'ax sat on a tiny chair next to a hanging hammock, I knew that I was entering an ancient and sacred place. Behind the hammock there was a wide bed with many layers of cloth, zarapes. The roof was low and uneven to my eye. The walls seemed moist and speckled with ash.

K'ayum Ma'ax stood up and asked me to take his place on the small chair and moved a few feet behind me. The way was being cleared for me to address Viejo Chan K'in, the house was being rearranged for my visit; each element was being positioned, intricately, yet with great care and ease. Koh II went to the back and sat on a bed against the wall draped with blankets and colored bedsheets.

At the center Viejo Chan K'in was lying deep in his hammock, on his side, facing me. His curled legs were covered by an old tunic, and his arms fell across his body like water. His hands were dark, hard, large, and crooked. I noticed something odd about his hands: They seemed to be frozen, and the fingers were pulled forward, fixed as if clutching an invisible weight, an eternal machete. His face was small and round, brown with eyes that glimmered; his gaze was gentle.

"He came here twenty-three years ago," K'ayum Ma'ax interjected as if to jump-start our conversation. Viejo Chan K'in stretched back, looked up at his son, turned to me, and said something inaudible.

"Yes, I came here about that time," I said as if I was clear about what he had said. "I came with a friend. We landed on a little runway out here by Jorge Paniagua's place. You were at the milpa. We came by cayuco across the lake, with cameras. You were in the milpa with the boys. They were cutting cane for hunting arrows. You were smoking a cigar and laughing with Jorge Paniagua."

"Yes, I was there. Oh, yes," Viejo Chan K'in said.

"How have you been?"

"The flu . . . it's been cold lately."

"That's what Antonio told me. He says the tobacco doesn't grow anymore."

"It doesn't grow anymore. It's gotten colder. I don't know why."

Viejo Chan K'in mentioned the cold. What was this cold they were talking about? Viejo Chan K'in and Antonio were telling me something very direct, and yet I couldn't grasp it.

"I brought some things for you," I said.

I dug into my old turquoise backpack with three Teenage Mutant Ninja Turtles sewn on the back. Pulled out the cigarettes. Koh II screwed her mouth and said that Viejo Chan K'in couldn't smoke now. I gave her the large cigarette cartons with a few packs missing. Nelly Maldonado had told me that Chan K'in loved mayonnaise; I brought the jar out. I had bought it at a supermercado next to the zócalo in San Cristóbal. Viejo Chan K'in smiled. This is his favorite, Koh II said. I found the Christmas rum cakes wrapped in airtight silver packages. A good choice—I could tell by Koh II's approving smile.

One of the thin dogs came in and sniffed at the embers by the small bright-haired boy near the entrance. The child had white skin and white hair. I lost the little balance I had achieved. He was the same boy who accompanied Leo, the man with the Travel All van, at Lake Nahá a few days ago. I hadn't realized that he was one of Chan K'in's youngest children.

The canvas sack of granola that my friend Jorge Herrera gave me in San Francisco was the best gift. Organic fiber with almonds and dates, raisins, and honeyed oats. K'ayum Ma'ax almost jumped up with excitement. He exclaimed to Koh II that this was what his father needed for his grippe. Viejo Chan K'in nodded his head and smiled. We spoke a few more words.

"Have you seen Trudi?" he asked me.

"Yes, I've been staying at Na Bolom."

"How is she?"

"She's not too well."

"Oh, not well."

"She can't talk anymore."

"Ah."

"She doesn't walk well."

"Ah."

Viejo Chan K'in's eyes sparkled and receded into another time. His frail body moved an inch or two to adjust his posture; he rubbed his hands and fell deeper into his hammock and looked away for a moment, coughed. Our meeting had come to a close.

"Well, I just wanted to come by and visit you," I told him. "Your son K'ayum Ma'ax has been very hospitable. I am leaving him an old movie about the days when I came here the first time. For you—thank you, Chan K'in, I just wanted to thank you. For everything."

I said farewell to Viejo Chan K'in and Koh II and walked back to La Ruta with K'ayum Ma'ax. Silent through the reeds and grasses. Tears began to well up in my eyes. Down the slope to the open gravel by the tiendita.

My things were already packed from the night before. It was an old habit from always living on the move. My wanderings as a child, alone with my mother, came to me again. My father's absences, his disappearance into the night, into his other family in New Mexico, my aloneness turned into a knot in my throat as I double-checked the few bags in my room. My keen ability to survive on sparse supplies and in almost any environment, my poet-on-the-run preparedness, had something to do with my early and fast and lonesome years as a child.

Visiting Viejo Chan K'in was a culminating point. Even though we spoke about very little, I felt that I had been filled with a set of truths too big to hold or articulate. My chest was tight as I walked over to K'ayum Ma'ax's wife, Nuk, and thanked her for everything. She asked me to stay and then gave me a red bean necklace. I thanked K'ayum Ma'ax, who had by now put on an indigo blue cardigan over his tunic. He looked more serious with the sweater, more distant.

By noon I stood at the edge of La Ruta, with my bags on the road, waiting for the Tumbo to take me back to the beginning.

JUNGLE BOLERO

What does it mean?
A point of arrival and I am early with everyone lost around me.
A point of arrival and I am late and surrounded
by the past.

Margarita Luna Robles, from
"What Is Called Dreaming"

The faded turquoise Ninja backpack was full of empty notebooks. The camera had barely been used. The only things that I wrote were some of my dreams. I knew I had abandoned the search, the study that I never formulated.

Market truck.

Leaned on a post and waited for the Tumbo. A week had gone by in a matter of seconds; everything was a wash of tropical sunlight, blue-black night skies and young faces, hand signs and televised blue-light figures.

Two young Tzeltales walked up to me with long machetes and Ladino clothes, their yellowed and ragged nylon hats angled to one side. They had smooth dark-rose skin, a prankish look, an agile poise. They asked if K'ayum Ma'ax was in. A few minutes later, after negotiating for ten thousand pesos, they began cutting down the tall weeds, bushes, and grass that spread out from K'ayum's modern house into La Ruta. Their arms swung the sharp blades making the leaves fly up and fall into small green tufts. I could hear them sharpen their machetes—clean, brisk sheets of sound that pulled me forward and backward.

A wave of music came from K'ayum Ma'ax's living room—corridos and boleros this time instead of Chicano classics or soundtracks from Spike Lee movies. At first I thought the music came from the stereo, but it was K'ayum Ma'ax playing his guitar, singing old love songs from the fifties.

> De piedra será la cama
> de piedra la cabecera . . .
>
> The bed will be made of stone
> of stone the headboard . . .

Water came to my eyes. Couldn't stop myself. The sun burned my face and tears flooded me. I looked over Lake Nahá and away into the mountains so no one would see them. I was caught in an odd mesh of sadness and loneliness, emotions I had wanted to avoid from the start. K'ayum Ma'ax's voice was prying into my well-sewn posture of poet on the prowl, man on the edge of the last Lacandones. El Próspero and its kicked-in campesino shacks had carved a hole into me, and K'ayum Ma'ax had seen this. As much as I pretended indifference, the music was dislodging my armature into jigsaw pieces as I leaned against the light pole in a faked whimsical stance, unable to place the overall picture into focus.

I blamed Viejo Chan K'in and his small pure stature, his centennial endurance, his collective penitence standing for everything I had wanted to rescue and love now gone to the Ladino hydra, the North American corporate gargoyle, and now the NAFTA tentacle; I blamed him for my angry sadness. I didn't want to accept that he wasn't anguished or that he didn't feel my petty losses. I blamed K'ayum Ma'ax for being so elegant and articulate, for being reserved and in control, for his Ladino style, his model home and his aloofness to the other Indians in the colonia, and yet I was the builder of my own little disintegrations.

I blamed the Tzeltales and the Ladinos for my little pain poems— how they encroached and pushed, guffawed at the Lacandones' attempts to speak in Spanish of the significance of their culture and who envied them for their bank accounts from selling mahogany and from engraving their names on tourist wood. And I blamed Frans and Trudi Blom for creating the Na Bolom Museum of Living Lacandón Mayas, for introducing the gifting of commodities into the selva in the forties, for sowing "civilized" culture-gadgets at the entrance of every village home, for escorting cool capitalism into the battered heart of the tropical forest peoples. I knew the blaming was another self-made sham; I too had echoed the colonial gestures and had fulfilled colonial expectations by giving green money, by laying down voice-activated recorders, by offering a cache of rock cassettes, by performing my own "missionary" do-good literary genuflections.

I wanted to let go.

Something else was pushing into me.

It was the selva.

Something was taking place in the green darkness that I never ventured to notice or step into. And now, as I crept back into American oblivion through the last arenas for hydroelectric oppression, the true picture seemed to leap out of the trees and crush me until every drop of my being was wasted, disillusioned, and meted out, unable to discern the grimacing wave of rebellion about to burst through the refugee interiors of la selva.

Leaving. As I had never left.

I was leaving in a busted wagon of busted Indians swinging swollen bags of corn and baby rice powder, beans and refined flour, cookies and large Cokes the color of iodine. They would get off at the dotted stop where their new colonias stood up like fancy billboards, with braided ribbons in their hair, with low machetes and high cheekbones. I was leaving in the raw Tumbo full of chickens tied at the feet and slabs of fresh

kill on the screwed wires where the luggage goes, where I would place
the hammock Doña América gave me, the one I never used. Rolling up
on the Tumbo, the way I leaned forward on the cayuco, to the other end
point of my soul full of marching songs and fighting women from
Chenalhó with star shapes on their rebozos, full of praying men and reflective leaves falling to shreds in front of the cathedral, kneeling and crying at the bishop's gate, on their own loose wire of certainty, full of word
herbs, of story traces, of child and boy selva laughter, of wandering
mules alongside Tzeltal machete teen men, of Nuk of la tiendita hovering over her small fortune, selling aspirins to the village, hovering over
her tiny fullness. I was leaving without answers, the only way I could
leave.

I was leaving with the well-kept designs of the PRI man and his
petrochemical posse out of my reach and with a premonition of an
ocean-liner force about to crash through one of the last villages of the
White Jaguar. All I had was a deep mix of despair and love for all the
Mayan faces I had seen, for the ones that had entered and visited me.

> La mujer que me quiera
> me ha de querer de veras . . .
>
> The woman who will love me
> will have to love me truly . . .

I was leaving in the Tumbo in an hour or two. I was the timber fragment about to roll into the waters going to El Norte, rootless and severed.

The bolero came from inside, from under my left shirt pocket. Roaring, it crossed back and forth through my occupations, through my separations, through my migrations, through my Americanness, my intrin-
sic global virus of American border-maker power, of deportations and
relocations, of imposed salvations and protracted usurpations.

Mountains into circles into chants and deaths, sudden disappear-
ances into the eternal hammock holding up the last and the first faces:
Mayas. Mexicanos. Ladinos and Chicanos.
North into South.

South into me.

A green bolero from Nahá. I carried it around my neck. A moist green
stone, a green voice fire with redness at the edges; it multiplied across

Latin America and the earth itself, whether Panama, Nicaragua, or El Salvador, whether Uruguay or Chile, or Malaysia, Thailand, or the Philippines. Nahá was there too—interchangeable, fluid; above smoke and cold ground below, global. Everywhere the trees spoke the same language, everywhere the shape of Viejo Chan K'in's hands, curled around a translucent machete blade; *caoba blood writing* with cold winds falling upon its lowland territories, through the Indian massacres, the raped forests, the dream-colored caoba memory.

Turned back to the village for the last time.

I could tell by the way people walked on the Ruta, carefree and determined, by how they looked into my eyes and the lightness of their voices, the selva light; I could tell by the fragments of chipped stone, the kind used for arrowheads thrown at the edge of the road, by the slowing speed of the Ladino vendor trucks stacked with blond chairs, avocados, squash, and hard rolls; I was leaving with this song about emptiness and revolution.

III

Jaguar Hotel

JAGUAR HOTEL

A serious thing has happened: a virus has lodged itself where
one would have least expected it, yet, in the very place it can
do the worst damage—that is, in the very center of anti-viral
battle—indeed, if I'm to stick with this metaphor, right
in the central antibiotic warehouse.
From scene 5 of *Temptation*, a play by Václav Havel.

Jag Performance Notes

This two-act play is dedicated to the Maya of Mexico and all Indians of the Americas. Mayan theater groups from Chiapas and San
Cristóbal de las Casas, such as Fortaleza de Mujeres Mayas and La
Fomma, are presently at work and will prevail. Although "Jaguar
Hotel" remains an unfinished and tattered enterprise, deep aprecio
goes to Margarita Luna Robles and Andrew Díaz for their critical and
creative feedback. Without the staged workshop reading of the original version by Theatre Degree Zero of Tucson and Bisbee, Arizona,
headed by John Sullivan and Michelle Rae, this piece would have suffered in large measure. Gratitude and a bottle of pox for Guillermo and
Mimi Retaña for translating this text into Spanish, so that it may journey into Mexico. Also I want to salute Charley Trujillo for his work on
Chicanos in Viet Nam, which inspired many moments in this performance project.

Fragments of current national and international "politico" news
may replace "Presidential Speech." An "open" scene—one the teatro itself adds to the play after reading the text—may be inserted in any section where the actors and audience feel it will enhance the performance
piece. It is up to the troupe and audience to determine the direction,
style, and tempo of the acts and scenes, to color and materialize the
sets. Key question: can the puzzle of capitalism versus spirit versus
magic versus revolution versus genocide versus stage versus writing
be solved?

Landscape

Busted hotel in a remote Mexican town in southern Chiapas, Mexico, oscillating between the mountainous highland Tzotzil-Tzeltal hamlets and the open lowland campesino colonias and Lacandón Mayan rain-forest villages. All characters are fictive.

The Hotel

Day and deep night rising. Various makeshift rooms. Sound of jets overhead. Crossfire and tanks. Tenants sit on floor, others stand, at odd angles. "Rooms" may be played out singularly or simultaneously; also, the hotel may have two or three floors or wings, labyrinths, infernos, caves. A fire here, two candles there, a bell, a neon lobby, thick religious Gothic gates, flowers, nets, artifacts, indecipherable misshapen monuments. The "rooms" may be represented so as to have marked differences or they may contrast subtly. The hotel and performance create an environment that inherits and battles against textures, structures, and atmospheres, netted to a Spanish fortress, an old colonial monastery, a humid European museum, and a set of Mayan ghost cayucos. One more question: Is there a way out of this smoldering depot of trapped seekers?

Personae

CANEK, a young Indian man, Chan Ma'ax Viejo's son; dressed in bitten-off white sheet tunic and rubber sandals, watch, and Walkman.

MATAL, young Indian woman, Canek's wife; wears cheap commercial skirt, an ordinary blouse, jelly pumps.

JACINTO, a very young Indian hotel security guard; faded fatigues, old rifle and huaraches.

NELLY, an older Ladina woman; long dress, blouse, shawl, shoes.

GRETA, a very old white woman, once a fiery political activist for Mayan Indian rights and conservation of the rain forest, now sickly after recent stroke and partially paralyzed; loses consciousness on occasion; founder of hotel; horse-riding pants and khaki shirt, boots.

OSCAR, a young and stout Mexican student; stone-washed Levis, O. J. T-shirt, loafers.

XUN, an old Indian man; traditional Zinacanteco attire, huaraches.

MARUCH, a young Indian student, Greta's personal assistant; Dõna América's daughter, Chamula blouse with ordinary Ladina skirt, pumps.

DOÑA AMÉRICA, a very old Indian woman; torn white blouse and long dress, shawl, barefoot.

CHAN MA'AX VIEJO, a village elder; grayish tunic, barefoot.

MARGARITA, a young Chicana political activist; political buttons, Frida Kahlo T-shirt, army pants, boots.

LIONEL, a middle-aged Chicano professor; slacks, white dress shirt, shiny shoes, cell phone.

CHUY, middle-aged Chicano, disabled Viet Nam vet; camouflage outfit, dog tags, soldier boots, in wheelchair.

LOLO, a young married Ladino man; sporty shorts, tennis shoes, watch, tie-dyed T-shirt, beaded sixties necklace.

CHAN RODRIGO, a middle-aged Indian man; old spotted white tunic, barefoot.

TEDDY, a young white writer from San Francisco; jeans and no shirt, string for necklace, watch, huaraches.

FIDENCIA, a middle-aged Indian woman; disheveled greenish skirt, blouse and apron, jelly pumps.

BEAU, a middle-aged white man in his fifties; khakis, plaid shirt, big watch, loafers.

PACHECO, a young Mexican Army soldado; camouflage pants and boots, big watch, no shirt, gold chain with gold medallion, machine gun.

ROSARIO, an older Mexican Army soldado; camouflage pants, big watch, tight tank top, scapulary, machine gun, and knife in one of his boots.

ANONYMOUS HOTEL GUESTS.

Act 1: The Day

Scene 1. CHAN MA'AX VIEJO

(In an abandoned rain-forest village palmita)

Dawn. He dreams in his hammock. Wind and far-away cross fire. Restless. Tosses and turns—terrible screams, frightened. Above him a video screen lights up. Gortari appears, then Zedillo, then Clinton, then Gortari, then Dole, then a generic man with a generic face. These "presidential" images repeat. He walks downstage, sweats, trembles, shivers—begins to pray in Maya. Retrieves a sacred clay incense God pot, to burn and make an offering. Kneels before the clay bowl, bowed with face covered by long black hair. The voices of the presidents form a fragmented collage of speech-making as Chan Ma'ax lowers his head. As he begins to speak, the speeches interfere and intertwine.

CHAN MA'AX VIEJO: I have a village. Once I had a village. It is called Bolom. I can hear them calling. Then it goes away. The caoba tree grows over ninety meters. Above the world. In the day it speaks with the sky crickets. About abandonment. The abandonment of the earth. At night it sends you its secretos in the form of little river winds. Hachakyüm, the creator of the Lacandones, breathes life through every leaf . . .

PRESIDENTIAL SPEECH *(in fragments, bombastic and seductive):*
    Actualmente.
    ante la inevitable construcción — de una carretera.
    escuchar y evaluar alternativas — corrientes grandes
    para escuchar. pero también — a sus lados.
    se discute la posibilidad de crear en las zonas campesinas
    aldeanas, un basurero.

CHAN MA'AX VIEJO: The red flesh of the caoba tree is green. At night, we speak. In our dreams, we visit. That's all I can tell you. Green air. Green water. Green spirit. My village is lurking somewhere. Sometimes I can hear it rise up. Raise its little paws. After the rains. After the bulldozers. After the malaria, pneumonia. After the split seed of the colonists. It still raises its jaguar head. Then something moves me. Something from the back . . .

PRESIDENTIAL SPEECH *(in fragments, bombastic and seductive):*
    diverse opinions — the most important and spectacular — yes
    a strategic plan — for the circulation
    sustained — the account embraces
    external organizations — it represents the region
    therefore — in the future
    protected — how can they ask us to cancel? — yes
    confrontábamos el problema, como presa base
    el impacto ambiental, los terroristas
    surgió la posibilidad, unir el estado
    diálogo, pero al mismo tiempo

en particular apoyamos la solicitud, la voz
finalmente creemos que, desde Ciudad Juárez
for our nation — we have analyzed
third — a committee shall be formed of — from Nuevo Laredo
the people of Chiapas have pointed out that
in the remainder of my administration
scientific organizations — a tropical — autobahn
tropical technicians — we hope — yes
podremos
minas e industria, tres aspectos fundamentales
para las hidroeléctricas múltiples, lo podremos hacer
configuraciones multiples, aquí se ha planteado
no afectaría a Guatemala o Chiapas, será parte integral.

CHAN MA'AX VIEJO: Who is it? Who can live back there behind all of this?
Who stayed behind? Behind all this devastation and beauty. Is it me?
Is it the women? Is it my own hair pulling at me from the womb of a
lake? Behind a tiny pebble, a firefly? I stand here. Next to the caoba.
There is someone inside. Knocking. Can you hear her knocking?

PRESIDENTIAL SPEECH *(in fragments, bombastic and seductive):*
the ecological and culural cost to construct dams
Mexico and Guatemala and — the sons of their sons
on the other hand — I find it quite reasonable — actually
the Usumacinta River — during decades
but rather let us speak of humanity — if we have opened
global recognition — the traces — yes
the most ancient civilizations — being part of
the Americas — our equilibrium — more
Yaxchilán — Piedras Negras — on our foundation
consideramos que debe haber congruencia, al mismo tiempo
biodiversidad, el camino, la conservación, sí
en todos estos proyectos, la importancia del ciudadano
y en esta ocasión quiero además, es necesario, actualmente
hacer, un billón, dos cientos mil millones, es necesario, sí
hacer, actualmente, debería . . .

CHAN MA'AX VIEJO: What is it? I cannot tell. There is no one to answer. I
stand here. Next to the caoba. Alone. My wife, Koh, pushes me, but
it's no use. My hands don't listen. My legs are deaf. Nothing listens.
I stand here. Awake with the roots. I know you walk there with me,

somewhere. Stars, so many stars, in black. I look for a fallen tree. I want to sleep there, in that fallen tree. My skin, my foot, my hand, my ears are stripes—spots.

Scene 2. BEAU AND FIDENCIA

(Early morning at the hotel, cleaning Beau's room as he shaves, the Metzabok Room)

BEAU: The old sewer pipelines don't work anymore. All you have now are tin pipes pushing out of the earth. You sit there. You empty yourself. Squat. So pitiful. You connect your insides to the insides of this nation. The old sewer pipes won't work . . . anymore. Portable toilets. That's next . . . portable.

FIDENCIA: Oh. Uh. Oh. Ahhh.

BEAU: My son has stomach cancer. They just told me this morning. I've got to fly to New Jersey tomorrow. Take a combi to Tuxtla as soon as the sun comes up. They told me at the kitchen, while I was eating. I can't eat anymore.

FIDENCIA: Sí. Ohhh. Cancer. Sí, sí . . . sí . . .

BEAU: A few blocks from the zócalo, a poor Indian woman from Tene-japa sells tortillas from a large basket. She weaves a thin cloth tied to her waist. I could tell she's from Tenejapa by the woven signature at the bottom of her huipil. Textiles, there's more than meets the eye of the turista. I study how they weave too. Mayan weavers map the motion of the universe with color and designs. The Earthlord and his musician, the toad, swirl in a cosmic dance of cotton. On the sleeves sits a scorpion. He brings rain by poking the clouds with his stinger. Bright red strings and electric blue silk-like thread. She pulls out from herself, against herself; she unravels the colors and weaves them with her little hands, looking down at them . . . from time to time.

FIDENCIA: Tortillas. Ahhh. Pues. Ahhhhh . . . sí . . .

BEAU: Today, I noticed that something was wrong with her eyes. They were yellow and full of fluid. She wove strings and sold tortillas. She said "two thousand pesos" in a weak voice. I gave her three thousand and took the soft stack rolled in a square of old paper.

FIDENCIA: Ahhh. Sí. Mmmm . . .

BEAU: Walked and chewed the tortillas . . . I tried to push the food down my throat. Even though I was ravenous, even though I chewed hard, I wrestled with the corn paste in my mouth; it went down in shreds . . . some of it stuck to the sides of my cheeks, lodged inside, some of it dissolved on my tongue and stayed there, the rest of it knotted itself in the middle of my throat. Couldn't swallow because something was bruising me and did not allow me to chew and swallow. It was forcing me—against my will—to spit everything out; most of all it wanted me to spit myself out. The tortillas wanted to turn me over, upside down, with the guts out, with the fluid out too, like the woman kneeling on the curb, pulling strings out of her belly, selling them as ribbons or belts; something didn't permit me to swallow, to fill myself, to become solid . . . it wanted me to spit, to drench myself, to scream, to empty myself with my body . . . Open.

FIDENCIA: Empteh. Empteh . . . empteh . . . ahhh . . .

Scene 3. CANEK AND MATAL

(Ocosingo Room)

CANEK: Matal, you think we can have breakfast in their little restaurant?

MATAL: Eggs, toast. Eggs toast. Eggs. Toast. Maybe.

CANEK: You know, they do have the best chorizo in town. When they sell our amber earrings and our little caoba statues . . . you know . . . maybe we can go into their little restaurant.

MATAL: Like Doña Greta used to say, "When you are ready, Canek."

CANEK: She named this place after us. Bolom. She learned our language. She taught us many things.

MATAL: Now she sleeps with her eyes open.

CANEK: It used to take days to reach this hotel. Even on a mule—days and nights. Pacho, her husband, caught a bad fever once, remember? We had to leave him alone in the selva with just a few things to eat.

MATAL: Now it's just three hours—from here to the jungle in three hours. The Mayan airlines. The Lacandonia buses. Maybe you could learn to drive one too.

CANEK: A chofer? A Lacandón chofer driving a Lacandonia bus to the Last Lands of the Lacandón? Me a chofer? You could drive a bulldozer. Haa!

MATAL: Bulldozers are different. Greta wanted to stop the developers from taking our land. So many things she wanted for us. She mapped our village, the ruins. She brought in clinics and campamentos . . . to be with us.

CANEK: To be with us? She hated us. We were nothing but safari Indians for her turistas. To be with us?

MATAL: How could you say that? So they could shoot fotos. So they could learn our language, keep us alive . . . That's what she used to say.

CANEK: Our language? So they could be our new white mothers. So we could suck their chi-chis and learn to grow like them. With tractors, with trucks. Bulldozers. Dragged. Around our lakes. Bulldozers are different, that's right.

MATAL: Why are you saying this? You've caught something? Your face is different. We are here now. We've been here for quite a while.

CANEK: Before we came here, my father, Chan Ma'ax Viejo, used to tell us about the red guacamayo, the white turtle, and how they multiplied off the shore of Río Jataté where there are roads now. Buses, Matal, bulldozers, oil factories sucking blood from the earth. Now the military search for our brothers and sisters. They think we are going to kill them. We can't even eat in the kitchen. Eggs, toast—nothing! Soon we'll have to pay rent.

MATAL: Your face is different. I don't know what to do with you. Your mother, Koh, is not here. She never wanted to come. She would scold you. And the money you made, she never bothered you about it.

CANEK: You want to know what I did with the eight million pesos Joaquín Chancala gave me?

MATAL: You talked to your father so he would sign over the timber rights to the Ladino timber company men, like Joaquín. I don't want to know any more.

CANEK: What did I do with the money? I am not going to tell you. Why should I tell you? We are here. Nowhere, doing nothing. Looking at each other make faces. I have nothing to say. I signed the paper, that's all . . . words on paper. We are not even here. So what!

MATAL: What did Chan Ma'ax say?

CANEK: I don't want to talk about it. They are taking away our trees anyway. With or without signatures. You know it.

MATAL: I don't know anything. We are here alone. No one knows anything

CANEK: I didn't say anything. We are here, sitting. That is all. Sitting. Just sitting.

Scene 4. CHAN MA'AX VIEJO

(In the village house alone, speaking to the burning God pot)

My children are different. They walk about kicking stones and cutting trees. I tell them, "Every time you bring down a tree, a star falls from the sky." I tell them, "the roots of all living things are tied together. When a tree dies you die." They laugh. They go about cutting the great caoba tree. They come back laughing. "Look, we cut it down and we're still alive, look!" they say. They carve little caoba statues, take them to San Cristóbal. Sell them in the hotels. They come back laughing, drinking cañabrava. All night—drink and laugh out loud into the black trees. They hire a Tzeltal indio with a busted truck to drive them in circles with their sad eyes out the windows. Laughing. They hire a mestizo taxi from Palenque, with the little they earn from selling arrows and red-bean necklaces . . . They do not know . . . that already they have begun to die. *(Lifts God pot into the air and places it back at the center of the floor)*
Ofrenda del pozol si el dios lo quiere
Ofrenda del pozol, si el dios lo quiere
Ofrenda del pozol si el dios lo quiere.

Tsula wa ku qatik yum
Tsula wa ku qatik yum
Tsula wa ku qatik yum
Tsula wa ku qatik yum.*

Scene 5. CHUY AND MARGARITA

(In the Chamula Room, door open)

CHUY: We got to keep this shit together. You know what I mean, all right?
MARGARITA: Chuy, you mean we got to be firme? Trucha?
CHUY: Tú sabes. You know what time it is. You can always count on me, chavala. Firme and brown down to the coffee grounds. I was there at the Chicano Moratorium commemoration last year. Man, you don't want me to get started, I know my shit. From San Antó to Saint Nam . . . tin tan . . . Firme and brown down to the coffee grounds.
MARGARITA: Me la rayo, to the bone, loco.

---

*Spanish and Lacandón prayer: An offering of corn stew, if the god wishes it.

CHUY: You're not bullshitting me, are you, Margarita? I mean . . .

MARGARITA: Like I said, loco. Firme, al alba. On the ball, jack. I know where you are coming from, ese. I've checked you out. I know when you're together. ¿Sabes? You think I've been painting my nails con mayonesa or what? Mira, my stuff's tight too, ese. Barrios Unidos in Austin, *Con Safos* magazine in L.A., Teatro de la Misión in San Fra, Centro Cultural in San Antó. You think I came down here like all those bullshit Mexican tourists, not to mention the pinchis gringos, Germans, Swedes, and Frenchitos with their Ninja backpacks full of Pepto-Bismol and traveler checks? Shit, it's time to make tight choices. We got to figure if la onda is about going in or staying out. Do we stay and lose ourselves? Join up with the Zapatistas, fall back into Guatemala and get the bigger action? Are we in the position to protect, to save, to change anything? To change ourselves? ¿Entiendes méndez?

CHUY: Simón.

MARGARITA: ¿Simón?

CHUY: Simón.

MARGARITA: ¿Simón?

CHUY: Simón. Simón!

MARGARITA: Simón what? Yes, what? Wake up, man. We're sixty kilometers from la frontera de Guatemala, the mother of all Tijuanas. So we met at the mercado, so I asked you to hang with me. So you've been looking for a good lay and some mota, way down here, three thousand miles from your drunken vet carnales taking their last swig of Jack Daniels while poppin' down whites with chocolate sprinkle doughnuts an' talking about the good ol' days at Cam Ranh Bay. Think you got huevos now? Times change, carnal. Got on-line Zapatista computer chat lines, back where I'm from. Yo estoy hecha de otro árbol, Chuy. Simón what?

CHUY: Uh, I heard you. Chill out—I got it.

Scene 6. CANEK AND MATAL

(In the Ocosingo Room)

CANEK: I wanted to stay, I told you Matal. Everyone's run to Palenque. They jumped the trucks, the buses. They left everything behind. Everyone is gone. I wanted to stay . . .

MATAL: Your father is still there. Your mother, Koh. But we've always come here.

CANEK: "The revolution," they said. "We'll lose everything to the Tojolabales, the foreigners, the Tzeltales, the Ladino colonists from Ocosingo . . . the soldados." I didn't want to fight, I mean, with what . . . with . . . I mean . . . I would lose everything . . . I mean . . .

MATAL: You could be killed, you and . . . then . . .

CANEK: You.

MATAL: We are here now, Canek. Here . . . now.

CANEK: This room. These walls. This door. This window that sees nothing. This floor. Dry tortillas. Lemonade. Chorizo. Queso de Ocosingo in the Ocosingo Room.

MATAL: Since you were a kid you been coming here. Since Greta brought you over with Pepe Chan Bor on a mule, when you were just nine, you've been coming here. When we got married, you said, "Wait till you see San Cristóbal, just wait. The bread, the longaniza, the streets." You met many people who paid you for words. From the United States. You rode on jeeps. You smoked cigarettes, you wore a watch. You used toilets like the Ladinos. Since you were a kid. I always wanted to be like you, Canek.

CANEK: What are we going to do now? The roads are blocked. My father is alone. Across the patio flowers, Doña Greta is dying in her room.

MATAL: She is the one who brought all of us here. Now she leaves us.

CANEK: We are neither here nor there, Matal. They will kill my father at any moment. Los soldados. Outside this hotel, I can hear the fires, the planes . . .

MATAL: They will kill us too . . . if we leave. You understand?

CANEK: My father is old, very old, the last of the elders.

MATAL: If we stay, nothing will happen.

CANEK: If we stay what will happen to us?

MATAL: We've been here for years.

CANEK: We've been here . . . for . . . years . . .

Scene 7. CHUY, in wheelchair, and Lolo

(In the garden)

LOLO: Did you hear about Woodstock? I wish I could have been there—man!

CHUY: Your wife wanted to go. I was at the first one, cabrón. Shudda seen Jimi Hendrix. That vato was flyin' like a chopper without C-rations.

LOLO: Yeah, I know—you told me. That was a few days before you went to Viet Nam, right? Did I get that right, hijín?

CHUY: You got it, carnalito. That was a few days before I got on the TWA.

LOLO: TWA? ¿Qué onda, hijín?

CHUY: The Wrong Airline—quivo?

LOLO: TWA—I don't get it.

CHUY: Simón, man. Imagine, a vato from San Antonio, only child and all that shit—todo católico y pendejo, altar boy at Our Lady of Guadalupe, Our Lady of Cholo citizenship, left-handed bell-ringer, left-handed masturbator with Coca-Cola glasses, buck teeth—and still, camarada, they drafted my Chicano candy ass all the way to Chicano Hawaii. ¿Quivo?

LOLO: There you go again. What do you mean, Chicano Hawaii? You never said that, hijín.

CHUY: What the fuck, mamón? When you come down on Nam, ese, when you jump off that fuckin' hotdog-shaped helicopter, the shit looks like Hawaii! ¿Quivo? And who the fuck is out there, puto? Middle-class college wimps studying the cranial size of your tío's ball-peen cabeza? ¡Chale! It's Cheekans, blacks, Okies, and Porto Ricans, quivo? I had never been nowhere, loco—not even Austin. From San Antó to Chicano Hawaii—quivo!

LOLO: But you took a little time out at Woodstock, ¿verdad, hijín? Hendrix, Santana, right? You told me, right?

CHUY: I was up near the stage, ese—that was my landing zone—with a red-haired loca from San José. A Chicana bien hinchada, you know what I mean? Anyways, she was on crutches 'cause her boyfriend, some puto from Salinas todo pedo on White Port con lemon juice, fell on top of her and cracked her ass on the way down the stairs. So anyways, carnal . . . here's Jimi wailing on his lira, man, then all of a sudden, he reaches down and takes la huera's crutch and jams with it. ¡Qué locote ese vato! Shit!

LOLO: Did you say he grabbed her crotch?

CHUY: Pinchi Mexicano puto, man—I said crutch, man. Agarra la onda, or I'll work it out with your jaina—toda preñada and everything.

LOLO: Contról, hijín. I never heard that stuff, Chuy! Hendrix, TWA—that was before my time. Soy de Comitán . . . me and my wife. My wife's very busy. In the Harvard Room. We've got a kid, you know. She's been competing for the job as assistant curator. You know.

CHUY: Oh, excuse me, tutti frutti.

LOLO: Tell me about Santana.

CHUY: Check it out. Ever since they brought in the new director, things have opened up. Red Hot Chili Peppers, The Stones—it all comes in now! Got a TV the size of an elephant's ass in the lobby. Satellite dish up on the hill. When they pipe Santana into this hotel—on the speakers, mira, una buena moteada, unos taquitos del mercado—you'll be on my landing zone!

LOLO: I tell her, "What about the kid?" What are we going to do about the niño? School, clothes, books, doctors—what do we do? I get up at night, take him out wrapped in a blanket, walk through here, from the patio to the supply room and back again. He's gonna get sick, cries all the time.

CHUY: Santana . . . man! He's still doing it. Bien padre, vato. I got my lira, it's always tuned up. Know some leads too. *(Lolo looks at him)* Come on. You know I can do the lead to "Black Magic Woman."

LOLO: You watched Santana? In the lobby?

CHUY: Red Hot Chili Peppers. All those cats! They got the works here, ese. Maíz, Santana, the jungle, the mountains . . . this is my Nam. That's all I need, fuckin' A. Fuck the big city. Fuck Los Estados. Fuck 'em with a pogo stick. I am still on a mission, ese. Anytime. Just waiting—for my orders to come in, you know what I mean? Just call my number. So they blasted my legs off—so what? I was carrying the M-60, we got into a firefight, sargeant asked, everybody all right? Started to move but I couldn't. When I looked back my legs looked like fuckin' hamburger. Shit, I was a fuckin' taquito de carne asada. Loco. All fucked up. This is my kinda place. Just breathe it in, cabrón. It's all here. I look out my window . . . just waitin' it out, carnalito. Tengo mi pistola, mi mota . . . y mis huevos. Nothing's changed.

LOLO: I want my kid to be in a rock band someday. He'll do what I say, too.

CHUY: I am sure your ruca's got other ideas, loco.

LOLO: She's out there. Leafing through the negatives that Greta has taken for the last forty years. Next week she's going to start on the Mujeres Zapatistas collection.

CHUY: Zapatistas? Come on, Zapatistas? You can't see their faces. Don't even know where they are. They'll kick your ass before you can say "Burger time"!

LOLO: Not the ones in the selva. Not those guys. Relax, hijo. The ones that rode with Emiliano. In the revolution, pendejo. Doña Greta met them after she arrived from Europe. In the early fifties.

CHUY: The revolution—yeah, the revolution. All right. Tell me about it, pendejo candy ass. "Wow, bien padre, man." What do you know about the revolution? What do your fucking turkey legs know about the revolution?

Scene 8. MATAL AND CANEK

(In the patio)

MATAL: There is an Americano in the Metzabok Room who is working on portable toilets for the Chamulas. He's a fat man with a heart condition, from New Jersey. I was talking to Fidencia, the maid . . .

CANEK: Chamulas? Bootleg liquor makers. One hundred thousand bootleg liguor makers. We're only five hundred. Remember that, Matal. Five hundred, not a hundred thousand. Fidencia's just another Chamula too, trying to pass for a Ladina with a broom.

MATAL: Chamulas—you can almost see them from the windows, in the mountains closest to the hotel. Sliding down further and further. Looking for work. They come down the mountain. We come up from the selva. Isn't that funny? They come down, we come up. Here we are, now.

CANEK: Next to the Jataté Room there is a photographer from Colorado that wants to adopt a boy from one of our villages—Chan K'in Jorge, the deaf mute.

MATAL: Adopt him?

CANEK: But of course, we are still welcome, honorary members of the hotel. How kind of them to show us their Mexican hospitality.

MATAL: You want to go back to see your father, don't you? You never talk this way.

CANEK: Mi casa es tu caspa.

MATAL: All of a sudden, things are upside down and you look strange and say strange things.

CANEK: Chamulas? I always said I hate them. We always said it back home. The Tojolabales too—all they're good for is cutting weeds with machetes.

MATAL: You left yours behind.

CANEK: Mi caspa es tu casa. Haaa!

Scene 9. CHAN MA'AX VIEJO

(In his palmita, burning incense in the God pot)

CHAN MA'AX VIEJO: The white jaguar comes back at times and visits
me. My grandfathers come back with him. My grandmothers come
back. The chicleros appear and vanish and the caoba stumps heal,
the sap glistens, the sky crickets stop their sad songs—for a moment. The Spanish come and go too, with terrible fever faces and
smallpox legs, with their empty words, they retreat into the underworld of Kisin, the devourer of what is below. The monteros appear, hunched . . . throw away their axes. The Jataté and the
Usumacinta Rivers whisper against the banks of the earth. No
longer are they stuffed with bleeding logs and machinery. The
white jaguar comes back for a while, then another jaguar appears,
of a different color. The motion of the dots on her body speak of another time, another universe spins in her heart. Is it the same universe? Is ours colliding? Are both jaguars the same one? Smoke,
columns of smoke rise from each rough dot and stripe. Blood and
smoke . . . Machine men and machine hearts gnash their engines. It
is not jaguar, maybe—it is the blue engine of the underworld. It is
Kisin. He comes to devour us, so few of us left—why? Where is my
universe blanket? I ask my wife, Koh. The one I use for the ceremony of the God pots, for the ceremony of the new year . . . On one
side of the blanket, all the stars, all the lives spin, the roots of all the
living beings. On the other side, it is mystery, it is on our body. Mystery covers us with fullness and emptiness. *(Chan Ma'ax Viejo goes
into a trance as the "Presidential Speech" begins. He begins to dance as a
jaguar, peaceful, then aggressive. When the "speech" ends he goes back to
the God pot, in low prayer.)*

PRESIDENTIAL SPEECH *(seductive, sardonic):* un plan estratégico, para la circulación

organizaciones externas, representa la región

posteriormente, en el futuro, sí, sí

confrontábamos el problema, como presa base

the environmental impact — the terrorists

the possibility became clear — unite the State

conciliation — to protect — a project
dialogue — but at the same time — yes yes
in particular we support the endorsement — the voice
some organizations — all the way from Nogales
actually — yes — yes
before the inevitable construction of a highway
to listen — to evaluate alternatives — global currents
to listen — but also — on the behalf of
the formation of peasant zones the possibility
aldeanas, un basurero, sí
diversas opiniones, el más importante y espectacular
un plan estratégico, para la circulación
organizaciones externas, representa la región
posteriormente, en el futuro
aldeanas, un basurero, sí, sí . . .

Scene 10. JACINTO *walks through the door and joins* CANEK *and* MATAL

(In the Ocosingo Room)

JACINTO: Did you hear what happened to Chan Ma'ax Viejo?

CANEK: They've done nothing to my father.

JACINTO: Nothing at all? Are you sure?

CANEK: Jacinto, I am not going to talk about this. Matal, she won't tell you either. You won't catch anyone from our village saying a thing. Do you understand this? Nothing has been said. Nothing has been done. Only the wind from the caoba trees knows. Got it?

JACINTO: You know something, don't you?

MATAL: Tell him about little Rosita of the Twisted Jaw.

CANEK: You never met her. You left your Chamula village the day she was born. She sells Bayer aspirin and big bottles of Sprite in our little tiendita. On La Ruta. It's a lovely little store. A few palmitas away from my father's house.

MATAL: Mexican tomato paste. Mexican crackers. Mexican salt. Anything you want from San Cristóbal. They even have . . .

JACINTO: I am not Chamula! My municipio is Zinacantán. Twenty thousand strong. A few days ago we celebrated the fiesta of San Lorenzo.

CANEK: . . . even a chair once in a while, in the tiendita—Mexican chairs. Anything you want. Chairs from Zinacantán! Haa!

JACINTO: Did you say chairs? Not from Zinacantán, no . . .

CANEK: You guys even have VCRs. You don't fool me. I've been around here. I just have a satellite dish in Nahá Sayab. You guys got more land than we do. Fertilizer, chemicals. You grow the milpa year round. Trucks, I seen them. I seen you drive your troques with your eyes bulging out from staying awake, all the way from Mexico City. Money in your chamorros. Chamula, you don't fool me.

JACINTO: Not all of us have VCRs. Or satellite dishes like you, Canek.

CANEK *(to Matal):* Tell him about the caps.

MATAL: When the guy from Ocosingo comes in his truck with his mestizo wife, he drops off a few chairs for Rosita of the Twisted Jaw. Avocados. Baseball caps.

CANEK: When we left they had Giants caps from San Francisco and one from los Cowboys, from Texas. A silver star!

JACINTO: Cowboys?

CANEK: Puros Cowboys! Ajuaaa!

JACINTO: In Zinacantán, I knew many things. Haven't been there for years. My mother was a widow. She came here to see, maybe she could keep me alive, me and my sister Pasquala. A drunk Ladino man raped her a few blocks from here, in el Barrio de los Mexicanos. She couldn't ever go back home again. In Zinacantán, I knew many things. I could tell you the difference between those with a "heated heart" and those that devour souls. Out here, nothing . . . My mother died so young. My sister? Who knows? She left for the colonias outside of Ocosingo . . . ¿quién sabe? I look up at the sky and remember nothing.

MATAL: There is nothing . . . to remember here.

JACINTO: I eat in the restaurant, you know, where Doña Greta has all her paintings on the wall? Where they give tours and they talk about how this hotel was once a monastery and how Doña Greta and her husband, Pacho, paid sixteen thousand dollars for it in 1950. It even had its own chapel and strange Ladino drawings . . . Eggs in the morning with thick slices of wheat bread . . . I'd rather have tortillas, tortillas right from the fire—like at home. Here? Eggs . . . Eggs, just eggs, too many eggs.

MATAL: The jaguar? Did you see the jaguar she has on the wall? "Bolom," I told her. That's how you say it in Maya. Bolom. Did you see it? She brought the jaguar plaque from Oaxaca. It's at the front gate, facing Calle Vicente Dugelay.

JACINTO: Bolom. Bolom? What jaguar? Where?

CANEK: Up high. Where you can't see it, Chamula.

JACINTO: If I can't see it, it's because it's not real. Maybe the Earthlord devoured it.

CANEK: This is the Ocosingo Room. In the back, past the gardens, they have the Quetzal Room, the Harvard Room. And a few doors from here, the Fray Bartolomé library with thousands of books and articles on us.

MATAL: They are rebuilding the library?

JACINTO: On us, books? The roof leaks when it rains.

MATAL: On us. Lacandones. A little on Chamulas. Hundreds of portfolios, full of negatives. You're in some of them.

JACINTO: I told you, I am not Chamula. I am from . . .

(Nelly comes in through the door.)

NELLY: What are you doing here, Jacinto? Didn't I tell you to keep quiet? Watch the hotel. No one knows where you are.

MATAL: We know.

NELLY: Tomorrow they are going to bring in the American Embassy. This is going to be the American Embassy. The town is up in arms. There are tanks on the street, more soldiers in the mercados. The bishop is fasting until things change. The cathedral is full of reporters from the States. Gortari is being extradited from Winnepeg. There's nobody in the streets. Roadblocks. Sandbags. No one can get in here. No one can leave.

CANEK: Ahhh. Roadblocks. Like in the selva. No one can get out. No one can get in. Just like the selva—haa!

NELLY: No more donations for the rain forest, that's for sure. El Viejo Chan Ma'ax?

CANEK: He's alone now.

NELLY: I don't know how old your father is—but it's true, isn't it? He still works la milpa? Greta lives too, but she is different now. She rarely comes out of her room. See, over there? The room with the "feliz cumpleaños" painted on the crown of the door, see it? Ninety-three years old. A couple of years ago she let go of this place, this beautiful house. She couldn't move around any more, you know. The hotel was taken over by that man—Armendaña, they call him. Then he

gave the administration job to a woman. Look at me. Yo me he en-
vejecido aquí. I have grown old here.

MATAL: Maybe you should have that job—you know, as the administrator.

NELLY: Things would be different. What can I do? I live in the back, a little farther back than your room. Behind the Chamula Room. Maybe I
could have gotten that job. You've seen the donation box in the reception lobby? People come from all parts of the world and put money in
it. "For the Rain Forest," it says. They come from all over the world.
Germany, Italy, France. From los Estados Unidos, from Sweden and
England. They put their money here, in this little box, for the rain forest. "See how pretty it's painted," they say. With a little yellow jaguar.

MATAL: Bolom!

CANEK: Bolom? No one's seen the jaguar. The money never gets there.
There is no rain forest fund of any kind. It is all a sham. You should
talk to the others.

NELLY: Have you met Oscar? He's here as a student—from la capital. He
gets free room and board as long as he gives full credit to the hotel
and leaves a copy of his research in the Harvard Room when he's
done. We always have some students staying with us. They study the
Indians. Right now, he's just back from Nahá Chan Sayab. He went
to visit Carmita, the only one in the village with rubber boots.

CANEK: What do you mean he went to visit Carmita? There's no Carmita
anymore! Right now, he's trapped somewhere on La Ruta, in some
Red Cross ambulance staring at a bag of water shoot into his arm.
There's a revolution going on out there.

JACINTO: Oscar is with Doña America. In the supply room.

MATAL: You remember Carmita? PEMEX came in two years ago and
gave us a load of money at Nahá Chan Sayab, like they did in all our
villages. They came to Lake Ocotal. Some of the Lacandones bought
TVs and radios. Carmita wanted Nikes. You bought two Walkmans
and a stereo, Canek. Remember?

CANEK: I am here now. You are here now. There is only this floor, that
floor, this window, this door. This, this. That is all.

MATAL: I am so glad we are here. Nelly, do you have anything to eat?
Some cheese from Ocosingo? A tortilla with jelly?

JACINTO: Here, have some cigarettes. When is Chan Ma'ax Viejo coming?

CANEK: Did you say Chan Ma'ax Viejo?

JACINTO: When is he . . .

CANEK: Forget about Chan Ma'ax Viejo. Study your books in Spanish, march in the mornings all the way to Guadalupe Real, the church on the highest mountain slope. Ask the Ladinos about the video cameras they carry from the States. Polish your boots. Get ready to blow someone's brains out very soon. Don't come here asking stupid questions that have been asked by every Ladino asshole we run into. You keep your nose clean. This is your town now. This hotel is yours too. Forget about the villages. Forget about the old ones. What do you care anyway, Chamula? You're not one of us. You are not even who you were. You left your Zinacantán years ago.

MATAL: Come outside. *(Leads Jacinto out the door into the patio)* Come.

Scene 11. GRETA AND MARUCH

(Outside in the patio)

MARUCH: So beautiful. The sky, really. And of course the hotel . . .

GRETA *(Speaks with difficulty. She's partially paralyzed; her words come out in bolts, stutters, and lucid phrases):* The sky. Did you say . . . ?

MARUCH: So . . . deep and strange.

GRETA: I would have killed them.

MARUCH: You what?

GRETA: Killed all of them. I would have done anything to save the rain forest. Its people.

MARUCH: Oh, yes, yes, everyone knows that—we can see. That's why we are here.

GRETA: But the fuckers never listened. The governor even gave one Lacandón the Chiapas Prize. Eight million pesos and a diploma.

MARUCH: Yes, yes, we know. It was an honor. You always wanted that. It was your dream. You told us we deserved much more.

GRETA: Eight million. Fuckers. The PRI.

MARUCH: There's a copy of the diploma pasted by the main gate, at the entrance to the hotel.

GRETA: They wrapped their cocks around every caoba tree and fucked every root in the earth.

MARUCH: Take it easy, Señora Greta. I am here with you. The day . . .

GRETA: When they came, their cock juice spat black oil and jizz all over the Indians' faces. The villages voted for them without even reading the papers they were signing. They stood up on platforms at the zócalo saying that it was for Mexico, for the future.

MARUCH: Think about the day, Señora Greta. It is better to consider the day.

GRETA: Energy, they said.

MARUCH: Development. They said the word "development." Remember when I couldn't even speak in Spanish? You've done so much for me, Señora Greta.

GRETA: You didn't vote.

MARUCH: Vote? They really don't want us Chamulas to vote. They call all Indians Chamulas. As long as they get their vote . . . No one in Mexico votes like Chamulas vote.

GRETA: You don't know.

MARUCH: You are wrong. The PRI came as always. With a bottle of pox, they sat down with the caciques. Made deals. Took our ballots and filled them out and stuffed them with more ballots. "Tacos," they called them. Tacos for Gortari. Tacos for Zedillo—taco votes . . . Let's enjoy the daylight.

GRETA: Pimps.

MARUCH: Señora Greta. You are not well. Let's go to your room.

GRETA: You don't know what you're talking about, Chamula. While you clean the flower vases, while you sweep up the dust from the bricks in the patio, when you change the linens in the second-floor rooms, I know you look down and spy on me. All of you—spies.

MARUCH: In your house? Look down?

GRETA: I heard you talking about how I keep you here. You used the word "museum." "In this museum," you said. I see you . . . Chamula.

MARUCH: You see? Me?

GRETA: But maybe there's more and you don't know. Just maybe . . . I look at you too.

MARUCH: What?

GRETA: *They* look at you too!

MARUCH: What are you saying, Doña Greta?

GRETA: The Ladinos look at you! At your ass.

MARUCH: Do they?

GRETA: They say you are a lamb chop with braids, a little Chamula Indian that went to the university in Tuxtla Gutiérrez. Bowl scrubber with a degree.

MARUCH: I know how they look at me.

GRETA: You can't fool them. You can't do nothing about it. You are still the same.

MARUCH: Fine. I am.

GRETA: Behind the Quetzal Room . . . they want to get you. Should I cut their throats? String up their little white cocks and their weak balls and mash them down their necks? Should I? I am too old, you think?

MARUCH: Your words escape you. You don't know. A crazy thorn burns in your heart.

Scene 12. OLD XUN and OSCAR

(In the reception lobby, Oscar with tape recorder and notes, eating a sandwich)

OSCAR: How do you say "brujero" in Tzotzil?

XUN: H-ak'chamel.

OSCAR: H-ak'chamel?

XUN: Yes.

OSCAR: And what does that word, h-ak'chamel . . . mean?

XUN: Someone . . .

OSCAR: Someone who makes . . . ?

XUN: Someone who gives . . .

OSCAR: Someone who gives?

XUN: Someone who gives sickness. Who sells portions of people's souls to the Earth Lord. Who appears . . .

OSCAR: Appears?

XUN: Sí. Appears . . . to the victim in the form of an animal, a spirit companion.

OSCAR: Animal spirit? Companion?

XUN: Yes.

OSCAR: Animal . . . spirit?

XUN: Sí, sí. Because he . . . is . . . a brujero, a . . . witch.

OSCAR: And what kind of animal spirits can . . . the h-ak'chamel turn into?

XUN: Well, whatever he likes.

OSCAR: Whatever he likes?

XUN: Sí. Sí, I believe so. Since he is a brujero, he knows how it's going to be. He knows. When it's one of us, we don't know what's going to happen, we don't know.

OSCAR: How do you say, Let's go wash our hands?

Scene 13. MARGARITA and CHUY

(In the library)

MARGARITA *(to Chuy):* Soon, we'll make a move, carnal . . . very soon. Maybe we'll hit the streets, catch a little air. Take in the sounds. Case the town out. Man, back home, they have no idea what's going on here. Everybody's gettin' big, high on their asses. Chicano studies has turned into welfare studies, La Raza's getting gypped. Black studies, ethnic studies, women's studies, "Native" American studies—oh, yes, Asian American studies . . . Who would have guessed that we were busy building our own segregation compounds. In Califas, migrant farmworker kids come all the way from tiny towns like Easton, Hanford, Selma, Shafter, Visalia to hear some chileno or argentino or a UCLA Hispanic tío-taco talk about Emiliano Zapata, the Treaty of Guadalupe Hidalgo, some vendido that's never even been near the local barrio liquor store, not to mention the real heavy trips that la Chicanada goes through. Day in, day out . . . I swear . . .

CHUY: You were in San Antó? Man, that's where my mom's from. Presa street. She opened up a flower shop last year. Me la rayo!

MARGARITA: You seen these guys! Making fifty, sixty, seventy, and eighty thousand mangos a year just to sit on their acculturated, self-serving, vendido chops—just to ogle the brown-legged twenty-two-year-old chavalas in their classes, masturbate in their pastel hospital green offices, cash in their feria, drive home in their metallic blue Celicas, finger their pepperoni slice.

CHUY: Selling root beers and flowers . . . Margarita, you should see my jefita. She says they even got a souvenir shop a block down with Cesar Chavez T-shirts and little sculptures of la Virgen de Guadalupe. ¿Quivo?

MARGARITA: What about the busted familias of Chicanos and Chicanas who really want to make a difference? What about them? Where do they run to?

CHUY: "Business is coming in, all of a sudden, a lot of people are interested in Mexicans," the jefita said. When the bolillos roll in to her little store, they freak out. You know—she still has John F. Kennedy and Jimmy Carter's carátula up on the wall. Kennedy right next to the nopales, el Santo Niño de Atocha, green candles, red candles with

archangels and all their holy artillery . . . serpientes, swords, and
moon goddesses—it's a fuckin' Chicano carnival. Esos bolillos, man
. . . bunch of candy asses.

MARGARITA: Man, this thing here is going to put a stop to all that hocus
pocus. Soon, Chuy, we're going to get things rockin'.

CHUY: Simón . . .

MARGARITA: We're gonna light the fuse and than blam! The whole
Christmas enchilada is going to light up, all the way from Brazil to
Pendejoville.

CHUY: My jefita . . . man, if it wasn't for her, I'd be locked up. She kept
me going. I just had to think about what she went through, that's
what kept my fire burning. She couldn't believe me when I got back
all busted up, in a wheelchair y todo. "Quintana came back too," she
used to tell me, todo enterito. "He's working in the fields to make
ends meet." She couldn't believe we ended up in the same can of shit.
When I look out these windows . . . I think of her . . . I am ready to
blow, Margarita. Just put the images together—back home en los
files, the Nam, and this fucked-up landing zone. Any leaf, any two-
tone ranchero babozo, any pinchi puto that looks at me the wrong
way is going to be chewing on my homemade detonation tamales.
Shit—you were in San Antó. Really?

MARGARITA: Yeah. Yeah, right, simón.

Scene 14. GRETA and MARUCH

*(In the museum, Lacandón "universe blanket" framed in background or
foreground)*

GRETA: How many times have you been in love?

MARUCH: What? What are you talking about? It's late. Maybe we should
go to your room now?

GRETA: When you sleep at night, whose arms do you embrace, what
color are they? Are they your color? How often does it happen? Tell
me. How many times?

MARUCH: OK, OK. That's my story. OK. That is my story. No one else's
but mine. Mine alone.

GRETA: That's why you are so miserable and lost.

MARUCH: Because they get me when they want to?

GRETA: So alone.

MARUCH: My mother is old, very old. Why should I trouble her? She's all I have. If it wasn't for you we would both be dead by now. Maybe if I was back in San Juan Chamula. Maybe, with my mother. With a father. This would all be different.

GRETA: Chamula . . . Chamula . . . Chamula.

MARUCH: I would come down the mountain with my mother and sell flowers, calla lilies wrapped on my back. I could barely carry them. Sometimes at the mercados the Ladinas would surprise us in the morning, break our eggs, steal our chamorros that my mother had sewn. Then we'd have to start all over. Come back again. And again. We couldn't survive. My mother would get up at three in the morning, make corn, give me and my brothers her share of tortillas. My father would leave for months, looking for work. She was so young. She was forced to marry him. When he didn't return, she came here. She lost all her relatives, friends. It was the Protestant church that led us to you. She's in the basement now, folding linen, checking out supplies. Maybe that's best. I've had to make up my own costumbres. You sent me to college. Once you leave your pueblo, you can't go back.

GRETA: Every other night, behind the Quetzal Room. They visit you. Soldados. They visit the little Indian schoolgirl and play Mickey Mouse.

MARUCH: I see you making words. You're making crazy words in the air. That's all. Let's go in now.

GRETA: Mickey Mouse. Mickey Mouse. Mickey Mouse.

Scene 15. LIONEL and MARGARITA

(Outside the kitchen)

MARGARITA *(Breathing in deep and exhaling):* Today is special, Lionel. Things couldn't be better. Lionel?

LIONEL: What? Oh yeah—they couldn't. I guess.

MARGARITA: We want this thing to work out smooth. Tú sabes, it's about the proceso. Not the producto. We want this whole onda to shine and buzz like hot salsa on huevos rancheros. No more pedos. Or fat-ass excuses by the políticos, the new governor of Chiapas, Ponce de Leon, the babozo presidente. Gortari in Boston drinking cranberry juice, eating pie à la mode in Amsterdam, the Sinaloa cartel cabrones eating our tortillas. If there's going to be any kind of new movimiento here, la cosa's gotta be solid—solid like us Indian women *(touches her heart)*, like an Indian heart.

LIONEL: You told me you could get me in touch with the indios here. I mean—I am on a tight schedule, you know . . . got to get back to the university . . . As a matter of fact, I should have left with the rest of the group, yesterday. I dropped them off at the Colón depot. To tell you the truth, I didn't know why I wanted to stay. I mean we had a good time, looked around, bought all kinds of belts and leather briefcases . . . But I just felt kinda empty or excited . . . I . . . I felt something. I had just met a man named Tucán, a fat indio man with reddish eyes, a suit—can you believe it, Tucán? When he told me he could easily earn one million pesos a month by making truck shipments, I said to myself, this thing is getting interesting. I could write about this stuff, I said to myself. I . . . I mean, it would be a first in the department—but I didn't know what or why or whom . . . you know . . . I . . .

MARGARITA: Indios are not what you think they are, man. If you think they are all on their knees selling chicles and waiting for Johnny Gordo, I've got news for you. Zinacantecos with their communal land tracts got a lot of bank credit from the Banco Rural, from the National Agriculture and Livestock Insurance Program. They even borrow from each other to avoid all the Ladino paperwork—of course at higher rates than the banco . . . So a number of them, like this Tucán guy, can venture out, make un chingo de feria—more than you got in your Indian briefcase, hermano.

LIONEL: I used to read about people like you. About Rigoberta and the Quiché in Guatemala. Four million Mayas from here to El Salvador— all that.

MARGARITA: I am not that kind of Indian. Soy india chicana. Get your notes straight. I am working on joining up with the Zapatistas.

LIONEL: Zapatistas?

MARGARITA: Revolution's in the air. That's all I can tell you. Suck it in.

LIONEL: I used to tell my class about people like you.

MARGARITA: In the air—that's all I can tell you.

LIONEL: I don't know what to feel right now.

MARGARITA: Whatever you are feeling is what you should be feeling.

Scene 16. OSCAR and MARUCH

(In the museum)

OSCAR: Oscar Mendieta de la O.

MARUCH: Maruch, Maruch, personal assistant to la Señora Greta.

OSCAR: You're Doña América's daughter?

MARUCH: I am, yes.

OSCAR: When I started my research on the Chamulas, she's the one who told me how to get to the highlands.

MARUCH: That's her life now.

OSCAR: She works in the basement checking out expedition supplies into la selva. I didn't expect to meet her like that . . . I know you . . .

MARUCH: You know me?

OSCAR: You are the one who cleans Señora Greta's diapers—you put her to bed, don't you? You are the one?

MARUCH: That's my life now.

OSCAR: That's it?

MARUCH: That's it.

OSCAR: You went to school to clean diapers? That's all?

MARUCH: To the university.

OSCAR: To work as a hotel maid? You're beautiful. You could do things, you . . .

MARUCH: I help my mother, Doña America.

OSCAR: Woooow! *(Joking)* I can read the future—"The New India de Mexico," featuring La Señorita Diaper Cleaner and her . . .

MARUCH: You're not funny. I am leaving.

OSCAR: Wait . . . I am conducting a survey in San Juan Chamula and Zinacantán, looking at changes in the market economy. Maybe you can help me. You know . . .

MARUCH: Investments in herbicides?

OSCAR: What?

MARUCH: Class differentiation.

OSCAR: Wait a minute.

MARUCH: New generations of entrepreneurs?

OSCAR: Nah, no way. You don't know that stuff. I mean . . .

MARUCH: You should study yourself. You're pretty ugly. *(Laughs)*

OSCAR: Look, maybe you and I . . . could . . .

MARUCH: You and I?

OSCAR: What? Right! Me, you, you and me! What? First you know everything, now you don't? *(Grabs her)* I said you and me.

MARUCH: You? *(Pushes herself off)* You . . . are very ugly. *(Leaves)*

OSCAR: Wait, wait a minute. Look, let's start over. How do you know
about herbicide investments? I study. That's *my* work. Come here!
Maruch, let's talk. Two bottles of pox, OK? You and me . . . uh . . . I
have a tape player . . . Hey, what did I say?

Scene 17. CANEK, MATAL, JACINTO, and NELLY

(Ocosingo Room)

MATAL: Are you awake, Canek?

CANEK: Always. A Lacandón never sleeps. Where's the beer?

JACINTO: Kitchen's closed. Too late. Nada.

NELLY: Maybe we can form our own club or something?

JACINTO: How do I look? Would I qualify?

CANEK: Club Culo en la Piedra.

MATAL: Salud!

JACINTO: Salut Don Culo en la Piedra!

CANEK: Salut Don Culíssimo en la Piedra!

NELLY: Such a delightful club.

MATAL: You are an honorary member. We voted already.

CANEK: We voted already. Honorary Doña Culito en la Piedrita.

NELLY: What did I do to deserve such an honor?

CANEK: You've been here longer than us. Haaa!

MATAL: I hitched a ride from Palenque, on the new road that curls
around our village.

CANEK: I got a ride on the Tumbo bus, that giant piece of shit with trac-
tor wheels, with slabs of steak and cheese doughnuts from Ocosingo
on the racks, and roosters and young Tojolabal Indian girls with ribbons in their hair, and their grandmothers with the same ribbons, full
of stench and smiles and holes and tourists with cameras asking for
arrows to take back home. "Fifteen thousand paysos," then "twenty
thousand paysos." Little caoba smoked black wax string arrows, ex-

cept this time instead of sitting on the Palenque pyramids selling beads like us, you sat on the steps outside your room looking very india with your culito on the stone. Or brick . . . like us.

JACINTO: Sí señorita, sí señorito.

NELLY: *(Playful)* I am a philanthropist, not an Indian. I am from California, New York. I give money to the little box in the lobby. I love the trees, the ones that are used for balché for the ceremony of the New Year. For the making of the God pots. Why don't you join me? Aren't I funny?

JACINTO: What happened to Chan Ma'ax Viejo? Does he still wear the universe blanket, the one he puts on in the ceremony for the New Year? Spots of stars and fire on his back.

CANEK: Don't talk about him. Please don't mention his name. Don't talk about the God pots. Whatever you do, don't talk any more. Maybe it's this room. Maybe it's the night and what hangs up there. Ready to come down. I said it many times already. Everyone here heard me. What do you know about our God pots? Maybe it's because these walls are made by Ladino hands. Maybe it's because a few feet from here there are watery sounds, muffled and watery blood sounds. I don't want to talk about Chan Ma'ax Viejo.

JACINTO: It's too late. You must say it.

CANEK: I must say it?

JACINTO: You've heard the marching outside. The wheels grinding. The camera men running. The new flags going up. You have it wrong. You have it all wrong. Your mother, Koh, would remind you. Matal told me everything. You've grown too comfortable with your new house in the village. Stereo, rap music, and other stuff that the American anthropologists and turistas bring you—the stuff you expect from any visitor. Your father never said a word to you. He saw you taking the French visitors to the caves where you keep your gods. And now after all that is happening, you want . . .

CANEK: What do you know—Chamula?

JACINTO *(Long pause):* I went for a walk the other day.

NELLY: What are you talking about?

JACINTO: I went for a walk the other day.

NELLY: What are you talking about?

JACINTO: Up there, by Tzontevitz, the sacred mountain.

CANEK: You were up there, with the rest of your boot-legging asshole
    Chamulas?
JACINTO: I looked down at this hotel, at this town. I saw lines . . .
NELLY: You saw lines?
JACINTO: I saw lines.
NELLY: You saw lines?
JACINTO: Lines of faces and babies dropping from their mothers' insides
    as they stood screaming in their huts . . . so many lines of Indians.
    Some with machetes, with strings, others weaving hats and leather
    briefcases for the foreigners. I saw them, some with one eye, stand-
    ing, selling, buying colored yarn from the Ladino, on the corners, go-
    ing down the sacred hill with pots and candles, flowers on their
    backs. I looked back at Tzontevitz, inside—the gods inside the moun-
    tain's heart. Then I saw a bird in the sky. It made me cry.
CANEK: It made him cry.

Scene 18. OSCAR

(In lobby; phone rings)

OSCAR: Helo . . . helo? They are coming tomorrow? OK. Who? Who? Oh,
    yes, yes. Mr. and Mrs. Who? Prepare the Tzotzil Room. At three
    o'clock. OK. Helo, who's there? Helo?
    (Hangs up, clicks on television. Presidential figures appear.)
PRESIDENTIAL SPEECH *(sexy and sweet):* no afectaría a Guatemala, será
    parte integral
    the ecological and cultural cost to construct dams
    Mexico and Guatemala and — the sons of their sons
    on the other hand — I find it quite reasonable — actually
    the Usumacinta River — during decades
    but rather let us speak of humanity — if we have opened
    global recognition — the traces — yes
    the most ancient civilizations — being part of
    the Americas — our equilibrium — more
    Yaxchilán — Piedras Negras — on our foundation
    consideramos que debe haber congruencia, al mismo tiempo
    biodiversidad, el camino, la conservación, sí, sí
    en todos estos proyectos, la importancia del ciudadano

OSCAR: It's probably another anthropologist from America calling . . . always calling . . . or one of those so-called Chicanos. They've been coming here for years. First it was the Harvard project, Señora Greta told us all about it. Pochos . . . Chicanos! That's why I am here. I mean, I want to study and get my degrees. Maybe I'll show them my work on the Chamulas. A mexicano sees things different, you know. They'll take me back with them—I wouldn't go, though. I am not like the rest. Mexico needs us. A Mexican student works ten times harder than those so-called Chicanos . . . and the rest of them . . . foreigners. They come here with their scholarship money and Jeeps, they get grants to study "their culture," "the dying culture." Then they go around getting drunk on posh, they stuff themselves at La Estrella . . . a vegetarian restaurant by the Santo Domingo church. They buy the black wool chamorros of the caciques from Chamula, go to the market on Sunday dressed like Indian clowns, drink gourds of chicha, and stumble back to the Hotel Santa Clara, or the one run by a Spaniard a few blocks from here, saying, "Orale, vato, simón, órale, loco, watcha, racha quatcha, óraleeeeeh . . . "

A Mexican student works hard. We know where Mexico is, what it's made of, and where it's going. Our government is not what the americanos and a few losers around here make it out to be. In the last five years we've invested over 750 million nuevos pesos into bringing about changes in Chiapas. Has anyone checked with the Secretariat of Social Development? New hospitals in Chiapas, eighty new clinics, four thousand remodeled schools, two thousand new classrooms, three thousand kilometers of new roads and highways, electric energy for twelve hundred communities that never had it, five hundred new systems of drinking water for the people. Has anyone cared to check the figures? Land? Do I hear that old revolutionary call for "tierra"? Ninety million hectares of land were doled out to the indigenous peoples, mostly in the last couple of years. We have even organized a program especially suited for the needs of the selva in the lowlands. Zapatistas? Indios? Revolución? A Mexican student doesn't waste time with fancy words. We know who the Indians are, we know about Chicanos. They are nothing but stripped-down gringos who think they are Indian. That's the problem—they come here acting Indian, looking for their roots— just like the French, like the anthropologists that publish in *Geo-*

mundo—they are really becoming white, in search of their white roots. We don't need imaginative types in Mexico. Anyone with an imagination is a colonizer, another evangelist on a search for more converts. What we need are chimpanzees with technology who'll do what must be done, what we decide. Build a new nation out of stones, follow the numbers, perform the proper manuevers . . . no fancy bullshit. Let me tell you, no one wants to be Indian. I don't. We don't. You won't catch a mexicano making that Chicano mistake. A Mexican student is serious about things. Mexico is in our hands.
Blackout.

Act 2: La Noche

Scene 19. CHAN MA'AX VIEJO in the village

(Before the clay pot, more smoke)

Ofrenda del pozol, si el dios lo quiere
Ofrenda del pozol si el dios lo quiere
Ofrenda del pozol, si el dios lo quiere
Ofrenda del pozol si el dios lo quiere
Ofrenda del pozol, si el dios lo quiere
Ofrenda del pozol si el dios lo quiere.

Tsula wa ku qatik yum*
Tsula wa ku qatik yum
Tsula wa ku qatik yum *(Senses danger)*
Tsula wa ku qatik?
Ku qatik tusla . . . ?
Tsula?
Wa?
Ku qatik . . .
Yum . . . ?

---

*Spanish and Lacandón prayer: An offering of corn stew, if the god wishes it.

Scene 20. CHAN RODRIGO and TEDDY

(In the kitchen)

TEDDY: Ssshhhhh, I said. *(Chan Rodrigo crying)* I said ssshhhh . . . be quiet!
(Chan Rodrigo crying, coughing) They're out there. Listen.
(Crying again) What the fuck is the matter with you?
(Chan Rodrigo coughing) Shit! I hauled your ass all the way from the
Nahá Chan Sayab . . .

CHAN RODRIGO: It doesn't matter anymore. *(Crying)*

TEDDY: "Look what they did to her," you said. "Just look at her," you said.
"Now I got it," you said. "Look at my arms, the spots," you said.
(Chan Rodrigo crying)
Just hold on! . . . Shut up! They're out there.

CHAN RODRIGO: I am not going to make it. It was such a foolish idea . . .

TEDDY: What? Did you say . . . did I hear you correctly. Did you say "foolish"? *(Chan Rodrigo crying)*
Did you say, "It was a foolish idea"? *(Chan Rodrigo crying)*
I suppose you are going to put on your plastic sandals and march out
of here, catch a nice taxi all the way back into the jungle, through the
military blockades in Huixtán, Las Margaritas, and Ocosingo. Look
at you!

CHAN RODRIGO: They won't treat me here. In the clinics. You know it. I
want to go back to her.

TEDDY: Is that all you can think about? They raped her, remember? Those
turds in blue suits that work at the Petróleos Mexicanos plant right
next to your house. Fourteen years old. Then she got sick, she got so
sick she ended up like a crazy leopard, full of spots on her face and
tits. Breast feeding with spots on her tit. Shit. Didn't I just tell you? I
am working on this shit. All right?

CHAN RODRIGO: You told me? I don't remember anymore.

TEDDY: Fucking parasites. Parasites from cattle, parasites from the guts of
seventy thousand refugees from Guatemala. From rancheros and their
lard-eating assholes. From the PRI billionaires. In the fucking water.

CHAN RODRIGO: All right. All right . . .

TEDDY: I'm working on it, OK? Do you think I came all the way over here
from San Francisco to jack off? Don't fuck this up. When my novel
comes out, everyone will know about those fucking spots. Now come
on, you probably don't even have it.

CHAN RODRIGO *(Shivers):* My wife died so quickly. The wind came down
    from the hills.
TEDDY: Hold on, OK?
CHAN RODRIGO: Ahhhhhhh. Uuhhhh . . .
TEDDY: Maybe we'll split tonight. I got a pal in Tuxtla.
CHAN RODRIGO: It's getting so hot and so cold at the same time.
TEDDY: Hold on, man. Come on!
CHAN RODRIGO: That's what Chan Ma'ax Viejo said. "The tobacco flower
    won't grow," he said. The leaves fall off as soon as you pass by. He
    just lay back in his hammock with his tiny black hands folded over
    his chest . . .
TEDDY: Hold on, I said . . . shit.
CHAN RODRIGO: . . . and then he went to sleep. *(Crying, then throws up)*
TEDDY: Fuck it.
CHAN RODRIGO: I want to make love.

Scene 21. GRETA and MARUCH

(In Greta's palatial room, Maruch undresses her and prepares her for bed.)

GRETA: *(Pulls out a small envelope from her bra, stutters as she speaks)* Here
    are the figures.
MARUCH: Ahhhhhh . . .
GRETA: Here are the figures!
MARUCH: Sí sí sí sí, Doña Greta, sí sí . . .
GRETA: I said . . .
MARUCH: Shhhhhhhh . . . shhhh . . .
GRETA: Here are the figures!! By 1980, in Chiapas
    11 oil wells pumped juice on a daily basis
    123,000 barrels of crude,
    384 million square feet of gas,
    4 percent and 12 percent of the national output . . .
MARUCH: Shhhhh, Doña Greta.
GRETA: By 1982, in Chiapas
    80 percent of the 198,622 families that resided in indigenous areas
        still subsisted on maize and beans
    100 percent of these same families didn't have milk
    10 percent on occasion ate meat and . . .

MARUCH: Sí . . . your legs . . . have you seen your legs lately?

GRETA: Today? . . . What about today? Fifteen percent with septic tanks, 15 percent . . .

MARUCH: Your legs are very sore . . . blisters . . .

GRETA: Thirty percent without electricity . . . more than 50 percent without sewer drainage, and that doesn't include the Indians!

MARUCH: Your back is bad . . . more sores . . .

GRETA: What of the Indian sexual abuse and servitude—or as they say, "derecho de pernada"? Tell me! What of the Indian dead? Say something!

MARUCH: I know, Doña Greta. I did the research for you.

GRETA: No electricity, no sewers, dead dysentery babies, 12 million Indians in Mexico are on fire, bulldozed into a mass grave . . . What are the real numbers now?

MARUCH: I know, Doña Greta. I did the research *(puts her in bed)*—remember?

Scene 22. JACINTO and MARUCH

(In the garden)

MARUCH: I am trembling.

JACINTO: Wait till the morning. It's going to be just fine.

MARUCH: Every room is taken. The hotel is full. People knock at the doors. Day in day out. From the outside they are pushing. Each room is too full, from the inside. Every room. The basement. We are all back to back . . . I . . . I . . .

JACINTO: Just wait—a little.

MARUCH: When Greta dies, someone will take her room too. Fidencia will come with her buckets and soap. Her husband, Toño, will fill up the fireplace with wood and make a neat little pyramid out of kindling wood like he does in all the rooms.

JACINTO: Look at me, Maruch!

MARUCH: I am looking.

JACINTO: You never look at me. Look! Do you remember when I was just a little kid selling Chiclets out there in the zócalo? Chicle! Chicle! Chicle! I'd get some black wool bags from your mother, belts sometimes—Chicle!!

MARUCH: I am looking.

JACINTO: They had just thrown your family out of Chamula. For being Protestant. We were kids.

MARUCH: Selling Chiclets. Downtown. Yerba buena . . . in el zócalo. Canela . . . canelaaaa!

JACINTO: Man, I always wanted to be like Poyín, with his cool hair, stone-washed pantalones. A chupón hanging from his neck. All the girls on the schoolbus would never look at me. It was always Poyín. You left to Tuxtla . . .

MARUCH: Poyín sells café Tzotzil by the highway on the way to Comitán, a few blocks from the boys' technical school. El Poyín . . . alone in a broken shack full of coffee sacks.

JACINTO: Look at me. I am ready, Maruch! Look at my face, am I ready?

MARUCH: I am looking. (*They kiss.*)

JACINTO: Am I ready?

MARUCH: You think this is a great place to be, don't you? Fun—you want to wear fun soldado pants, don't you? A fun Ladino soldier shirt. A fun teething toy, a chupón around your fun neck, a light see-through pink one. Hanging on your fun neck. Soldado style, elegant soldado shoes. Fun words. That's what you want? Words? More words. So you can be filled up with soldier fun. You love it, don't you? Being filled up with fun words. Everything that fills you up . . . Capitán Jacinto.

JACINTO: I see you. You wear jeans! The americanos leave you things. French cologne, Calvin Klein, Obsession, T-shirts with Charlie Sheen and Madonna. You wear fun clothes too. I see you. In the Quetzal Room, at night I see . . .

MARUCH: My head is not full of fun, my heart is here. (*Touches her heart*) That's all.

JACINTO: I am out, Maruch. I am on my way. No kids. I am the only chavo around here with no kids! Lolo's got a kid, another on the way . . . Look at me! Maybe I'll go to Veracruz, eat shrimp off the tables like Mr. Armendaña, the new hotel manager . . . listen to marimbas, eat tamales de mumú, drink guanábana, dance all night, get a girl, have coffee in the cafeterias like the Ladinos. That's heart, Maruch. Rolling Stones, like Lolo. That's heart.

MARUCH: Tomorrow, you'll be free. Everything will work like you say. You'll be alive. You and Lolo, you'll look up into the sky and you won't hear a sound. It'll be a real sky with a real bird flying through it, Jacinto. You'll walk into a crowd of turistas in Veracruz, the sea rolling in fancy colors like your pants.

JACINTO: What about you?

MARUCH: Me?

JACINTO: You . . . and me. *(They kiss again.)*

Scene 23. CHUY and XUN

(By the main gate)

CHUY: What are you doing here?

XUN: Waiting.

CHUY: Waiting?

XUN: Waiting.

CHUY: For . . .

XUN: You.

CHUY: What?

XUN: I've been waiting for you for two hours.

CHUY: Oh, uh . . . uh . . .

XUN: You said you would buy two servilletas. Did you get the money?

CHUY: Uh, come on.

XUN: You said they were for your mother back home.

CHUY: Come on, man, I didn't say that.

XUN: Ten thousand for the pair.

CHUY: It's too late.

XUN: You know how far it is to Zinacantán?

CHUY: Beat it, viejo.

XUN: Eight thousand. My wife is sick—for the medicine, at least.

CHUY: Don't tell me that. That's what you tell the turistas—don't tell me that. Who do you think I am? I see you every day with thousands and thousands of pinchis pesos of merchandise. "La señora Greta says I can sell these here, la señora Greta said I could bring my daughter to sell her chamorros and huipiles." I've seen you, man . . . with your son, Mariano. Driving in his truck full of flowers. "All the way from Mexico City," you said. Don't you dare tell me your old lady is sick.

XUN: I haven't had any breakfast.

CHUY: I said beat it—fuckin' candy-ass Indian.

Scene 24. LIONEL and GRETA

(In Greta's bedroom. Greta paces and sees something through her windows, screams.)

LIONEL: Are you upset? I heard you scream. I . . .

GRETA: Perhaps you'll kill me later in the night. Don't you think?

LIONEL: What? You're upset. I know . . .

GRETA: Will it be up to you? Or is there someone else with you? Someone's behind you. Outside. A handsome soldado? A tiny man with a thick back? Another PRI fucker? Maybe someone from the INI? The Ministry of Social Development? Or is it you? Did they send you here? I am sure of it. I can tell. They sent you, didn't they?

LIONEL: Ahhh?

GRETA: Just tell me. Can you do that? We are alone here.

LIONEL: Easy, Señora Greta. Easy.

GRETA: It's you. What do you want? The kitchen is full of things. The chapel. There in the Harvard Room. Do you know why it's called the Harvard Room?

LIONEL: Ahhh. Wait. Please. I don't know what you are saying. I can't understand you. You're talking too fast.

GRETA: I met Chan Ma'ax Viejo when I was forty. I had worked against Hitler in Germany, I was arrested in France as a subversive. I fought for women's rights in the United States. When I met Chan Ma'ax, he was my new beginning. The forest was bleeding and I wanted to stop the blood.

LIONEL: Maybe we can start an exchange program? The department would just love it. Take care of things, you know. We'll even keep the Harvard Room. Did you say the Harvard Room?

GRETA: You fucking whore.

Scene 25. MARGARITA and MARUCH

(Upstairs in the Jataté Room)

MARGARITA: Orale, Maruch! Get on down to the coffee grounds, esa.

MARUCH: You and me—right?

MARGARITA: Simón. We're going to walk down Vicente Guerrero past Calle Diego Dugelay, check out the old marimberos in their studios, studying up for the next quinceañera. All the way down to el Hotel Ciudad Real!

MARUCH: Right in the center of town? In el zócalo?

MARGARITA: Simón. 'Cause we got huevos, Maruch. You and me. Las dos. ¿Quivo? ¿Washusay, chavalona?

MARUCH: Right across from la catedral?

MARGARITA: Bien firmes. The rest of the pinchis pendejos can kiss our ass. You know, you're looking good.

MARUCH: Uh—you're looking too.

MARGARITA: Me? Chale. I am here for the pleito. That's all. Pleito. P-L-E-I-T-O. That spells chingazos.

MARUCH: It doesn't work like that, Maga . . . I was never . . . beautiful.

MARGARITA: Let's go! Andale!

MARUCH: You said your lover left you.

MARGARITA: My what?

MARUCH: Your lover—you said.

MARGARITA: He can kiss my Chicana ass any time of the night. Vamos.

MARUCH: You shouldn't have come here. You're lost.

MARGARITA: I got values, chavalona. You think 'cause I wear my hair high up like a tipi I am some kind of payasa. There's just a few questions to answer, es todo.

MARUCH: You got questions. Here? Questions?

MARGARITA: Are we going all the way? Or are we going to kiss ass? Nice and short. Al punto. Al dente. ¿Me entiendes?

MARUCH: I see. You got questions.

MARGARITA: The pinchi pendejo couldn't hang, OK? He came here for other things. His dead mother. His dead father. His stupid wives. The alcoholic from Santa Cruz. And the other, some vendida from Chicago, coke sniffing, high-tone politickin' baboza with tenure at Yale. He came to get away from all that shit. From himself. It's just me and you. Las meras meras! Vámonos.

MARUCH: It's too dark out. It's . . . too dark. (*Margarita touches Maruch's leg and they hold eyes.*)

Scene 26. Lolo, Chuy, and Jacinto

(*In the old chapel, Christ figures, saints, candles*)

CHUY: Seventy-nine dollars.

LOLO: That's right. Seventy-nine and pow!

CHUY: Right. From Juárez to La Capital, Mexico City. One way, express. No mess.

LOLO: It's not one of those old jalopy buses with tortilleras hanging on your ass, on the windows. Not on this bus. Straight, carnal—Juárez to La Capirucha. Eighty bones and you're there. Ochenta virotes!

CHUY: Mexico's changing. No more santos on the dashboards. That's for the oldies. No more fucking gallineros on your maseta.

LOLO: That's for the veteranos. No more santos on the dashboard, right? We got TV, video, a wet bar in the back, cabrón. Seventy-nine varos!

CHUY: Just a hop, skip, and a panzazo and you're here, carnis. Dallas Cowboys in Mexico City. Who ever imagined?

JACINTO: I never been in one of those buses.

LOLO: Wet bar in the toilet? Is that right, hijín?

CHUY: It's bigger than you, cabrón. Plush. Lean back and suck the breeze. Chrome panels. Radials. Shines like a puta. Music. Maldita, La Lupita, Selena, Café Tacuba. Red leather seats. There's a morenita that comes to you. She wears black Wranglers and has teeth that shine like a tiger's. Make you hard. Make you right, carnalito. Drinks, she says. Aperitifs, she says. Martini, Evian? It's artistic. It's all inside. With you. Napkins with an eagle stamped on them. Todo. The light comes softly. You turn it on. It turns you on. Whatever you want to see, vato. No one offends you. No mamón to push a tortilla down your oreja. You don't have to ask any questions. It's bilingual. Inglis and español. If anyone messes with you, the chofer will kick his ass. Fácil. Música all the way. Caldo con chichi. Aprende. Just seventy-nine bolas, cabrón. You already got two.

LOLO: All you need is seventy-seven more!

JACINTO: No santos on the dashboard? None?

CHUY: No cilantro, no chorizo. No midnight stops with your ass against the glass. I've been there, camarada. My jefe's de Tucson. Eight hours to Juárez. I been there. Man. You should have seen la gente rolling to Nogales the day they passed NAFTA. Man, la raza—they ran like cockroaches. You should have seen them. Cockroaches from the south. Cockroaches from el norte. Man, me la rayo. It was a fucking cockroach festival. Cockroaches with toasters—you know the ones with extra-wide slots—boxes of Pampers, cartons of Weenstones, galones de Kalúa. The cockroaches never spent so much feria in such a short time. But they got a lot of cockroach credit on the border. They took the bus. In Juárez, it's pure. It's cool like a block of ice and diamonds.

LOLO: Esencial.

CHUY: Fundamental.

LOLO: Evolving.

CHUY: Central.

LOLO: The new wave.

JACINTO: I am sorry. Excuse me. But I have to have santos on the dashboard.

Thank you.

Scene 27. MARUCH and GRETA

(In Greta's bedroom. Greta has a nightmare. Screams and sits up in bed, trembling. Maruch runs in.)

MARUCH: Doña Greta . . . ?

GRETA: By 1980, in Chiapas

10,000 oil wells pumped juice on a daily basis

123 million barrels of crude, 750 million. Do you hear me?

MARUCH: What?

GRETA: What are the numbers, Maruch? What are they, Chamula?

MARUCH: Shhhhh, Doña Greta.

GRETA: 90 percent, 80 percent, 97 percent, 84 percent, 88 percent, 79 percent, 91 percent . . . Maruch! 839 65 percent percent percent. Now!

MARUCH: Sí . . . sí . . .

GRETA: I forget . . . Did I forget? What did I forget, Maruch? Did I get it right? What did I miss? I know I missed something. What was it? How did I start? What did I say? Do you remember? What was it? What was I saying? I was saying something, Maruch . . . I was saying something? Was . . . I?

Scene 28. TEDDY

(At the main gate. Teddy attempts to open door; someone is knocking.)

TEDDY: Sí? Who is it? Wait. Por favor. Just a minute. *(Caught off guard by the television voices in the lobby nearby)*

PRESIDENTIAL SPEECH *(military voice):* se discute la posibilidad de crear en
　　　las zonas campesinas
　　　aldeanas, un basurero, sí . . .
　　　un plan estratégico, para la circulación
　　　sostenible, cuya cuenta barca, sí . . .
　　　the environmental impact — the terrorists
　　　the possibility became clear — unite the State
　　　conciliation — to protect — a project
　　　dialogue — but at the same time — yes yes
　　　in particular we support the endorsement — the voice
　　　finally we believe that — all the way from Ciudad Juárez
　　　for our nation — we have analyzed
　　　tercero, se creara un comité de, desde Nuevo Laredo
　　　los chiapanecos han señalado que
　　　en el resto de mi administración
　　　organizaciones científicas, autopista moderna
　　　mines and — industry — three fundamental aspects
　　　for multiple hydroelectrics — we — can — do — it
　　　multiple configurations — we propose this
　　　it would not affect Guatemala — it would be an integral part
　　　yes yes

TEDDY *(to audience):* Only amusements stop us from dying for real. That's
what a good book is all about. I mean, who's going to tell the real
story? Do you think everything is going to change, just like that? Get
outta here, you think things are gonna go from blood and disease and
famine into a giant velvet ball! Fuck! You think a writer gets off easy?
I know about American writers. Believe me, there's something sad
about American writers. They don't give a damn about what they're
gettin' outta life—nothing, zero, nada—they don't care. Why should
I? Why should they? We're sitting on top of everybody else's bleeding carcass. We write about it once in a while, get a little tingle in the
crotch, get a card, a check, maybe. And the readers? They'll buy our
books so they can go to sleep, sleep no matter what. Bloated worms—
no trouble in their clean-cut and trim yards, no frothy putrid mess in
their dotted nighties and Calvin Klein jockey shorts. So what! So I
help them sleep better. I am an alarm clock with snooze control. So I
write, show them a little more life—at a distance—let it fall on their
worm heads like a truck of cement.

Scene 29. GROUP

(Outside supply room)

GRETA: Maruch, I am going now. To my room—Maruch?
OSCAR: Maruch, are you listening?
MARUCH: Please stay—a little.
MATAL: It's late.
CANEK: The wind comes down wherever you are.
JACINTO: I like it here. I am used to it. It's like home.

st wait until my orders come in. Me la rayo, just wait. Pow!

vant to say something.

m speechless.

nyone seen my wife?

late.

to be different. I've become old here. It wasn't like that. We
nt. I have to say it. We were different. This place. The
en the rooms were filled with a different smell. I would
the morning and the ocote would wind its smoke out
n windows and float all the way back beyond the ring
here they say the gods and goddesses used to live.

CHA...: crosses. Crosses and fog on those mountains.
BEAU...: on . . . You know, five cancer tumors . . . in the
sto
MARUC...: and a voice in the leaves. With a mask wrapped
arou.
JACINTO: e you an honorary member of our secret club.
Tonigh... w your heads. Repeat after me . . . Actual-
mente, s...
TEDDY: Wha...
MARGARITA: ...don't repeat after nobody.

Sc... AX VIEJO in the village

(Invoking the go... re)

I can hear it rise up.
Raise its little paws. After the rains.

The caoba tree grows over ninety meters. Above the world.

In the day it speaks with the sky crickets. About
abandonment.
The red flesh of the caoba tree is green. At night, we speak.

In our dreams, we visit. That's all I can tell you. Green air.
The abandonment of the earth. At night it sends you its
     secretos
in the form of little river winds.

My village is lurking somewhere. Sometimes . . . let's see—
After the bulldozers. After the malaria, pneumonia.

After the split seed of the colonists. It still raises its jaguar
head. Then,
something moves me. Something from the back . . . ahhhh.

Hachakyüm, the creator of the Lacandones,
breathes life through every leaf. Green water. Green spirit.
I have a village. Once I had a village . . . let's seee—

It is called Bolom . . . ahhhh.
I can hear them calling. Then it goes away.
Then it goes away . . . uhhh . . .

Scene 31. LIONEL, MATAL, DOÑA AMÉRICA, and CANEK

(Canek is severely wounded. Lionel on cell phone. Jets roar overhead. Rain.)

LIONEL: Just wait, just wait. Someone will answer.
CANEK: Just wait?
LIONEL: Just wait. I am calling, but there's no answer.
CANEK: Just wait? All this blood. No answer?
LIONEL: Just wait, OK?
CANEK: Just wait . . . just wait.
LIONEL: Look, man, I've been calling for the last hour. That tourniquet on
    your leg should do it, OK? Come on. It wasn't my fault. I am bleed-

ing too, you know. You got the bright idea to go back to Nahá Chan Sayab. Right? Man, you didn't even make it to Ocosingo. When I found you, you were holed up in an upside-down combi, all blown out, you and two dead Mayan kids with filed-down shovels. "Going back to get my father," you said. So Matal comes knocking on my door. Said maybe they wouldn't harm a professor from the United States. That's what I was waiting for, I guess, that was my piece of excitement! I should have left weeks ago when I was supposed to. The department probably has an all-points bulletin on me. School's started. I am in a mess—they probably think I'm in a morgue in Veracruz. Shit! "Going back to get my father," right? I don't know how we made it back. If it hadn't been for one of those *(mispronouncing)* Chamuls or Zincantecos or whatever they call themselves, I wouldn't have been able to drag you back here.

CANEK: The soldados asked me if I was with the Zapatistas. They said it the way they say "indios." "What about the amnesty, the diálogo?" You said—they let you go because you're from . . .

LIONEL: Los Angeles. California. Look at my arm—and tell me how they let me go.

CANEK: Because you're from Los Estados. Where am I from?

LIONEL: Come on, look at my arm.

CANEK: Where am I from?

LIONEL: You're losing a lot of blood. I told them I was with you, didn't I?

CANEK: You told them.

LIONEL: I told them.

CANEK: Los Estados.

LIONEL: I told them. OK?

CANEK: Where's Matal? Is she back?

LIONEL: She went to see Doña América. Maybe she can help you. I think I got a line open. Hello? Bueno?

CANEK: Hah.

LIONEL: Yes. Yes. This is the hotel, I mean the embassy. I mean, uh, look, we've been hit bad. This is the hotel, you know—the only one with a golden plaque on the outside. Look, I am a tourist, I have papers . . . Lionel Quintero Clark. Uh, California. I have a man here, an indio . . . He's bleed— Hey, hey! Hello? Hello?

CANEK: My father . . .

LIONEL: What?

CANEK: Where is he? Is he alive? Where's my mother?

LIONEL: What?

CANEK: Forget it. Señor Quintero Clark.

LIONEL: The Red Cross. They're coming.

CANEK: They told you "they're coming"?

LIONEL: As soon as I get a line.

CANEK: The Army is not going to let them in. They're telling them that we're Zapatistas. We have machine guns . . .

LIONEL: What? You're crazy. Machine guns?

CANEK: THEY'LL PLANT THEM ON US. THEY'LL SAY WE'RE KILLERS.
  (Knocking)

LIONEL: I'll get them back on the phone. We're not going down. I'll explain everything. Just wait.
  (Knocking)

CANEK: Matal! Get up and answer the door, Don Lionel. Matal!

LIONEL: What if it's them? I am not going to answer. I don't want to die.
  (On the phone) Hello?

CANEK: Matal? I am here! Open! Open the door. Matal!

LIONEL: Wait, I think I have a line open. Hello, hello?
  (Door opens. Matal and Doña América enter with a box of Chiclets.)

CANEK: Matal? Matal? I am here. Down here. Matal?

LIONEL: Hello? Yes, yes. The room? What room are we in, Canek? What damn fucking room is this?
  (Matal sits next to Canek and tightens his tourniquet.)

DOÑA AMÉRICA: ¿Chiclets? ¿Chiclets, señor? ¿Chiclets, jóven? ¿Ayúdame con unos chicles?

CANEK: Matal? I can't get up.

DOÑA AMÉRICA: Buenas noches, Señor Lionel. Mil pesos. Señor Lionel. Mil. Pesos. Tenemos sabor a yerba buena y canela.

LIONEL: What? Crazy vieja. Get down. Doña América! What room are we in? Is this the Harvard Room? This is the Harvard Room. Right? Don't you know where you are? Get down. Don't go near the window. Hey?

DOÑA AMÉRICA *(Looking out the window)*: Chicles. In the zócalo. Chicles in the catedral. Chicles in the mercado. Maruch, ten, llévate esta cajita. ¡Pero ahorita! Si la vendes te compro un biscocho y un atole de vainilla. Chicles, señor. Maruch, mi hija.

LIONEL: I said get down! Now!

DOÑA AMÉRICA: The soldados . . . took her. In front of my eyes, Don Lionel. They held her up and grabbed her. I had to look at her, Don Lionel. I knew it was going to be the last time. She was out with Margarita. In San Juan Chamula. Look at her, Don Lionel. Out there in
the zócalo. *(Cries)*

CANEK: Matal. Please. My leg—is it there? I can't feel it!

DOÑA AMÉRICA: They ripped out her fingernails, Don Lionel. Burned her
face with cigars. See? Hanging on the tree. "Indian piñata puta," they
shouted, grabbing themselves. In front of the kiosko. In the zócalo.
Look.

CANEK: Is that true, Matal?

DOÑA AMÉRICA: All those years I watched over her. Borrowed and
saved. Since she was a tiny girl carrying calla lilies to the mercados.
With the help of Doña Greta, I sent her to school in la capital. For
what, Don Lionel? She was everything I had. Now who will take care
of Doña Greta? Who will take care of me? Maruch?

LIONEL: Hello? Hello? Hello?

DOÑA AMÉRICA: Canela . . . yerba . . . buenaaaaaaa . . .

Scene 32. CHAN MA'AX VIEJO in his palmita

(Offering prayers to God pot. Rushes, forgets things, breaks the God pot.
Frantic.)

AAhhhhh . . .
ehhhh . . . shhhhh . . . ahhh ooohhhhh
mmmm . . . shhhhhh
ahhhh ahh ah ah ahhh noooooooo
no no no
uhhhhhh . . . No!

Scene 33. DOÑA AMÉRICA

(Offering Chiclets to anonymous hotel guests passing through lobby)

My daughter . . . Maruch . . . had a beautiful body . . . they all wanted her
. . . all of them . . . they followed her as they followed me . . . they wanted
to smell her as they wanted to smell my hair . . . all of America followed

her into the room, wherever she was . . . they were there too . . . watching . . . waiting . . . smelling . . . taking . . . they pulled, they trapped . . . they opened . . . they opened . . . they wanted her after they had her . . . before they saw her . . . they wanted all of her . . . as they wanted me . . . the day I walked here from my village . . . they had already seen me . . . before she was born . . . they had already touched her . . . they followed her as they followed me . . . all of America followed her . . . they wanted her body . . . that is all . . . the stars and the levels of the heavens, the red and the torquoise, the green and the white, the underworld . . . all of her . . . the sun and moon being born, the terrible accidents of the universe making rain, they wanted all of her . . . to take her luxury, all of her wealth . . . this small flame . . . this . . . motion from the heights of the god mountains, they wanted her . . . they stole her and never feared . . . and never . . . will they . . . ever . . . return her.

Scene 34. FIDENCIA, TEDDY, and CHAN RODRIGO

(In supply room)

FIDENCIA *(With mop):* What you doing here?
TEDDY: Looking for bandages. What do you mean—doing what?
FIDENCIA: Nada.
TEDDY: We've met before?
FIDENCIA: Nada.
TEDDY: We met.
FIDENCIA: He dying?
TEDDY: We've met before?
FIDENCIA: Touch him . . . here. *(Touches her heart, then touches Rodrigo's heart. Chan Rodrigo rises slowly, moves softly, and dances. He takes on the characteristics of a fierce animal and begins to stalk both Fidencia and Teddy. He attacks Teddy. Teddy dies. Rodrigo dies.)*

Scene 35. CHAN MA'AX VIEJO in his palmita

(Desperately invokes the shattered God pot in his hands)

I have a village. Once I had a village. It was called . . . ? It was called . . . Uhhh . . . what was it called? I have . . . I had . . . then . . . it goes away

... There was a tree ... once ... a village ... in the day ... above the world. I could hear— No. No ... I had a village ... ninety meters, ninety ... It was called ... I can hear them calling, then it goes ... it goes? It was about abandonment, yes ... the sky, I think. There was something in the sky? Rivers? There was something about the rivers. I had rivers. Once, the village, once ... I forgot how this goes. I have it all wrong. The creator of the Lacandones ... The creator? It was about you, that's it, it was about you, the leaves, about the crickets—the crickets? No, no. It was about me ... no. My son Canek would remind me—where is he? Where is everyone? My wife, Koh—where is she now? Is it night? I am forgetting ... where is Matal? So alone, my village had a name. I stand here. Was I praying? Oh yes, the prayers ... The prayers, so many prayers. I am hearing things my words, men, fires, someone, there is someone behind me ... above the rest of the world ... Next to the caoba. Someone must be knocking ... but I can't hear. My daughter, she would tell me. Someone out there. Here? I had a village ... once ... This is all I can say.

Scene 36. ROSARIO, PACHECO, MARUCH, MARGARITA, and JACINTO

(Quetzal Room, where the soldiers keep a cot, guns, food, a TV, radio, and liquor. The music of Carlos Santana plays in backgound. Margarita is strapped to a chair, gagged; her face bleeds.)

ROSARIO: Pacheco—préndela, cabrón. *(Turns on TV so as not to be heard)* Sshhh *(to Margarita)*.
PACHECO: Ssshhhh ...
ROSARIO *(To Margarita):* Mira, los monitos, ¡haaa!
PACHECO *(To Margarita):* ¡Monitos! Look. How do you say monitos?
ROSARIO *(Points to Pacheco):* That's your Tío Goofy. Like Goofy?
PACHECO: And that's *(points to Rosario)* your other tío, El Pato Pasqual.
ROSARIO: And that ... *(points to the presidential faces on the TV)*
PACHECO: That is Porky Pig!
ROSARIO: And this *(unbuttons pants, zipper)*, this is your favorite pet, El Pluto.
PACHECO: Be nice to El Pato. He says you haven't seen Plutito in a long time. *(Margarita struggles and loosens the mouth gag.)*

ROSARIO *(to Pacheco):* Mírala, qué bonita.

PACHECO: Qué pretty.

ROSARIO *(to Margarita):* What were you doing with our Maruch, our Chamula?

MARGARITA: Uhhhhh. Ahhhhhh . . . Chamula?

PACHECO: You can tell your Tío Goofy.

ROSARIO: What were you doing outside? You knew about the curfew . . .

PACHECO *(To Rosario, pretending he hears a noise):* Is someone knocking, Comandante Rosario?

ROSARIO: Yes, I believe so . . . Comandante Pacheco.

PACHECO: I think it's coming from over there. *(Points to closet)*

ROSARIO *(To Margarita):* Can you hear it? It's so loud, who could it be?

PACHECO: Maybe it's Mickey Mouse?

ROSARIO: Mickey? Nah . . .

PACHECO: Is not Bugs Bunny?

ROSARIO: Nahh . . .

PACHECO: Doesn't sound like Dumbo.

ROSARIO: Nahhh, can't be Dumbo. He's got no manners—haaa!

PACHECO: I think it's Mickey Mouse.

ROSARIO: Mickey? Nahhh, he's too busy!

PACHECO: Of course . . . It's Mickey—your wife!

ROSARIO: Yes, yes, how could I forget her?

PACHECO: After so many years . . .

ROSARIO: Yes, yes, now *that* I remember. We got married, right here in this room. Me and La Mickey Mouse.

PACHECO: Shall I show her in, la Señora Mickey Mouse?

ROSARIO: Please show her in, Comandante Pacheco. Mickey works hard.

PACHECO: Oh, of course . . . *(Drags Maruch's bloodied body out of the closet)* Just got back from the candy store. The piñata store—haaaa!

ROSARIO *(To Margarita):* Remember Mickey?

MARGARITA: Uhhh . . . ahhhhhh . . . uhhh . . . uhhhhuhu . . . *(Pacheco twists her head toward Maruch at Rosario's request.)*

ROSARIO: What were you doing with that Chamula!

MARGARITA: Uhhhh . . . Uhhhhh?

ROSARIO: You've been involved in subversive activities for quite some time. We heard things—huh, Pacheco?

PACHECO: Tings, we heard—tings, Comandante Rosario. Many tings, we heard.

ROSARIO: Think of your tío, El Pato. Maybe I can help you.

MARGARITA: El Pato ahhhhhhh . . . ?

ROSARIO: You got mixed up with the wrong people, the church . . . with a communist church and a communist bishop, eh?

MARGARITA: Communist!

ROSARIO: Indios pendejos, they don't know what they got.

PACHECO: It could be worse.

MARGARITA: Uhhh . . . ahhhh . . . uhhh . . . *(Struggles to free herself)*

ROSARIO: This is Mexico. Chamula . . . *(points to Maruch)* on a beautiful night like this . . . *(Unwraps the gag around Margarita's mouth)*

PACHECO: You want a Fanta?

ROSARIO: Pepsi? It will make you feel bilingual.

PACHECO: Pep . . . si? Get it? Haaahaaaaa!

ROSARIO: Let's have a party, okeh?

MARGARITA: Uuuhhhhhhh . . . ahhhhh . . .

ROSARIO: You, me . . . Goofy, Pluto, and Mickey—right, Goofy?

PACHECO: Pos, let's party. *(Puts machine gun to her head)* Try this party sombrero on.

ROSARIO: Looks good on her, eh? Don't you think, Comandante Pacheco? *(To Margarita)* What were you doing with Mickey Mouse? Where where you going?

PACHECO: Last time, okeh.

MARGARITA: I was uhhhhh . . . uhhhhhh . . . I was uhhhh . . .

ROSARIO: Yes, we're listening . . . go on. You look a little goofy, but go on.

MARGARITA: Ahhhh . . . I was goin' . . . to show her that I could . . .

PACHECO: Make tortillas?

ROSARIO: Tamales?

MARGARITA: Uhhh . . . uhhhhh . . . ahhhhh . . .

ROSARIO: Go on, please. Pacheco, help her *(mock French)*, poir favoir.

MARGARITA: Uhhhh . . . that I was . . . that I . . . could . . .

ROSARIO: Try on the sombrero again. *(Signals to Pacheco)*

MARGARITA: That . . . uhhhhhh . . . I could walk . . . alone.

(Pacheco gets behind Maruch's slumped body as if it were a puppet.)

PACHECO: Look at me. *(Pointing to his new head)* This is Goofy. Tell Goofy that you are not afraid.

ROSARIO: Good girl. *(Takes body from Pacheco and copies gesture)* This is El Pato. Look at me. Tell El Pato to come outside the hotel and play, OK?

PACHECO: This is Presidente Porky. *(Same as before)* Look at me. Tell your Presidente that you can do whatever you want, that . . .

ROSARIO: This is Goofy *(again)*, your long lost cousin. Tell him that you can walk in the dark—and make a big escándalo. Say you're going to change things around here—change, right? *(Drops Maruch's body and slaps Margarita)*

PACHECO: Esmuski, excuse me *(to Maruch on floor)*, did you hear anything, Mickey? Esmuski? *(Whispers into each of Rosario's ears.)* Now listen to Uncle Pato, he's smart.

ROSARIO: Uncle Pato says Pluto wants to see you, he's very thirsty. *(To Pacheco)* Amárrala . . . la boca watcha . . . *(To Margarita)* Listen to Uncle Pato, now listen closely . . . *(Drops pants)*

PACHECO: Listen carefully . . . órale.

ROSARIO: Actually, my wife Mickey won't mind. You know how that is—just like in the United States. No problem.

PACHECO: Orale, let's put on some party music. *(Turns on radio; Santana's "Black Magic Woman" is heard. Rosario attempts to rape Margarita; Pacheco mimics Rosario and prepares to rape the dead body of Maruch. A loud knocking is heard; they stop, alarmed. They scramble, unable to get their machine guns. Rosario signals Pacheco to open the door as he pulls a knife from his boot. Jacinto breaks through and pushes Pacheco to the floor. They wrestle, and Jacinto knocks out Pacheco. Rosario knifes Jacinto; Margarita picks up Jacinto's rifle and aims it at Rosario. He runs out into the night. Jacinto manages to get up; he takes the rifle from Margarita and goes after Rosario. Music blends into "Presidential Speech" sequence. Margarita steps over to Maruch, holds her hand, then lifts her up and embraces her.)*

PRESIDENTIAL SPEECH *(From hilarious to sexy, then polite)*:

actually — yes — yes
before the inevitable construction of a highway
the formation of peasant zones the possibility
at the margins, the villages — a trashcan — yesyesyes
therefore — in the future
protected — how can they ask us to cancel? — yes
confrontábamos el problema, como presa base
el impacto ambiental, los terroristas
surgió la posibilidad, unir el estado
conciliación, proteger, un proyecto
diálogo, pero al mismo tiempo

en particular apoyamos la solicitud, la voz
algunas agrupaciones, desde Nogales
finalmente creemos que, desde Ciudad Juárez
pare nuestra nación, hemos analizado
tercero, se creara un comité de, desde Nuevo Laredo
los chiapanecos han señalado que
en el resto de mi administración
mines and — industry — three fundamental aspects
for multiple hydroelectrics — we — can — do — it
it would not affect Guatemala — it would be an integral part
yes yes
the ecological and cultural cost to construct dams
Mexico and Guatemala and — the sons of their sons
on the other hand — I find it quite reasonable — actually
the Usumacinta River — during decades
but rather let us speak of humanity — if we have opened
the most ancient civilizations — being part of
the Americas — our equilibrium — more
Yaxchilán — Piedras Negras — on our foundation
consideramos que debe haber congruencia, al mismo tiempo
biodiversidad, el camino, la conservación
en todos estos proyectos, la importancia del ciudadano
And on this occasion, furthermore, I want — it is
necessary — actually — to make a billion — two
hundred thousand — million — it is necessary
es necesario — hacer millones un billón — actualmente
actually
Blackout.

IV

Anahuak Vortex

ANAHUAK VORTEX
(Mexico City, 1995)

Black muscles, bronze coins
    & the statue of Coatlique—you appear

between Our Mother of the Serpent Skirt & the shrunken
head of a three-piece Zedillo banker, you come luminous—
the one who devoured me, who left me sightless,
blue bastard with a doodling gypsy hood &

a parenthesis in my skinny pocket, my small town north
of Mexicano Meaning, the one who rocked me with your
dead pagan hands & Catholic skin beads—awkward,
off my feet, certain and riddled by incomplete searches,

the weight of your blood bones, uncertain, in this zócalo
abuela brujería, the search shatters you say, I too fall, my
swollen heart, this bad gauze bundle roving being—
with mercado sinew fools—with your border death blood

hey—you, yes, you, you say—goof rag, sweltered in
absence, toothless into swaying abandon and continental
abcess, yes—you, gave birth to me, this launch, nocturnal
and peering emptiness, smoke of your Revolución

suicide hair between night & death, cruel dust, I rumble
in my teen-age Tojolabal girl gait, alien with the face in
primal suffering, of Ocosingo in rape; did I say Tojolabal,
fake myself, lush rape—again,

the heads of Zedillo's green-eyed corporate monteros, you
will identify them & kiss this mump empowered eternity

233

as the world flies off its axis, do I remember, was it you
doubled up against the corn stall goo, a torn priestess

robed in El Paso, Second Ward salt cans & bruised
washerwoman knees—Stanton Street, Mt. Franklin,
deportation brothels, gasolined, vaporized from
Chihuahua—your city rolls up with sugary sweat,

beneath this sludge &
                    long ago,

left pocked, left Latin, left America, shredded now,
swollen amphibian tongues with the skin cross-hatched
in Soldado Sanskrit, in PRI grammar, Cantinflas &
Morrison rise too in neon plastic & Guadalupe

Solar Angel Estampas, Morrison Cantinflas, Mexico,
flayed under a Che Guevara poster infra-blue, wand,
one thousand bulbs suspended from the trees; still,
they read "Felicidades Zedillo, Felicidades Mexico"

there are no awakenings, no avengers, this alligator
nation, wavers, trembles, for a second or two, amputated,
half in slime, half in the sky, half in music, half in scream,
half in tenderness, half in a terrible twist of accidents

& your little hand calls me, your desolation carriage
flayed, until it reaches my forehead, the one you blessed
with abandon, drowned longing—or was it magic, this
quasi Aztec block, reshaped and carved into the infinite

circular ruin up, at midnight, glittering, I stand
at the Gates of Zedillo Ponce de Leon, America's last
Prince of PRI, with Gortari henchman in columns,
trained on pigs, in reddish masks & Swiss banks,

                    severed wombs
                        from El Niño Perdido,
                pus down their ears,
                        a high official's wife, Juana,
                            La Loca—

estranged and zombied, imprisoned, in this marvelous
synapse & language fails, it struts with its tiny ass, maybe
this blood platoon is all, these dried sausage horse-bone
muscled faces of the slum-millions, these mercado tortilla

eating drooler saint crazies, gooey in half-light, they burn,
rise, through the presidential aquarium, oil, sinew, petro-
uterus & urethras, stripped into demon maguey thorn
cadavers with honey breasts at the tips, they saunter,

shop, they order tortas de lomo, jamón con queso, flan,
pan integral, naranjas de California, mangos de Manila,
tomates de Arizona, papas, yes papas de Idajó,
burn back baby, to moss skeletons & guerrilla forest shadows,

this subversive swamp in vigil, angled to the masses,
a slash & burn rosary, a parade of Tzotzil ulcers, holy
memory in procession, forward with Hidalgo's crazed
eyes, backward with Kahlo's ripped pubis; I amble

                toward this new Dracula
                    timeless nothingness archipelago—
                below me,
                    or is it above me,

my baroque fountains, dwarfed with Nahá, pillaged
patterns, shrapnel echoes & ricochets green with loss,
a ditch with three broken Tzeltal soldiers, this selva
brain peers at me wherever I go, as in this skin torch

docile split fool, in search, always in search, my Llorona
in Chicano accents, my Llorona in American corrosion &

hybrid politeness, watery scarves in concrete, angelic
jibberish rivers & pour down like porridge from the sky,

Mexico, DF—this swirled neon track of diviners; my
Indian mother, you turn back, you who devoured me,
with your suffering,

      I walk the Zone, boy lovers
        with long hair spill on the floor
    & flirt, smoke Winstons
      over me & blow

your fog of Lost Souls into my excited ears, fatigues & wet
eyes, John Lennon spectacles, Guess jeans, tiny diamond
purses, Victorian formless Passion runners, black ant
colonies of maquiladora & plantation peasants: you

who fell when Mexico rumbled & ripped your Singers,
your needles & strings, your uneven patches of electric
metro track, 30,000 miles of skinny skulls, nixtamal
tracheas & polyester float below me, kerosene ancients

with famous faces, from La Obrera, from the back yard
steam house Huichol barrios of shriveled yellowish
embryos, offerings, unfortunate branches, green smeared
candles & shrunken angels to la colonia Corn Goddess—

    Tatei Werika Uimari, I lean,
      stapled to you,

to sardonic mercado walls, fall deep, where you happen
& give birth, La Alameda, the colonial fountains, New Spain
in phosphor drag night city-stand deliriums, earthquake
eagle ghost and demolition sex teams, a still-life,

my infantile Rivera synthesis, with my third eye bombed,
the Thing is alive, that is all, frozen, dipped erotic through

Chiapa de Corzo, through Tapachula coffee, cotton,
banana and finca drool, gestapo sperm, a tiny piece of rain

pasted with a forbidden & forlorn tear of Martí, young
lovers stroll & finger my wiry California heart, vendors
with hotcakes, porno kitchens—cancel me, through
worms in plastic see-through cones, here is Domingo

Xun, from Oxchuk, they say, the blindfolded Ladino
Indian who sells his clairvoyance to the French tourists,
here is Armodia H. from Atizapán de Zaragoza, a lawyer
waiting for love, "O$_{\iota}$ tattered selva," I want to pray,

"O, shambled municipios & milpas," I want to say,
O, deaf walking stick of coffee healers, last refugees across
Finca Flor de Cacao, wrapped in xate palm leaf,
in tortuga blanca steadfastness, in Rigoberta's fire

"Where is Mexico?" I want to utter these terms, ask you,
but I am stroking myself, my dead face Braille, this clap
clap, the writer they say, the reader without a head, fleeing
from America toward an obscure disaster, milky,

                    drummed, enchained in apocalypse,
              the language is hidden and mute,
        that is—
              a devoted river of cancer

at my feet, spores and industries of square-eyed State
Pontiffs, in your blood again, I taste lies,
in your splayed & ceaseless DNA aborted, a military
deluge without a primal cause or dictator

staked out or silenced, you only prepare death for me,
Zedillo rolls, through la selva Ruta Maya, as he betrays
his own lost criollo spirit of rebellion & pulls up against
Zapatistas, from La Torre, you can see the Mexican Army,

cut through Bachajón and Pichucalco, fueled with US
Pentagon news, they burn toward Montes Azules,
a "circle of death" into Zapatistas & Guatemala, into
Guerrero, Aguas Blancas—17 dead, campesinos

de la Sierra Sur: because you beg for fertilizer,
because you ask el Señor—Governor of Guerrero,
the President's compadre—fall into Ajuchitlán,
cut to Cuxmala, more Indian dead, campesino dead

Mexico in brown paste muslin, rubble shade, rouge
jazz that expands, nausea mixed guns that contract—
Aztec, Spanish, Mayan, Mestiza, Americano Mestizo,
Nothing—you, below Xochimilco, students demonstrate

in two generations, against Mayan genocide, please track
this word *genocide*, my torso gyrations, my blood
disasters—only, all, peer down, all of us—seven
thousand feet above the rest of the world, Smog Eaters

& true Hunger Artists of the universe, bent & bloodied
stone shoes, October the second, 1968—under
the Chihuahua building of Plaza Tlatelolco, you too,
rise again, die again, a score of helicopters drop flares

rise again, die again under the banner: Concilio Nacional
de Huelga, a surprise attack by the police and military,
the modern towers of Tlatelolco swing back, ghost
brigades write & sing again—electronic, continental

>"Free the political prisoners, no grenadiers,"
>they say, against the wall,
>*Ho Chi Minh Brigade,*
>   *¡Presente!*
>*Che Guevara Brigade,*
>   *¡Presente!*
> *Frank Pais Brigade.*
>*¡Presente!*

reassembled, international: "Todos somos Marcos,
Todos somos Marcos," zócalo howl chant, zócalo
student newspaper poetry fire from the dented mouth
125,000, sing, a wry smile in the corner of my lips,

upstairs, Technocrats for the Post-Modern, new catagories,
fluid in snake benevolent camouflage, military envoys
from Fort America, this smoky hut from Waiting &
Floating Never Arriving, this convex pyramid of Indian

Desire, this Techno—Bourgeois—Democracy, viral,
howler monkey love, lyrical & impossible language,
coffined, awake—dead students in the yards, they burn
again, the Bishop of San Cristóbal is stoned down

by Ladinos on Avenida Utrillo, "Drink water from
the streets, cry for peace, find the heart," he says,
more students cry for Gortari's head, raped old ones with
slime woolens, they love again, next to their last candles

to San Martín Caballero, slaughtered, Indian soldiers
with copper faces, they bleed again, ambushed
cuartel sargentos with guttered asses, they sing of Mexico
again, spin the Host, they kneel, Chols in acid wash

    & dark soldados in Suburbans,
    four wheel drive, your amber sap
    is up to my thighs,
        campesinas
breathe—Marta of the Twisted
    Jaw—you blur to a flat board school
in splinters & dream in malaria
    trouble hammock, the soundtrack slips,

    centuries escape me, images tumble
w/o text, on their own,
        without relation, again,

flesh caoba juice & military fauna steel, San Francisco,
Tijuana, Tenejapa, Lacandonia USA, a sign on Avenida
San Juan de Letrán sinks into the rubble, into a rock,
Lotería Nacional Presenta—PEMEX y El Tajín,

a neo-Rousseau flare, in mahogany skin, alive,
I am upside down Siqueiros, carved in Paris or
am I a Tamayo dot stretched on a beggar child's feline face
where the Indian introduces me, a cloud of dust:

    Oh, excuse me, escuse my literary leprosy, electricity
    Oh, excuse my tiny dictator, the one on my nose
    Cream-faced and mestizo, kill him, please, that is all
    Torture him, make him look skyward, with his
    Thick Iowa hands inside his camera—excuse him
    He is blind, incorrigible, an orphan, his veins show,
    He likes you, he likes White Indian maidens to
    Serve him at the PRI Goddess Café, to haul honor
    & archeology, almost bare-breasted, he likes, to be
    A writer, in wake, silvery symbols, Palenque
    Phosphor, he likes to drag up to the Stone Mother,
    He refers to her at the beginning of this passage, he
    Will refer to you too, excuse him, his sacred lust,
    His global cock, his red-black tongue PRI,
    PEMEX, Banamex, NAFTA, MXPYTRZ, scramble it
    World Bank—for him, his robust gods without

    a face, or
        a flowery vagina,

my voice scrawls sideways, my small & perfectly shaped
travel feet, stroll The Thing-Against-Itself, this Jaguar
America & a jangle of opalescent crucifixes, go down:
babies, go down into this spliced consciousness, blistered,

Mexico ≠ Mexico, syntax is out of synch, popped &
scorched, into another century of anthro excreta hashed,

the-object-into-oblivion, eyeless in El Próspero, left eyeless
in Huixtán, left bloodless in a Simojovel petro-brothel,

    my whirling ulnas & your blackish husk
        femurs of Chenalhó, more half-words;
    this is my ink,
           feel it run down my cheeks,
      down the arms, this spirit mud,
           motherless slime, this drift of being.

V

Mayan Drifter

LETTER TO K'AYUM MA'AX
(via Palenque)

Dear K'ayum Ma'ax,

What has happened?

Mexico is bleeding. At both ends of its flowery boundaries, thorns burst, people pass into shadowy light. The northern territories blur, the ones so much in love with the American Quixote, the oblong persona who commands the glamor and flash of corporate credit and piña colada teen-age stomps from the upscale San Diego hills into Tijuana. Yes, the border fuse has been set; one gun blast to the brain and the other into the solar plexus of Sr. Luis Donaldo Colosio, the PRI presidential candidate. An old Mexico ended with him; destruction at the northern line of power versus powerlessness.

At the southern edge of the nation the serum flows into Guatemala and crosses back into a continuous and smoldering Mayan Indian and campesino revolution. Mexico grows reddish liberation spikes across its breast and at its feet while the stock market tumbles and European magazines resurrect Zapata, the mustachioed Indian peasant warrior from Anenecuilco. And almost out of impulse, the kind of conqueror's reflex invented by Cortés, the United States doles out billions to stabilize and lure back Mexican dependence and the psychic armature of some ancient fissure that cannot be healed with gold.

If you stand on the open dirt roads of Lomas Taurinas, the last Mexican colonia that Colosio walked upon, you can see Río Tijuana, a concrete labyrinth of boutiques and compressed iron statues of forgotten Aztec warriors and Mexican heroes. You can see the open pit where the center city boils up with its velveteen canvas portrait shops of Elvis and Madonna, O.J. Simpson and the Dallas Cowboys. The old jai alai game building still props up the figure of a well-groomed man dressed in white carrying the world globe on his back. But the clothes are bloodied now. If you look closely you will see the tiny threads of dirt roads, more

Mayan drifter

endless little trails that blend into countless brown-skinned colonias of desolation and death; up there by the hills of La Obrera, on the other side of El Valle del Rubí and farther south by the little white crosses on the road to Ensenada, the old land of the Cocopá Indians. This is Tijuana, the Great Horror Belt for the Indian ambling to El Norte; at night you can probably find a few Lacandones huddled with Huichols, Mayos, and Mayas, sleeping on blue plastic tarps on the main street, La Revolución, by day selling friendship bracelets and chakira bead rings, saving up for the Great Coyote Journey to the States. Except this "revolución" is soaked with alcohol instead of blood, guitar shops and zarape stacks instead of guns and flour-sack T-shirts that read Viva Mexico instead of Viva la Muerte. This is Tijuana, where the Greatest Laser Border Wall on the earth looms over maquila worker shanties and tilted human shack stacks, manufactured and conceptualized in the United States to keep Mexicans out of the country; the most expensive U.S. border patrol fortress on the globe. And still, the blood juice runs deep and pulses forcefully across the border lines. This is our lot and maybe this is where you and I come together as we stumble through the words for freedom and power.

What to say? How are you?

How is your family? Viejo Chan K'in and Antonio, your wife's father? Sorry it's taken me so long to get back to you. Since the day I left, the journey to Nahá has been on my mind. Writing, rewriting, that's all I have been doing, it seems; locked up in a tiny room in Fresno facing east. Day in, day out—in between my classes at the Chicano Studies department in Fresno State—I come back to the southeastern lowlands of Chiapas, to Nahá, la selva . . . on paper.

I've been trying to reach you. I called Larry, the photographer at Na Bolom who was in charge of Trudi Blom's photography archives. He told me that you and the rest of the village have run to Palenque. You are staying at your cousin Chan K'in's place in the city, he said. I didn't know that old Mateo's son had a small house in Palenque. When will you return to Nahá?

Larry said you are running from the Zapatista National Liberation Army, which recently cut through the selva and marched up La Ruta to Ocosingo, Altamirano, Las Margaritas, and into San Cristóbal de las Casas, who have been holed up in San Andrés Larrainzar. Military cercos surround them as they surrounded campesinos in El Salvador a

decade ago. Now they fall back to Montes Azules as the military stalks
this new and glamorous prey. This is all Larry knows. He is an American who has adopted a son from the southern Lacandón village of Lacanjá Chan Sayab and is trying to get back to San Cristóbal. I met his
small-framed son, Chan Bor, at Na Bolom. As a matter of fact, Chan Bor
invited me to Lacanjá Chan Sayab, but I told him I couldn't go because I
was headed to Nahá. He was gracious and wandered back to his room
at Na Bolom. Later, in San Cristóbal, I bumped into him outside a textile
shop. Chan Bor was with his wife, who stood to one side and looked
away from me as we talked. This is when I discovered I truly was a
Ladino. Larry made it as far as Palenque since he couldn't get in through
the highlands.

You must know Na Bolom is no longer what it used to be; it is the
American Embassy now. Everyone has drifted into different places, in
one swoop; everyone and everything have blurred into the Other Side.
Mayan refugees from la selva have come to the cities, Guatemalan
campesinos have crawled out of their border bunkers in the jungles next
to Yaxchilán and Bonampak. The PRI dynasty tumbles under conspiracy
plots for Colosio's assassination. The lowlands have migrated into the
highlands. Instead of pushing tourists through the mountains, the
Ladino choferes and taxistas are transporting journalists and members
of Indian treaty councils and human rights groups from the United
States to the hidden towns and surrounding colonias. Campesinos have
picked up guns and dropped their machetes. Nuns have let go of their
ablutions and call for revolution. Students in Mexico City have organized "Rock for Peace in Chiapas" concerts, American-made helicopters
used for antidrug campaigns in Mexico have sprayed the highlands with
missiles, Chamula women vendors are selling masked guerrilla dolls instead of their usual dusty clay figures. Many Ladino merchants have
shut themselves into the small rectangles of their high-walled houses;
they are hiding from snipers and passers-by—for once. Other Ladinos
are funneling their money into the Zapatista cause. The same Emiliano
Zapata posters carried at the Chicano moratorium against the Viet Nam
war in 1970—on Whittier Street in East Los Angeles—are now toted by
Indian woman in San Cristóbal. As the "process of dialogue" is installed,
refurbished, and reinvented by the new government and the church,
landless campesinos outside of the Ejército Zapatista movement block
roads and dig into their new trenches, without rhetoric or agendas, and

landowners in the north are breaking into banks claiming their piece of change.

I keep seeing images of San Cristóbal, Ocosingo, la Ruta Maya, and la selva on television or in the newspapers, every other day—the incredible Ruta, the road of two hundred thousand displaced Indian and refugee campesinos. Has this green desert road serpent of Quetzalcoatl and Kukulkán reached a new cycle, the Sixth Solar Age of the Aztecs, the New Mayan Light Source from the East? Does Hachakyüm, cosmic overseer of the Lacandón Mayas, say it is time to shed the old skin and face the global winds? Will the Tzotzil-Tzeltal Earth Lord blow retribution through the sacred mountains of Tzontevitz and Kalvaryo? Will the flurry that arrives from southeastern Chiapas shrivel the old sociocultural centers of oppression? Suddenly there is no news. Chiapas does not exist.

Things have drifted out to their opposite. On your TV, there must a blank. La Ruta must be a military parade. In 1970, a cop from Tuxtla Gutiérrez, the capital, would come and tour San Cristóbal for a day, watch the bicycle races in the zócalo, then head back. Now San Cristóbal is an armed fortress; the Mexican army stalks the city and surrounding hamlets. The campesino champitas, mud-house hamlets, and indios with sticks and machetes in the highlands have become the target. Since the beginning of '94 the local campesinos and indigenous groups have taken up arms; Chamulas since '93. They seem to look the same: high cheekbones and rough eyes from seeing too much squalor, and yet they point to each other expecting fullness, redemption.

The other day my wife, Margarita, and I went to San Francisco to look for news of San Cristóbal and found none. Maybe, we thought, the media networks from southern Mexico had reached the Mexicano and Latino communities in the Mission District like they used to in the seventies. Nothing. Only outdated papers usually purchased for the sports section. We came back to Fresno disgusted, with empty hands. Jorge Herrera, my friend in San Francisco, sends me photocopies of La Jornada from Mexico City. Remember I told you about Jorge, how he gave me the granola that I brought for your father? Just the other day he said that there is an underground Mayan collective called Grupo Maya. They even have a fax machine in their basement headquarters. These are the only resources that I have.

I am sure you are hearing the accounts day by day in the Palenque radio news. Salinas de Gortari has taken off his celebration tuxedo, Zedillo and his shadow men have withdrawn into nervous talk and hidden quarters as the PRI traces its hollow belly and skull. Maybe they won't ever lose, they'll just transform into another party, another mask with bitter ends. Clinton and his advisors watch closely. They are the ones noting la selva on the tele. In another room the Republicans take notes as they prepare more electoral landslides. Remember when we saw Gortari and Clinton on your twenty-seven-inch color screen in Nahá? And you mimicked them while we ate fried rice? Maybe la selva has grown back into the capital of the States, maybe things have truly reversed.

Even the priests and the bishop of San Cristóbal are giving talks out here about what is taking place, calling us to action. They come and go. They fast. Talks in the States, talks in San Cristóbal. Their words ring true. They seem to be the only reliable voices we have.

I didn't tell you about the maids at Na Bolom, Lupe and Fidencia. Where are they now? I wonder. How have they been changed and reversed? And the thousands of Indians on the streets of San Cristóbal, in the mercado—where have they run to? Back to the sacred shawls of their mountain god, Tzontevitz? How could they, if the military carried out air strikes and volleyed missiles into their hamlets? Where are the maids now?

All of a sudden, the sky itself is upside down, the blue has drifted into gray, and you are in Palenque, sitting on stone—"con el culo en la piedra," as you said—somewhere peering out of a small shack in the city, waiting to see if anyone is coming after you: the gendarmes, the promotores from the Instituto Nacional Indigenista, people with camera faces and recorder fingers.

Your son-in-law, Juan Carlos—did he bring enough string, wax, and bamboo so he could make arrows and sell them to the tourists? What else is there now but to follow the young husbands into the tourist mercados? Am I supposed to tell you to take up arms, to turn back to Nahá? We never talked about how your group, along with the other Lacandón villages, received exclusive timber revenue rights from the government, how you helped push out the colonias of campesinos and Mayas who had settled in the Montes Azules bioreserve in the selva. Is this why you are running from the Zapatistas?

How is Juan Carlos and your daughter, Angélica? I'll laugh if his old palmita is still standing when you return to the village and your laminated house has fallen. I'll laugh a little—I am rambling like a horieyit. This means asshole, right?

I am out of place too. Drifting.

Now I am looking back. And what I am looking for is not there. Mexico itself has collapsed into a flat and jagged desert of crossings, takeovers, and killings. What dream are we in? I want to ask Chan K'in José, your son's friend, the boy who carried me across Lago Nahá, in his dugout cayuco, rowing through the waters as if crossing into another light source. Who is visiting us in the night winds this time? A foreign platoon of revolution advisors? A mixed Indian and campesino refugee legion of resentments, a Ladino payback in the shape of dislodged bridges, barracks—the phosphor ghost of Colosio at the border line? Have "el hombre de la selva" and "la mujer de la selva" finally come out into the open after all these centuries? I'd like to know what your father and mother say.

Carlos Enrique and I talk about you too—Carlos Enrique, the Mexican anthropology student I met at your house in Nahá. He finally turned in his dissertation on Lacandón notions of body and self to the National Autonomous University in Mexico City. Can you believe it? But he's out of work and wandering around in Mexico City. He was on his way to visit Leo in Ocosingo, he said. I can still picture Leo in the shade at the end of Lake Nahá, leaning on his large van, talking about how much he's going to charge the Tzeltales for cabbing them to Palenque. He's in jail now, charged with killing his Lacandón wife. You must know this in detail. He beat her to death, Carlos Enrique said. It was in the papers all over Mexico City: the story of a white man in a Lacandón tunic crouched in the darkness of the Ocosingo jail while a rebellion smolders around his cell; this is Leo's world now. A feminist group in Mexico City has denounced him as an assassin of Mayan children. All this has happened since I left.

You remember Luz María, the other Mexican anthropology student visiting Nahá with Carlos Enrique? She is busy preparing a boletín in Mexico City on the various political and social movements that have taken place in la selva. She will send it to me as soon as she can, Carlos Enrique said. At night I wait for my dreams to give me direction, but nothing comes.

Carlos Enrique surprised me. In the fall of '92, a few weeks before I met him at your place, he had visited Marqués de Comillas, the colonia at the Guatemala boundary, not far from Nahá. He talked to a young man in a small village there, Flor de Cacao, who told him that he and many others from the Frente Sandinista, the Tupamaros, and other Central and South American resistance groups were planning to take over, to push through and fight for the indios and the peasants. Fully armed, the young man said, they were going to rally against the injustices perpetrated against the campesinos and the Indians. "I thought he was a fanatic," Carlos Enrique laughed as he told me. Then both of us grew quiet on the phone. We spoke of the tortures, murders—the Tzeltal, Tzoltzil, and Tojolabal Indians lying on cold ground with their wrists cut and their faces crushed by the Mexican military. Mexican Indians and campesinos on Mexican soil waging their own revolution with sharp sticks instead of automatics. Who would have thought of la selva as the new ground for the future of Mexico and the entire continent? Luz is on the right track. What do you think?

The cayucos are probably still there in the same place, floating on Lake Nahá, as empty and stark as the PEMEX campamentos a few yards across La Ruta, except the cayucos move with the winds and the waters.

Trudi Duby Blom is dead. It is true. She died on the twenty-third of December, a couple of weeks before the rebellion. I can't help wondering about the timing of her death. It was as if an era came to an end and another started. Trudi's struggle for la selva over the last five decades and its owners, the Hach Winik—the True People, as the Lacandones call themselves—came to a full stop. Or was it a struggle to contain you, a museum gesture? Did she fight for you? Or did she and Frans commit the same ethnographic sin: did they profit from you too? What will happen to Na Bolom, the Lacandón Maya refuge and research center in San Cristóbal? The archives? Was all this transformed into another cause, a more violent and direct one? The "research" comes back to la selva in the form of ashes and bullets. I don't know, but you must know. Maybe this is what she was trying to tell me, the last time I saw her at Na Bolom, as she gesticulated and struggled to lift her voice out of her throat. The stroke she had suffered wrapped her into stupor. Maybe she wanted to tell me about these ashes, maybe she wanted to repent, maybe she wanted to warn me—to run or to fight?

Why are you in Palenque? Was it because of the sheer numbers—two thousand Zapatistas to two hundred Lacandones? Or the twenty-three thousand military troops? Was it because you too had left yourself behind, because you had grown accustomed to the Ladino bank account given to you for caoba timber and Mayan artifacts? Or do you think the

Zapatista movement is another intervention into El Próspero, as the Spanish called your land, envisioning riches and paradise? Is this one more finely tuned invasion into the Mayan lowlands, in the name of the Mayas?

When the papers out here reported an organized rebellion in Chiapas, one claiming the name of the Lacandones and the Mayas, I was stunned. How can this be? I asked myself. I walked around pinching myself; it was as if everything that I had seen since the early seventies had followed me and blasted out of the papers and the television. Even out of the mouths of people who had never pronounced the word Maya—or Chiapas or Mexican selva or Lacandones or indios de México—la selva broke through, through all boundaries, in all forms, in all media and language; a language temblor was in motion. A new mind.

What does Viejo Chan K'in say about this, about the Ejército Zapatista, Palenque? What does your wife, Nuk, say? Have the Zapatistas come to cure the cold your father and old Antonio spoke about, the cold descending on the land, the frío that won't let the tobacco flower blossom, the cold mist that enters the body and freezes the blood? The cold figures with firearms, the cold skin with a new PRI nose? I must tell you, I believe in the Zapatistas as I believe in you.

The papers here have quickly abandoned the issues of la selva and Mexico and gone back to news of California fires, Los Angeles earthquakes, terrorism in Japan, slaughter in Africa, and of course more mortar shells and peace talks in Sarajevo. War and peace and in between, nausea. It's as if we open the window in the morning and the entire world falls into our bedroom, in pieces and tattered faces. We have grown accustomed to this morning horror ritual. I don't want to become wary and numb to violence. I grieve for the people in Sarajevo and Africa; I tell my creative writing students to write poems as feverishly as they can; I ask them to tear through drywall as if they were breaking through stone and chipping out a new hieroglyphics—in the name of the dead, in the name of the shattered earth. They look at me and try to fathom what I am saying. Something reaches them, so they carve into the cardboard chalk walls and they use a long shiny nail to rip out their words. We talk about you and la selva. We draw, write, carve. They breathe deep and carve deep. Artwork. How far can art carve?

The whole earth is conversing violently. Hachakyüm, protector of la selva and the Lacandones, is shouting through mineral, concrete, mud slime, and stone; we are all aghast. La selva, Sarajevo, Japan, Burundi, Zaire, Chechnya, Chiapas, Mexico—north and south, east and west—and thousands of tiny earthquakes in our lives and houses and streets. And yet I know I can stroll back to my house, close the door, draw the shades, and lose myself to the blue nothingness in the corner of the room, propped up as a little square god with its opaque and busy electric face of many lives.

The other day, Margarita bought a set of frying pans on sale for nine dollars. I threw the old ones into the trash. For a millisecond, I imagined the battered pans coming back at us with angry handles and snarling Teflon faces; I imagined them throwing themselves at us for discarding them as useless and disposable, after years of service. This is our plight in the States; we discard old fixtures and fashions, trade them for new ones, as the world kicks itself out in the shape of a more virulent phantom.

Mexico. Indios. Campesinos: I say the words to myself.

I thought Mexico and its corporate self had accepted the Indian as a necessary exploited class. A five-minute walk through any Mexican state capital will prove this to anyone. I was sure the conquest screws were solid and dug in, that everyone had acknowledged Indian exploitation as a cornerstone in the new edifice for Mexico's development in the global system of trade, power, and cultural influence. Of course, all this acknowledgment was embedded in elevated terms of homage to Indian heritage. This is especially true in the United States, where we walk around with armloads of ponchos and gourds, tequila gallons and Kahlua syrup on our faces, fat guitars strapped around our shoulders, and twisted mariachi hats on our heads after visiting border towns and border huts to haggle for the best price because we read in some tourist book that this is the custom, because Mexico is a global junk wholesaler for American and European corporate enterprise.

No one thinks about Indians and campesinos here.

Indians in the U.S. mean there's nothing we can do about it; Indians here mean it's all over, all in the past; Indians and campesinos here mean there are exceptions to this statement. So what—next question? Imagine what Indians-in-Mexico mean here. Actually, I can tell you: more border networks, more money for bigger and better border fortification systems, computerized guards, vans, masks, night scanners, helicopters, and U.S.-Mexico interagency networks all with the same mission: to spend billions to capture and return Mexicans running from the abyss of famine, disease, corruption, and global corporate abuse—Indians, in short, with nowhere to run, Indians on a night flight to the macroworld of being and true positioning as fully realized human beings, in America. They are building a wall along the two-thousand-mile border from Tijuana to Matamoros, a new Berlin Wall with Spanish, Bostonian, and Moorish flourishes at the main gates. So goes our mythic quest as we drift from south to north and eventually stutter back to the abyss again. Some come back with a wad of greenbacks and California trinkets stuffed into a girdle or watches rolled up the arms, the way my Uncle Fernando used to do in the fifties—or like my Aunt Teresa in the sixties with what she thought were expensive dresses packed in aluminum petacas that she shipped but somehow never reached their tawdry destination on la Calle Uruguay in Mexico City.

In all my years in the university, working with arts groups, community centers, and in alliance with national networks for change, I had never come across anything about the plight of Mexican Indians. Usually we talked about Central America, Chile, and Brazil—the Miskitos in Nicaragua, the Mapuche in Chile; we scrambled for truth in the far reaches of the continent and the world. We eulogized Che Guevara, we sang with Victor Jara's accent, we painted murals with the face of Frida Kahlo. We fought hard for the installation of Queztalcoatl statues in our parks. We crashed the time barrier from pre-Columbian to post-Columbian in our search for our subjugated self, toward the Huichol in Nayarit, the Quiché in Guatemala, toward a tiny beggar child-woman from Chenalhó. Rigoberta Menchú had brought Guatemala, its fincas and the atrocities committed against the indígena, up against our breast. But Guatemala somehow seemed to be a million miles from Mexico. Mexico was amorphous, invisible—a friendly neighbor without a face or heart or brain; a wax figure waiting to be filled with North American corporate consciousness, as always, ready to be taken to the Land of Oz ovens and cooked and fine tuned with the proper organs, one of which was called NAFTA. This NAFTA was to be placed under the eyebrows, to be utilized as a nose or a mouth or an eye socket so that the eyes could find focus and the nose detect the proper direction of New Age tribute and servitude. The sad thing is many of us wanted that new nose. After the signing of NAFTA, we ran across the border towns and packed our minitrucks with bags and boxes and knotted muslin bundles of provisions sneezed by this facial feature. We felt good, strong, honored—at last. Mexican multimillionaire technocrats loosened their backstrap loom–woven belts, gave a lyrical toast, and belched.

Maybe I was the one who had accepted and acknowledged and pledged that you should remain in the same small shape of Nahá, in the lowlands of southeastern Chiapas, with your laminated roofs, algae depths, and white-glued caoba picnic tables, and with MTV shooting bluish rays into the toothless faces of small Mayan children. Maybe I was the one who wanted to own the last tracts of moist land and the oil derricks and cubicle housing so I could return and kneel on the raw gravel of la Ruta Maya and cry out my sadness, so I could come back released, transformed. Maybe this is why the Lacandón woman turned away from me in the San Cristóbal night, noting my Ladino penchant for polite paternalism and tragic redemptions. Maybe I wanted things to stay the same so I could blow out my own rhetoric and feel worthy. And maybe I was the one who didn't want the jungle to come alive like in your favorite movie, *Predator*, where the crab-faced lagoon monster swishes stylized war instruments and a self-invented body at the megamen from civilized America.

Maybe this is a story about movies and celluloid characters, about misshapen plots and torn-out climaxes, about shoddy cut-and-paste conclusions and amateur beginnings; an evil Gortari—Zedillo—Bush—Clinton screenplay workshop gone awry, a PRI-Republican Internet Goldrush hotline (PRIG) gone neon and global because their predecessors and followers deserve better—these Great Movie giants of How Mexico Should Be Won.

In the meantime this is something I put together for you, a group of photos and a book I wrote. You are going to laugh because you are in the book and many things you said are in there too. I'll send it to that hotel you told me about, the one that wanted to exhibit your paintings in Palenque. And I'll wait for your book, the one you said would be the true book on the Hach Winik. Also, I am including a poem I wrote a few years ago, the only one that I ever wrote about Nahá.

I didn't tell you that I've been talking to my children, Joaquín and Joshua and Alma, whom I haven't seen in years. We have been living separate lives since they were born, but just recently we started to write to each other and talk on the phone. Alma invited me to her high school graduation in Tempe, Arizona. My stepchildren, Marlene and Robert, are going about their own ways too—becoming more independent. Mar-

lene started City College, and Robert spends most of his time practicing
break-dancing moves; he says break dancing is back in style. Do you still
have the rap cassettes? Probably not, right?

I wonder where you are now, whether you are drifting toward
Palenque or ambling down La Ruta again, back to your lakes. Are you
stepping toward the north or the east, toward Tenosique, toward Veracruz? Is Juan Carlos selling arrows in Tuxtla Gutiérrez, or has he gone
farther, like the Chamulas and Zinacantecos have done, to Mexico City,
across Tehuantepec, the Isthmus? Have the young husbands and wives
branched out, alone, into the cities and mountains, as in the stories by
Juan Rulfo? Have you caught a train and blended yourself into the outskirts of Mérida? Into Lomas Taurinas in Tijuana? Is that where you are
now—with your father and mother, Koh II, who stood so proud outside
her palmita the day you took me to visit them on my last day in Nahá?

Have you gone out into the crazy, uncharted terrain of Mexico into
the U.S., where it becomes a ruby haze of fast arms and empty eyes, nothing but a reddish light pouring down from all the angular faces and all
the skies, where the blue-green of the selva finally breaks into its opposite? Are you and I exchanging positions? I know I am saying this all
wrong.

The dream of the black ocean liner comes up often, the dream I had
in your old house. An ocean liner, smoothing the horizon, a terrible and
beautiful force from afar, quiet, with unknown passengers and destinies.
I was hanging on a wire fence, alone with a strange woman, both of us
on the edge of the slippery wires. With shocked faces we saw the dark
ship coming, ominous and billowy as a rainstorm sky. I think of the story
of el hombre de la selva and how the foreigner who asked about the story
fell to the ground, almost dying, after he wrote down los secretos—the
stranger who begged your father, Viejo Chan K'in, to use the exact language so he could quote him properly and then fell and convulsed. I
think of how your father brought him back to life with songs and prayer.

The taste of rice comes to me too, rice steamed with Knoor tomato
powder bought at little Nuk's tiendita on La Ruta and fried with jungle
onions on your Campesino stove, spiced with garlic and tossed into a
bowl of speckled squash. Roll up a salted tortilla like a flute and drink
down a tiny glass of cañabrava, Mayan tequila; wash it down with Modelo beer from the six-packs that you keep in the back rooms. It is all
around me—the redness and the greenness, the light palma fragrance.

I know I am fooling myself with food, language, and colors; I haven't touched on the legs or the stomachs or the yellow-white in the eyes of the children, have I? Haven't mentioned the emptiness on La Ruta, the family of eight surviving on the smallest seed and a Coke bottle, on the run, crossing in zigzag patterns through the scraped mountains. La Selva, Chiapas, Guerrero. Every six months the temblor reaches another state. This is something I haven't mentioned, something that won't come up on the camera or the recorder or even the pages of Mexico or America. I use that word "America" with irony. This is something larger than the rebellion of your brothers and sisters, Mayas and campesinos, and Colosio's last step in the hills of Tijuana; is it about Mexico, drifting—contracting, rising and collapsing into a new figure or a last Dis-figure on the eyeteeth of its own technohungers and coyote billionaires, of the United States and the new wave of globalized capitalism?

I use the word "Chicano" with irony too. Here I claim it again; it is a half-step between Ladino and Indian, a jump start from apathy into commitment. The questions come back: will the business talk subdue all of us, will our private spaces and murmurings stop us cold, will the multiple horrors and earthquakes around the planet break the edge off—the Mexican, American, campesino, and Mayan edge where for the moment we meet again?

I have flowers for Tijuana, for the northern borders, as I have flowers for the Maya in the south. Tijuana, the rumbling city where I used to roam as a boy; where I searched for a doctor to heal the never-ending pains of my mother, Lucha; where I felt alive in the mercado prisms of green and red plexiglass lights; and where as a teenager I grooved at the Blue Fox cabaret with the first Chicano poets I ever met. Here are the flowers, these unwrapped words, for the highlands and lowlands of Chiapas, for the Maya, for your land, for our land where I jaunted and lost myself on your road in order to come back to the starting point.

GLOSSARY AND SELECTED READINGS

GLOSSARY

abuela brujería	grandmother's witchcraft
agarra la onda	get the message; get the drift
aguacate	avocado
Amárrala	tie her up; **Amárrala . . . la boca watcha** Tie her up . . . her mouth, take care of it
Anahuak	Nahuatl name for the Valley of Mexico; land surrounded by water; Mexico City
apartado postal	post office box
aprende	learn
atajadoras	Indian and Ladina women who steal the produce of Indian market women
avenida	avenue
¿Ayúdame?	Can you help me?
azul	blue
babozo, baboza	stupid fool
bajareque	wall structure made of thin woven sticks packed with a mud and grass mixture
balché	Lacandón Maya alcoholic ceremonial drink made from the bark of the balché tree
bien firmes	really fine, "together"
bien padre, vato	really cool, man
bolas	dollars; "balls"
boletín	bulletin, newsletter
bolillo	bread roll; also Chicano Spanish for a white person
bolo	drunk
brecha	opening, break
brujería	witchcraft
brujero	witch; wizard
bueno, buena	good
cabeza	head
cabrón	stupid
café	coffee
calabaza	squash
caldo con chichi	easy, "a bowl of cherries"; soup and breast milk
calle	street

camarada	dude, pal, friend
camino	road
cañabrava	sugar cane liquor
canela	cinnamon
caoba	mahogany
Capirucha, La	the capital, Mexico City
carátula	face, façade
caribal	a small Lacandón settlement
carnal (carnala, carnis, carnalito)	term and variants popularized during the Chicano movement of the 1960s and suggesting brotherhood, sisterhood, friendship, community membership
cayuco	dug-out canoe
cebolla	onion
cedro	cedar
cerco	military blockade surrounding a village or community; fence
chale	no way, never
chamorro	highland men's outer jacket, a wool poncho
chapay	small rain-forest palm used for the roofing of houses
chavala	girl; young
Chicana bien hinchada	a "well-built" Chicana
Chicanada	a Chicano "crew"; the Chicano community as a collective whole
chicha	fermented corn liquor
chicleros	the chicle tree (**sapodilla**) workers who, at the peak of the chicle industry between the 1920s and the 1950s, razed the rain forest to provide ingredients for chewing gum enterprises located mostly in the United States
chingazos	blows, fights
chingo de feria	a hell of a lot of money
chofer	driver
chorizo	sausage
choza	hut
chupón	baby teething toy
Coatlique	Aztec earth goddess
colibrí tzacatl	hummingbird native to Chiapas rainforest, *Amazilia tzacatl*
colonia	settler village
¿Cómo está?	How are you?
compañero	companion
con	with
Concilio Nacional de Huelga	National Strike Council, one of the organizations formed during 1968 student demonstrations in the

	Tlatelolco Plaza of Mexico City, where hundreds were massacred by government forces as they called for free speech, educational change, and human rights
corrido	Mexican historical ballad sung with guitar
cosa	thing
c.p. (*for* **código postal**)	zip code
criollos	first-generation Mexicans of Spanish descent
culo en la piedra	ass on stone, an ironic expression used by Lacandón Indians to refer to the way they spend their lives sitting at the pyramids selling tourist ware
derecho de pernada	the implicit right to rape and sexually abuse women finca workers
D.F.	Distrito Federal (i.e., Mexico City)
dulcería	candy shop
ejidatario	person who holds "title" to land in ejido tracts, usually vested in communities and managed by an ejidal committee
ejido	communally held land tract
¿Entiendes méndez?	Know what I mean, jelly bean?
esa	home girl; personal address to a woman; **ese** dude, man
escándalo	scandal
Esmuski	play on phrase "excuse me"
Estados, los	the States, the U.S.
estandarte	banner
esta noche	tonight
estar al alba	to be up to date
Es todo	That's all
EZLN	Ejército Zapatista de Liberación Nacional (Zapatista Army of National Liberation), which made history on January 1, 1994, in the Lacandón jungle by decisively announcing its armed struggle for Indian rights in Chiapas and throughout Mexico; a Chiapas-based social, political, and human rights movement that continues to the present
fácil	easy
fajina	overtime work schedule for campesinos, usually without pay
febrero	February
felicidades	congratulations
feliz cumpleaños	happy birthday
feria	money, spare change; a festival
finca	country property, farm, ranch

firme	firm; being "together, solid," organized, aware
flan	cream caramel, egg custard
flecha	arrow
fonda	small makeshift restaurant
galera	a low-quality, oppressive, open-air living space occupied by four to five hundred coffee plantation workers and their small domestic animals. The only covering is of palm or banana leaves.
gallineros	chicken coops and cages
galón	gallon
gaván (*pl.* **gavanes**)	a commercially woven cotton or wool zarape that fits over the head; also known in the States as a "poncho"
gente	people
guacamayos rojos	red macaws native and once plentiful in the Lacandón rain forest, *Ara macao*
guanábana	tropical pineapple-like fruit
guatapil	small palm leaf used in the lowlands for animal feed as well as for roofing material
Hachakyüm	Our True Lord, the Creator, principal deity of the Lacandón
Hach Winik	(*Lacandón Maya*) a true person
H-ak'chamel	sorcerer in the Mayan highlands
hermano	brother
hija, hijo	daughter, son
hijín	dude, brother, man
huera	light-skinned woman
huevos	eggs; "balls," courage
huipil	blouse used by women of the Mayan highlands
Idajó	Idaho
indígeno, indígena	indigenous
Inglis	English (standard spelling is **inglés**)
jabalí	wild boar
jaina	girlfriend, woman
jamón con queso	ham and cheese
jefe	father; boss
jornalero	day laborer
jóven	young man
kiosko	kiosk; a circular platform used as a performance arena for social and political events, usually located in the center of town

Kisin	Lacandón god of death, He who causes death; the devil; the earthquake
Ladino	person of mixed or Spanish descent not a member of an Indian community, or an acculturated Indian; usually carries negative connotations
lago	lake
las dos	the two of us
lira	guitar; lyre
mamón	sucker, fool
más	more
maseta	head; vase
¿Me entiendes?	Do you understand what I am saying?
Me la rayo	"I am down with it"; Check it out; Right on
menudo	tripe
meras meras, las	the true ones, the main ones
mercado	market
Mi casa es tu caspa	My house is your dandruff (*play on words*)
mil	a thousand
milpa	cornfield; any cultivated area; **milpero** maize grower
Mira, los monitos	Look, the cartoons
Mira, una buena moteada, unos taquitos del mercado	Look, a good marijuana high and tacos from the market stalls
Mírala, que bonita	Look at her, how pretty she is
mojarra, mojarrita	small fish, sardine
montería	an encampment of woodcutters
montero	worker engaged in the felling of trees
morenita	little brunette
mota	marijuana, "grass"
moteada	marijuana high
movimiento	action; also the Chicano social and political movement of the 1960s and 1970s
mujer	woman
municipio	township
nada	nothing
NAFTA	North American Free Trade Agreement
naranjas	oranges
niño	child; **niño perdido** lost child
nixtamal	lime and corn mix used for making tortillas
noche	night; **buenas noches** good evening; **esta noche** tonight
nopales	cactus plants

Norte, El	the North (generally the United States)
nuestro	our
ochenta virotes	eighty dollars; eighty bread rolls
ocote	kindling wood
onda, la	the "in-thing," the key idea, the plan; **agarra la onda** get the message; get the drift
Orale	"Right on"; "What's happening?" Watch out; Wow
oreja	ear
palmita	residence roofed with palm leaves; little palm
pan dulce	sweet bread; **pan integral** organic bread
panela	soft cheese
panzazo	belly flop; last-ditch effort
papas	potatoes
Pato Pasqual, El	Donald Duck
payasa	female clown, fool
pedos	problems; farts; **todo pedo** all loaded, drunk
PEMEX	Petróleos Mexicanos, Mexico's large petrochemical company
pendejos	fools; **Pendejoville** Fool City
petaca	case
pinchi	damn
pleito	fight, rumble
pochos, pochas	pejorative term for Chicanos or Chicanas; "half-breed"
por	for
pox (*or* **posh**)	distilled cane liquor
Préndela	Turn it on
PRI	Mexico's Institutional Revolutionary Party, currently undergoing internal fragmentation and probable collapse because of its history of corruption and deception
promotor	Indian bilingual teacher usually instrumental in promoting assimilation into Ladino society; sponsored by the Instituto Nacional Indigenista
pulquería	neighborhood bar and manufactory where the indigenous fermented and undistilled cactus-juice liquor (**pulque**) is made and sold
punto, al	to the point
puta	whore
puto	fool; dude; pejorative term for male homosexual
¡Qué locote ese vato!	That dude is crazy, wild, great!
¿Qué onda?	What's going on?
¿Quién sabe?	Who knows?

quinceañera	Mexican coming-out ceremony for a fifteen-year-old girl entering into womanhood
Quivo	How are you? What's up? How about that! Right on! Get it?
raza	Chicano people; race
rebozo	shawl
reducción	settlement of converted Indians
reina	queen
Robo-Ladino	sell-out. My way of referring to a Mexican national who is interested more in the profits and advances of technology than in the native peoples of Chiapas. *See also* **Ladino**
ruca	girlfriend, female lover; older woman
¿Sabes?	You know?
sabor	flavor
santo	saint
saraguato	howler monkey, *Alouatta pigra*
sargentos	sargeants
secundaria	secondary school
SEDUE	Secretaría de Desarrollo Urbano y Ecología (the Secretariat for Urban Development and Ecology), a Mexican federal ministry
selva	jungle; **Selva Lacandona** Lacandón rain forest
servilletas	cloth placemats decorated with hand-woven floral patterns Indian-made for tourist consumption; napkins
simón	yup, yes; right on!
sol a sol	sun to sun
soldado	soldier
somos	we are
Soy de Comitán	I am from the city of Comitán
Soy india chicana	I am a Chicana Indian
tamales de mumú	seafood tamales wrapped in banana leaves
taquito de carne asada	steak taco
Tatei Werika Uimari	one of the various female corn deities in Huichol Indian culture of central Mexico
Tatewarí	Grandfather Fire for the Huichol Indians
Tenemos sabor a yerba buena y canela	We have spearmint and cinnamon flavors
Tengo mi pistola, mi mota, y mis huevos	I've got my gun, my marijuana, and my balls

tienda de abarrotes	neighborhood sundry-goods store
tiendita	small make-shift store
tierra	land
Tin Tan	Blam blam; also the stage name of the Mexican comedian and movie star of the 1950s
tío	uncle; **tío taco** a sell-out, two-faced liar, an "Uncle Tom"
todo	all; **todo católico y pendejo** all Catholic and stupid; **todo enterito** all in one piece; **todo pedo** all loaded, drunk; **toda preñada** all pregnant (a negative term)
T'o'ohil	the Great One, a Lacandón spiritual leader and guardian of the Mayan tradition; **t'o'ohil** a teacher
tortas de lomo	pork loin sandwiches
tortilleras	female tortilla vendors
tortuga blanca	white tortoise, *Dermatemys mawii*
Trucha	Listen up! Be aware, on the ball, vigilant
Tú sabes	You know
Vamos, Vámonos	Let's go
varos	dollars, pesos
vato	dude
vendido, vendida	sell-out
¿verdad?	true?
viejo, vieja	old; old person
Washusay, chavalona?	What do you say, girl?
Weenstones	Winston cigarettes
xate	palm leaf harvested in the Lacandón jungle, mostly as a floral industry export
xatero	someone who harvests the xate palm leaf
yerba buena	spearmint
Yo estoy hecha de otro árbol	I am made from another tree; I am not like that; I am different
y todo	and everything
zócalo	central plaza in cities and towns throughout the Americas, usually adjacent to local religious and political administrative centers
zopilote de cabeza amarilla	yellow-headed buzzard, *Cathartes burrovianus*

SELECTED READINGS

The following is a short list of books and articles that assisted me in rethinking my own experience en route to the lowlands of America—en route to America.

Acosta, Oscar Z. *The Autobiography of a Brown Buffalo.* New York: Random House, 1989.

———. *The Revolt of the Cockroach People.* New York: Random House, 1989.

Alarcón, Francisco X. *Snake Poems.* Chronicle Press: San Francisco, 1992.

Almodóvar, Pedro. *Patty Diphusa and Other Writings.* Winchester, Mass.: Faber and Faber, 1991.

Alvarez, Robert R., Jr. *Familia: Adaptation and Migration in Baja and Alta California.* Berkeley: University of California Press, 1987.

Alvarez, Robert, and George A. Collier. "The Long Haul in Mexican Trucking: Traversing the Borderlands of the North and the South." *American Ethnologist* 21, no. 3 (1994): 606–27.

Anuario estadístico de los Estados Mexicanos. Aguascalientes: Instituto Nacional de Estadística Geográfica e Informática, 1994.

Anzaldúa, Gloria. *Borderlands* = La Frontera: The New Mestiza. San Francisco: Spinsters/Aunt Lute Press, 1987.

Blom, Frans, and Gertrude Duby. *La Selva Lacandona..* Mexico City: Editorial Cultura, 1955.

Bruce, Roberto D. *El libro de Chan Kin.* Mexico City: Instituto Nacional de Antropología e Historia, 1974.

Brunhouse, Robert L. *Frans Blom: Maya Explorer.* Albuquerque: University of New Mexico Press, 1976.

Burciaga, José Antonio. *Spilling the Beans: Lotería Chicana.* Santa Barbara, Calif.: Joshua Odell Editions, 1995.

Burgos-Debray, Elizabeth, ed. *I, Rigoberta Menchú: An Indian Woman in Guatemala.* New York: Verso, 1992.

Canby, Peter. *The Heart of the Sky: Travels among the Maya.* New York: Kodansha International, 1992.

Castellanos, Rosario. *Balún-Canán*. 3d ed. Mexico City: Fondo de Cultura Ecónomica, 1961.

————. *A Rosario Castellanos Reader: An Anthology of Her Poetry, Short Fiction, Essays, and Drama*. Ed. Maureen Ahern. Trans. Maureen Ahern and others. Austin: University of Texas Press, 1988.

————. *Another Way to Be: The Selected Works of Rosario Castellanos*. Ed. Myralyn F. Allgood. Athens: University of Georgia Press, 1990.

Castillo, Ana. *Xicanisma: Massace of the Dreamers*. New York: W. W. Norton, 1994.

Cervantes, Lorna Dee. *From the Cables of Genocide: Poems on Love and Hunger*. Houston, Texas: Arte Público Press, 1991.

Chávez, Denise. *Face of an Angel*. New York: W. W. Norton, 1994.

Cisneros, Sandra. *Woman Hollering Creek*. New York: Random House, 1992.

Collier, George A. *Fields of the Tzotzil: The Ecological Basis of Tradition in Highland Chiapas*. Austin: University of Texas Press, 1975.

————. *Seeking Food and Seeking Money: Changing Productive Relations in a Highland Mexican Community*. Discussion Paper 10. Geneva: United Nations Research Institute for Social Development, 1990.

Collier, George A., Daniel C. Mountjoy, and Ronald B. Nigh. "Peasant Agriculture and Global Change: A Maya Response to Energy Development in Southeastern Mexico." *BioScience* 44, no. 6 (June 1994): 398–407.

Collier, George A., and Elizabeth Lowery Quaratiello. *Basta! Land and the Zapatista Rebellion in Chiapas*. Oakland, Calif.: Institute for Food and Development Policy, 1995.

Davis, Olena Kalytiak. "Thirty Years Rising." M.F.A. thesis. Montpelier: Vermont College at Norwich, Spring 1995.

Ginsberg, Allen. *Reality Sandwiches*. San Francisco: City Lights Books, 1963.

Gómez-Peña, Guillermo. *Warrior for Gringostroika*. St. Paul, Minn.: Graywolf Press, 1994.

González, Ray. *Memory Fever: A Journey beyond El Paso del Norte*. Seattle: Broken Moon Press, 1994.

Gossen, Gary H. *Chamulas in the World of the Sun: Time and Space in a Maya Oral Tradition*. Cambridge, Mass.: Harvard University Press, 1974.

Gutiérrez-Holmes, Calixta. *Perils of the Soul*. New York: Free Press of Glenview, 1961.

Harris, Alex, and Margaret Sartor, eds. *Gertrude Blom: Bearing Witness*. Chapel Hill: University of North Carolina Press, 1984.

Havel, Václav. *Temptation: A Play in Ten Scenes*. Trans. Marie Winn. New York: Grove-Weidenfeld Press, 1989.

Hernández-Cruz, Víctor. *Red Beans*. St. Paul, Minn.: Coffee House Press, 1993.

Instituto Indigenista Interamericano. *Anuario indigenista* 33 (1994). Mexico City:
    Instituto Indigenista Interamericano.

La Botz, Dan. *Democracy in Mexico: Peasant Rebellion and Political Reform*. Boston:
    South End Press, 1995.

Marcus, George E., and Michael M. J. Fischer. *Anthropology as a Cultural Critique:
    An Experimental Moment in the Human Sciences*. Chicago, Ill.: University of
    Chicago Press, 1986.

Martínez, Rubén. *Other Side: Fault Lines, Guerilla Saints and the True Heart of Rock
    'n' Roll*. New York: Verso, 1992.

Martínez, Víctor. *Caring for a House*. San Jose, Calif.: Chusma House, 1992.

Menchú, Rigoberta, and the Comité de Unidad Campesina. *Trenzando el futuro:
    Luchas campesinas en la historia reciente de Guatemala*. Donostia (Gipuzcoa,
    Spain): Tercera Prensa/Hirugarren Prentsa, S.L., 1992.

Morris, Walter F., Jr. *Living Maya*. New York: Harry N. Abrams, 1987.

Novakovic, Yosip. *Apricots from Chernobyl*. St. Paul, Minn.: Graywolf Press, 1995.

Perera, Victor, and Robert D. Bruce. *The Last Lords of Palenque*. Boston: Little
    Brown and Company, 1982.

Riding, Alan. *Vecinos distantes: Un retrato de los mexicanos*. Mexico City: Joaquín
    Mortíz/Planeta, 1985.

Robles, Margarita Luna. *Tryptich: Dreams, Lust and Other Performances*. Santa
    Monica, Calif.: Santa Monica College Press, 1993.

Rodríguez, Abraham, Jr. *Spidertown*. New York: Hyperion, 1994.

Rodríguez, Luis J. *Always Running: La Vida Loca, Gang Days in L.A.* New York: Si-
    mon and Schuster, 1994.

Rosaldo, Renato. *The Remaking of Social Analysis*. Boston: Beacon Press, 1989.

Sáenz, Benjamin Alire. *Calendar of Dust*. Seattle: Broken Moon Press, 1992.
———. "I Want to Write an American Poem." In *Currents from the Dancing River:
    Anthology of Poetry, Fiction and Essays by Latinos*, ed. Ray González, 522–36.
    New York: HBJ, 1994.
———. *Carry Me Like Water*. New York: Hyperion, 1995.

Sánchez, Ricardo. *Canto y grito mi liberación*. Pullman: Washington State Univer-
    sity Press, 1995.

Silko, Leslie Marmon. *Almanac of the Dead: A Novel*. New York: Penguin Books,
    1991.

Toledo, Sonia Tello. "Simojovel: La lucha actual contra la servidumbre agraria." San Cristóbal de las Casas: Centro de Estudios Indígenas, Universidad Autónoma de Chiapas, n.d.

Trujillo, Charley. *Soldados: Chicanos in Viet Nam*. San Jose, Calif.: Chusma House, 1990.

———. *Dogs from Illusion*. San Jose, Calif.: Chusma House, 1994.

Van Den Bergh, Pierre L. *The Quest for the Other: Ethnic Tourism in San Cristóbal, Mexico*. Seattle: University of Washington Press, 1994.

Vásquez-Sánchez, M. A., and M. A. Ramos, eds. *Reserva de la biosfera Montes Azules, Selva Lacandona: Investigación para su conservación*. Publ. ocas. Ecosfera (edición preliminar). San Cristóbal de las Casas, Chiapas, Mexico: Centro de Estudios para la Conservación de los Recursos Naturales, 1992.

Vladislav, Jan. *Václav Havel, or Living in Truth: Twenty-two Essays Published on the Occasion of the Award of the Erasmus Prize to Václav Havel*. Winchester, Mass.: Faber and Faber, 1989.

Vogt, Evon Z. *Fieldwork among the Maya: Reflections on the Harvard Maya Project*. Albuquerque: University of New Mexico Press, 1994.

———, ed. *Los Zinacantecos*. Mexico City: Instituto Nacional Indigenista, 1966.

Vos, Jan de. *La paz de Dios y del rey: La conquista de la Selva Lacandona por los españoles, 1525–1821*. Mexico City: Gobierno del Estado de Chiapas, 1980.

———. *Oro verde: La conquista de la selva lacandona por los madereros tabasqueños, 1822–1949*. Mexico City: Fondo de Cultura Económica, 1988.